Climate Change and Political Theory

And Political Theory series

Climate Change and Political Theory

Catriona McKinnon

polity

First published in 2022 by Polity Press

Polity Press
65 Bridge Street
Cambridge CB2 1UR, UK

Polity Press
111 River Street
Hoboken, NJ 07030, USA

ISBN-13: 978-1-5095-2165-4 (hardback)
ISBN-13: 978-1-5095-2166-1 (paperback)

A catalogue record for this book is available from the British Library.

Library of Congress Control Number 2022932598

Typeset in 11 on 13pt Monotype Bembo
by Cheshire Typesetting Ltd, Cuddington, Cheshire
Printed and bound in Great Britain by TJ Books Ltd, Padstow, Cornwall

The publisher has used its best endeavours to ensure that the URLs for external websites referred to in this book are correct and active at the time of going to press. However, the publisher has no responsibility for the websites and can make no guarantee that a site will remain live or that the content is or will remain appropriate.

Every effort has been made to trace all copyright holders, but if any have been overlooked the publisher will be pleased to include any necessary credits in any subsequent reprint or edition.

For further information on Polity, visit our website:
politybooks.com

Contents

Acknowledgements

While this book was being written I took up a new position at the University of Exeter, moved house (twice), lost my dad, and we all navigated a global pandemic. As a result, I missed deadline after deadline. I am very grateful to George Owers and Julia Davies at Polity for their patience. Much of the material in this book was tested on my Climate Justice students at the University of Exeter. Their enthusiasm and idealism are a beacon in what can be a very dark place. I feel privileged to see them galvanising for action on climate change.

I received very thorough and helpful reports on the manuscript from three anonymous reviewers, and from George Owers at Polity. I would like to thank them for the time and care they put into this feedback: it greatly improved the book. I am also grateful for Henry Shue's eyes on the manuscript, which saved me from some embarrassing blunders

My lovely family – Matt, Caelan, and Bria – are the best in every respect. I would get nothing done without them, mostly because nothing would be worth doing.

Abbreviations

BECCS	bioenergy with carbon capture and storage
CBA	cost-benefit analysis
CC	climate change
CCS	carbon capture and storage
CDR	carbon dioxide removal
COP15	Fifteenth Session of the Conference of the Parties to the UNFCCC
DACS	direct air capture with storage
GDP	gross domestic product
GHG	greenhouse gas
IAM	Integrated Assessment Model
IPCC	Intergovernmental Panel on Climate Change
LDC	less developed country
MCB	marine cloud brightening
MDC	more developed country
MNC	multi-national corporation
NDC	nationally determined contribution
NESS	necessary element of a sufficient set
NET	negative energy technology
NGO	non-governmental organisation

R&D	research and development
SAI	stratospheric aerosol injection
SCoPEX	Stratospheric Controlled Perturbation Experiment
SRM	solar radiation management
UNEP	UN Environment Programme
UNFCCC	The United Nations Framework Convention on Climate Change
VSL	value of a statistical life
WFP	World Food Programme
WTP	willingness to pay

In memory of my Dad, Jim McKinnon, 1931–2020.
He lived his life in love.

1

Introduction:
An Unprecedented Challenge

Climate change and political theory

Climate change is often described as the most serious challenge faced by humanity. We have made great strides in understanding the climate system. In many countries, schoolchildren are now taught the basics of climate change. Public awareness of – and expressed concern about – climate change is significant (UNDP and University of Oxford 2021). However, the dominant narrative around climate change remains as stated in the first sentence of this book: climate change is a problem for all of us. The reality is that climate impacts will be (and already are) much worse for some people than for others: for example, the world's current poor, indigenous people, and women, are already being hit harder by climate change than those with less vulnerability. And lack of effective action on climate change is likely to exacerbate the vulnerability of future people. These facts illustrate how climate change raises questions of ethics, politics, the evolution of socio-economic systems, and histories of exclusion and domination. This lens is far less well known than the story of how the climate system has been seriously affected by human emissions of greenhouse gases (GHGs), and can be set back on track by concerted and coordinated political action to reduce emissions.

In recent decades, political theorists have done much to highlight the social, political, and ethical dimensions of the climate problem. In particular, the idea of climate justice, and a constellation of associated important concepts such as responsibility for climate injustice, has been articulated by political theorists so as to deliver a normative language in which the climate crisis can be properly framed. These framings reveal the crisis to be not only a matter of our climate system operating differently because of our GHG emissions but, more fundamentally, a product of historical injustices, current inequalities, institutional inadequacies, and the abuse of power. Political theorists have enabled us to see the climate crisis as a challenge to some of our most fundamental convictions about what makes for flourishing societies, successful economies, meaningful individual lives, and healthy politics. This book will trace arguments and analyses in political theory that have enriched our understanding of the climate crisis in these ways.

Speaking very broadly, political theory is an approach to questions of how we live together that prioritises normative perspectives. A 'normative perspective' is one that focuses on questions of how things ought to be rather than how they are. Sometimes this means making optimistic sets of assumptions about how people behave, and how political institutions operate,[1] in order to justify principles to govern the ideal society. For example, John Rawls' arguments for his theory of justice as fairness famously proceeds on the assumption that all people are willing to propose and abide by fair principles of social cooperation (Rawls 1999). There is an important place for this kind of 'ideal' political theory (Hamlin and Stemplowska 2012; Swift 2008). However, most political theorists accept that normative thinking about climate change will have a very different character given the radically non-ideal circumstances in which the crisis is accelerating (Heyward and Roser 2016). Very often, non-ideal political theory addressing climate change focuses on second, third, or fourth best solutions, and very often the focus is on reducing climate injustice rather than achieving climate justice.

Non-ideal political theory addressing climate change is empirically engaged and informed. Political theorists of climate change frame their work by reference to: the realities of the climate system and evolving scientific understanding of it; the history of climate politics and policies at multiple scales, and the latest research by policy analysts, legal experts, and theorists of institutional design; the economics of climate change, and its hidden assumptions; and the cultural meanings of the climate crisis.

This book's tour of political theory's most important contributions to thinking about climate change will include these empirical matters as it evolves. For now, I shall give a very brief overview of some key concepts in the science of climate change, and a potted history of international climate agreements, as the background against which the more topic-focused discussions to come take place.

What is climate change?

Anthropogenic climate change is a result of increasing human emissions of GHGs since roughly 1750. The process by which GHGs cause warming is called 'the greenhouse effect'. A portion of the heat from the Sun that reaches the Earth is trapped by GHGs in the atmosphere, and has a warming effect. This natural warming process has been massively intensified by the release of large amounts of GHGs into the atmosphere as a result of human activity, with the result that the Earth is warming at an unprecedented rate and speed.[2]

There are two primary physical drivers of current climate change: human emissions of GHGs, and human destruction of carbon sinks. On emissions, there are a variety of GHGs, all with different properties. One of the most significant of these properties is the length of time the GHG remains in the atmosphere after it has been emitted. For carbon dioxide (CO_2), which accounts for 76% of human emissions (IPCC 2014): 40% of today's emissions will remain in the atmosphere for 100 years, 30% will remain for

1,000 years, and 10% will remain after 10,000 years. In contrast methane (CH_4), which accounts for 16% of human emissions, stays in the atmosphere for only ten years or so, although its warming potential is 25 to 30 times more than that of carbon dioxide. The fact that CO_2 in particular stays in the atmosphere potentially for very long periods of time explains the 'lag' in the climate system: CO_2 emissions today will have an effect long into the future, especially given that emissions accumulate over time.

On carbon sinks, these are Earth systems and processes that absorb and store more carbon dioxide than they emit.[3] Forests, soil, and oceans all serve as vital carbon sinks, enabling the Earth's carbon cycle to stay in balance. Our large-scale destruction of carbon sinks, combined with our ever-increasing and accelerating emissions of GHGs, are the causes of the climate crisis. The roots of both these drivers are in the Industrial Revolution (beginning around 1750 in England), which generated an unprecedented demand for energy (satisfied by coal, oil, and gas) and land-use changes (for agriculture, timber, animal farming etc.) that have now reached every part of the globe (Ritchie and Roser 2013).

In 1750 CO_2 stood at 277 parts per million (ppm).[4] With some peaks and troughs, this is roughly the level at which CO_2 concentrations have been for the last 800,000 years.[5] CO_2 presently stands at over 400 ppm – the highest concentration in three million years. Emissions globally, and in all regions of the world, continue to grow.[6] Global average temperature has increased by 1.1C since 1850 as a result of these emissions.[7] However in some places, especially the polar regions, average temperature has increased by 2C. Many scenarios for future warming suggest rises of 3C–4C by 2100, with worst-case scenarios of over 5C.

The modelling that delivers these scenarios is well established, but it is important to uncover two assumptions made in the models that could render them highly conservative. The first relates to positive feedbacks in the climate system that could rapidly shift it from one state to another. Known as 'tipping points', these feedbacks are not included in models generating future climate scenarios, and passing one tipping point could cause a cascade of points to be passed (Carrington 2021; Lenton et al. 2019; Steffen et al. 2018).[8]

For example, if the West Antarctic Ice Sheet were to melt (at risk at 1C–3C of warming), this could cause sea-level rise that would increase the rate of melt of the Greenland Ice Sheet (at risk at 1C–3C of warming), and the influx of freshwater resulting from this could increase the likelihood of a shutdown of the thermohaline circulation in the Atlantic ocean (at risk at 3C–4C of warming). If this current were to shut down, the Gulf Stream would cease to warm Northern Europe, which would experience a huge drop in temperatures as a result. Tipping points could push the world's climate into a new state, and some of them could accelerate warming already underway (e.g. if the Siberian permafrost were to melt and release its methane). All these changes would be irreversible. And we know that the Earth has passed many climate tipping points in its history (National Research Council 2011; Ditlevsen 2017).

The second important assumption that affects temperature rises in scenarios modelling future climate change is 'climate sensitivity'. This is the amount of global surface warming that will occur in response to a doubling of atmospheric CO_2 concentrations compared to pre-industrial times. Crudely, the higher the value of climate sensitivity, the more warming we are likely to see. Scientific best estimates of climate sensitivity range from 1.5C–4.5C, with some studies suggesting a higher value of 5.2C.[9] Climate sensitivity is perhaps the biggest uncertainty in climate science. If climate sensitivity is higher than 5C – and some recent studies suggest we ought to take this seriously (Watts 2020; K. D. Williams, Hewitt, and Bodas-Salcedo 2020) – then warming is likely to accelerate much faster than expected, bringing with it catastrophic climate impacts and much increased risks of passing tipping points in the climate system.

Throughout this book I shall make reference to the Intergovernmental Panel on Climate Change (IPCC).[10] This important body was established by the United Nations (UN) in 1988 to provide policy relevant information on climate change for governments and beyond. The IPCC publishes periodical assessment reports that summarise the latest science in a range of climate-relevant domains. The IPCC published its Fifth Assessment Report in 2014, and the Sixth Assessment Report is in the process of being published (due 2022). The IPCC does no independent research: its Working Groups review, assess, and synthesise independent research done in the assessment period. IPCC scientists are not paid.

Many of the impacts of warming of 1C upwards (i.e. the warming we have already exceeded) will be discussed throughout this book, with a focus on what they mean for the planet's human inhabitants. These impacts include mass drought and food shortages, extreme weather events, huge numbers of people displaced by climate impacts, increased disease burdens and greater risk of pandemics, interpersonal and state conflict over scarce resources, death from temperatures higher than the human body can withstand, severe impacts on mental health, and – in very worst-case scenarios – the risk of human extinction. The temperature rises to which we are already committed, given atmospheric concentration of GHGs, make some of these impacts unavoidable; indeed, many of the world's most vulnerable and disadvantaged people are already being hit by these impacts. Political theory focuses on how people ought to live together in political societies, as well as other forms of community, even in the worst of circumstances. Without political theory we cannot make headway on identifying and justifying routes out of the climate crisis.

At this point I note that my focus in this book is only on human beings, and how climate change causes them damage. This focus is narrow and excludes all the other living things on the planet, which bear no responsibility for climate change and are already suffering its worst consequences. The scientific consensus is that we are in a sixth mass-extinction event, with rates of species extinction ten to 10,000 times higher than the expected background (or 'normal') rate of extinction (Barnosky et al. 2011; Bradshaw and Saltré 2019; Ceballos, Ehrlich, and Raven 2020). Climate change is a significant driver of the sixth mass extinction: current and projected warming changes habitats at a speed to which most living things cannot adapt. The destruction of the nonhuman natural world by climate change is a moral disgrace (McShane 2016; Nolt 2011b, 2021; Palmer 2011; Tschakert et al. 2021). I regret that I cannot do justice to this topic in this book.

What is the UNFCCC, and the Paris Agreement on Climate Change?

Moving through the book I shall discuss many specific examples of political, social, legal, and community action to address the climate crisis. This action is happening at all scales, from individual decisions to eat less meat, local decisions to create community green spaces and allotments, metropolitan transport policies, to regional and national climate action plans (Agyeman et al. 2016; Schlosberg 2009). Here, I will give an overview of the international agreement between states within which other multiple-scale efforts are ultimately embedded.

The UN Framework Convention on Climate Change (UNFCCC) was adopted in May 1992 and opened for signatures at the Rio Earth Summit in June that year.[11] The Convention entered into force on 21 March 1994. The UNFCCC is a multilateral treaty that recognises climate change as a global problem and commits its 197 parties to take action. The Earth Summit was a moment of cosmopolitan optimism and ambition: the secretary-general of the summit, Maurice Strong, opened it with the words: 'We are either going to save the whole world or no one will be saved. One part of the world cannot live in an orgy of unrestrained consumption where the rest destroys its environment just to survive. No one is immune from the effects of the other' (Brown 1992). The subsequent history of climate negotiations between parties to the Convention – at the Conference of the Parties (COP) meetings – have not delivered on the promise of Rio. The state of the climate in 2022, with emissions still rising and temperatures increasing, shows multilateral action on climate change within the UNFCCC to have been inadequate.[12]

The agreement that presently governs the cooperation of states within the UNFCCC is the Paris Agreement, adopted on 12 December 2015 at COP21 in Paris.[13] The key features of this Agreement are as follows, The Agreement states a commitment to keeping global average temperatures well below 2C, and preferably below 1.5C, and to achieve a global peaking of GHGs as soon as possible. The Agreement has a 'pledge and review' structure, whereby countries commit to making emissions reductions (and taking other action on climate change), and collectively review progress over time. These pledges are made in countries 'nationally determined contributions' (NDCs). NDCs cover a five-year time period and contain conditional and unconditional commitments.[14] Parties to the Paris Agreement are legally required to submit their NDCs but there are no legal requirements for them to make any specific commitments in those NDCs, and the contents of NDCs are determined entirely by national governments themselves. NDCs must state how countries' efforts will promote equity (understood in the UNFCCC as a commitment to 'common but differentiated responsibility' for climate change), but there are no external standards according to which NDCs can be judged in this regard (Okereke and Coventry 2016).[15] Unlike the Kyoto Protocol, the Paris Agreement makes no distinction between what is required of more developed countries (MDCs) and less developed countries (LDCs).

How are we doing on these climate ambitions? The UN Environment Programme (UNEP) publishes an annual report on the 'Emissions Gap' (UNEP 2021).[16] This gap is the difference between emissions reductions actually undertaken, and reductions that would have to be undertaken in order to achieve the Paris temperature goals. The subtitle of the most recent (2021) report is 'a world of climate promises not yet delivered'. The report notes that the most recent NDCs only take 7.5% off predicted 2030 emissions, whereas 55% is needed to achieve the Paris goal of keeping temperature rises below 1.5C, and 30% to achieve 2C. The unconditional pledges in the most recent NDCs put us on track for a temperature rise of at least 2.7C by 2100. The decade 2010–2020 was the hottest on record.[17] Defenders of the Paris Agreement are likely to point out that it is still early days, and the Agreement is designed to ratchet up ambition over time.[18] The United Nations Environment Programme (UNEP) tells us that '[t]o stand a chance of limiting global warming to 1.5C, we have eight years to almost halve greenhouse gas emissions: eight years to make the plans, put in place the policies, implement them and ultimately deliver the cuts. The clock is ticking loudly.'[19]

Let me introduce a key concept here: that of the GHG budget. The GHG budget is the amount of GHGs we can 'safely' release into the atmosphere for any given temperature threshold. Ignoring the interests of humanity and all the other living things on the planet, the GHG budget is expansive; perhaps it is unlimited. The Earth will persist in some form (even if Venus-like) regardless of the atmospheric concentration of GHGs. It is only because we want, quite rightly, to take into consideration the interests of the Earth's living things that the GHG budget is constrained. Focusing just on the interests of human beings, we know that above certain temperature thresholds life on Earth is very likely to become painful, miserable, or impossible for very many people. The GHG budget for a given temperature threshold captures what remains of the absorptive capacity of the atmosphere if we are to have a reasonable chance of staying below that threshold. The higher the threshold, the greater the budget.[20] The size of the remaining GHG budget depends, inter alia, on climate sensitivity. Climate sensitivity of 5C+ would make catastrophic worst-case climate futures much more likely and would massively shrink the remaining GHG budget, giving us even less time than we thought we had to cut emissions and ramp up adaptation. The GHG budget or, limited just to CO_2, the 'carbon budget', has provided a very useful frame for thinking about ethical and justice questions raised by climate change, as we shall see.

What is this book about?

This book shows the fundamental contribution of political theory, political philosophy, ethics, and moral philosophy to our approach to the climate crisis. I shall start in the next chapter by showing how an understanding of the climate problem as a moral crisis offers deep insights into the maddening question of why we have failed so badly to avert it. In Chapter 3 I explore the multiple victims of climate change, and the ways in which the damage done to them by climate impacts raises questions of justice. Chapter 4 engages with questions of why we should act on climate change, despite the many deep uncertainties we have about future climate scenarios, and considers the type of approach that should guide climate policymakers in these conditions of uncertainty. Chapter 5 considers where responsibility for taking this action falls most heavily. Chapter 6 considers routes out of the climate crisis, given that we have not, and are not, doing what we ought to do. Chapter 7 considers the perils and promises of some suites of new technology being proposed as routes out of the climate crisis. In Chapter 8 I conclude with a brief consideration of hope and despair in the climate crisis.

This is where an introduction to an introductory book on a normal topic would usually end. Climate change is not that type of topic. In the fifteen or so years I have been working on climate justice, the news has gone from bad to worse to almost unbearable. The only frame for the climate crisis that shows its true urgency, madness, stakes, and meaning is an ethical one. I hope this book convinces you of that.

2

Why Haven't We Achieved Climate Justice?

Why have we failed so badly to avert the climate crisis? An obvious answer to this question is that climate policymaking is a hot mess of powerful fossil fuel interests, ambitious politicians with their minds on the next election, public apathy, and institutional inertia. People are greedy, short-sighted, and ignorant; and it is very hard to change the course of any ship of state. All of this is true. But it is not enough by way of explanation. Humanity has risen to enormous challenges in the past despite our flaws and cumbersome institutions. For example, by agreeing the Montreal Protocol in the 1980s, nations worked together effectively to fix the 'hole' in the ozone layer; and in 1980, as a result of sustained and coordinated global efforts by the World Health Organisation, the world became free of smallpox.[1] Is there something different about climate change that makes it especially hard to tackle with even minimally just policies?

As we will see in subsequent chapters there is much disagreement about the full demands of climate justice and on whom these demands fall most heavily. That said, there is a core of agreement on the minimum content of climate justice. This core is given by consensus across the views of theorists, who accept that justice is possible and important to achieve in climate policy. It involves:

- A requirement on at least states and regional bodies to radically reduce emissions and enable adaptation.
- Commitment to protect the world's most vulnerable people from climate impacts that will exacerbate their disadvantage.
- Adoption of a long-term frame for just and effective climate policy that inter alia recognises the interests, needs, and claims of future people.

This core is minimal indeed. In the coming chapters it will be filled out to make it more ambitious and demanding. However, before that, we can see that current climate policy fails even these minimal standards for climate justice. Present reductions in the rate of GHG emissions are far lower than what is needed to minimise the risks of catastrophic climate change (Steffen et al. 2018). The world's most vulnerable people – those with the lowest average incomes, least wealth, and worst health – are not well protected from climate impacts by climate policy. In fact, the reverse appears to be true: the world's least advantaged people are most at risk from climate impacts, now and into the future.[2] And, current climate policy-making has a remarkable 'presentist' bias: political institutions and decision-making processes on all scales fail to represent the interests of future people. This is evident, for example, in the fact that dominant economistic approaches to climate policymaking heavily discount harms to future people, as we shall see in Chapter 3. Concern for future people as a matter of justice is at best rhetoric to adorn the preambles of political agreements that otherwise fail entirely to take account of them.

Why have we failed so badly to achieve even minimal justice in political action on climate change? Is the achievement of climate justice a pipe dream? Or, once we identify the source as a nature of our failures, can we make progress by employing our human creativity, inventiveness, and sociability to transform existing political and economic institutions to achieve climate justice? Many thinkers committed to climate justice believe so. But the scale of the transformation needed must first be acknowledged.

In this chapter, I will survey three influential analyses of the political and social challenges created by climate change. Each of these approaches aims to explain why progress towards climate justice is almost non-existent. What differentiates them are the sources of intractability they identify. On the first approach, our failures are explained by a failure of collectively rational use and governance of the atmosphere's capacity for absorbing GHGs. On this picture, climate change creates extremely hard coordination problems. The second approach advocates a more fine-grained way of thinking about the sites of action on climate change that could solve this coordination problem. On this approach, our failures can be explained by too little focus on the variety of cooperative endeavours to tackle climate change, which, taken together, have great potential to feed upwards into large-scale climate agreements in ways that maximise their effectiveness. The third approach treats climate change as presenting a snarl of ethical challenges. These combine to generate morally corrupt reasoning, leading to end-lessly inadequate climate policymaking that is almost irresistible to those with decision-making power, as well as those positioned to agitate for change. On the third approach, just solutions to climate change have been beyond our grasp, either because of the ethical inadequacies of those who could have made a difference or, worse, because our moral theories are simply not up to the task.

Is climate change a failure of collective rationality?

No one owns the atmosphere, and everyone depends on it for survival and flourishing. In particular, all human beings across time rely on the atmosphere's capacity to absorb GHGs within a range that keeps average temperatures on the surface tolerable for us. There was a time when the Earth's forests were similarly unowned and indispensable to human flourishing. International waters in the oceans are protected against the claims of sovereignty by UNCLOS.[3] Both oceans and forests are massive carbon sinks. Resources that are freely available to all, and cannot be withheld from some and made available to others except with great difficulty, are known as 'common pool resources'. Some common pool resources are not essential for survival or a good life: for example, silence is pleasant but the lack of it will kill no one nor ruin their lives.

The common pool resources of carbon sinks and the absorptive capacity of the atmosphere have a different significance. When GHGs, particularly CO_2, reach a certain concentration in the atmosphere, life-threatening climate impacts become much more likely. Deforestation and pollution of the sea, for example by plastics that destroy marine life (*Plastic and Climate* 2019), exacerbate the risks. A scenario in which maintaining common pool resources at a quality or quantity threshold necessary for the continued survival, or minimal well-being, of a group was famously called a 'tragedy of the commons' by Garrett Hardin (Hardin 1968). The key features of any tragedy of the commons are captured by Hardin as follows:

> Picture a pasture open to all. It is to be expected that each herdsman will try to keep as many cattle as possible on the commons . . . [T]he rational herdsman concludes that the only sensible course for him to pursue is to add another animal to his herd. And another; and another . . . But this is the conclusion reached by each and every herdsman sharing a commons. Therein is the tragedy. Each man is locked into a system that compels him to increase his herd without limit – in a world that is limited. (Hardin 1968: 1244)

How does this apply to climate change? The absorptive capacity of the atmosphere and carbon sinks are the commons. Each agent damaging the sinks or emitting GHGs serves their own self-interest, narrowly construed. They externalise the true costs of their conduct by imposing them on everyone else through their degradation of the commons. The agents in a tragedy of the climate commons could be individual people, corporations, or states. These agents act in the belief that the benefit they gain from disposing of single-use plastics, logging in the Amazon rainforest, or building a further runway at an airport, outweighs the damage that could befall them as a consequence of how their conduct depletes carbon sinks and/or increases GHG stocks. From the point of view of their own rational self-interest their choices are justified. But the outcome of billions of individuals, thousands of corporations, and hundreds of states reasoning in this way is climate catastrophe for the collective. With respect to common pool resources necessary for human survival or minimal well-being, the tragedy is that '[r]uin is the destination toward which all men rush, each pursuing his own best interest' (Hardin 1968: 1244).

Is there a solution to this tragedy? Famously, Hardin proposed forms of 'mutual coercion, mutually agreed upon' in order to limit damage to the commons upon which we all depend. He accepted that the restrictions on individual freedom required by this coercion might be unjust but thought that '[i]njustice is preferable to total ruin' (Hardin 1968: 1247).

Explaining the climate crisis as the inexorable outcome of an ever-expanding human population on a planet with limited common pool resources necessary for their survival has a simple elegance. If the explanation gets things right we should nevertheless question Hardin's assertion that coercive governance to protect the climate commons would involve unjust limitations to freedom. This assertion holds only if freedom increases as restrictions on conduct reduce. On this 'negative' view of freedom it consists in doing whatever one might want to do without interference from other agents such as the state (Berlin 2002). But it is not obvious that this is what we value when we prize liberty. Arguably, what matters to us is the freedom to live with dignity by exercising our fundamental human capabilities in various ways (Sen 2001). Given the centrality of the ecological commons to this end, restrictions on conduct degrading them could instead be a way to enhance our freedom.

Putting this to one side, is it really the case that we are doomed to collectively foul our own nest (Hardin 1968: 1245) without meaning to do so? Apart from making humanity a particularly pathetic species (which we might well be), some thinkers have worried that Hardin's analysis does not capture the collaborative ingenuity that human beings can show, given some assumptions that are better attuned to the realities of human interaction than Hardin's 'rational choice' model. By focusing on this we might have more reason for optimism about the climate crisis than Hardin's model suggests.

Should we multiply sites of action on climate change?

Elinor Ostrom makes the case that our options for tackling climate change are not best thought of as imposed as a result of 'mutual coercion mutually agreed upon'. She argues that the 'conventional' theory of collective action that delivers Hardin's climate tragedy depends on assumptions that are not empirically supported for many sites of cooperative action on climate change, and that the conventional theory overlooks the potential benefits to participants of such cooperation (Ostrom 2010). The key starting points for Ostrom's 'polycentric' approach to climate governance are as follows.

First, many groups capable of acting together to tackle climate change are composed of members who communicate with one another and learn (sometimes very fast) from one another's trials and errors. This enables them to understand the possible unintended consequences for the collective of their individual conduct, and to modify that conduct in effective ways. Second, the gains that can be generated by individual conduct should not be understood in purely material terms or short-term gains. Reputational benefits can be generated by participation in a cooperative effort to achieve a collective good. As cooperation is reciprocated, trust builds up between members of the group, which supports further cooperation and learning. On this 'bottom-up' model for climate governance what matters is securing social, political, and economic conditions in which people can build trust and learn from one another in ways fit to feed into larger, perhaps global-scale forms of cooperation that minimise collective irrationality and free riding. 'Mutual coercion mutually agreed upon' is a top-down strategy that is not only unnecessary but also potentially damaging to cooperation at multiple smaller-scale sites that could combine to support a significant effort to tackle climate change. As Ostrom puts it:

> What we have learned from extensive research is that when individuals are well informed about the problem they face and about who else is involved, and can build settings where trust and reciprocity can emerge, grow, and be sustained over time, costly and positive actions are frequently taken without waiting for an external authority to impose rules, monitor compliance, and assess penalties. (Ostrom 2010: 555)

A polycentric approach to climate governance recommends a multiplicity of governing authorities at different scales, with diverse functions, and distinct capabilities. These units can be as small as the family or as large as an international regime (Ostrom 2010: 552). When large-scale climate governance is – at least to some extent – driven and informed by forms of cooperation at smaller scales the problems of free riding and noncompliance that worried Hardin can be more easily addressed. On a bottom-up approach, free riders – and other agents whose conduct creates obstacles to effective and fair climate action – can be more easily identified and disincentivised from non-contribution. Ostrom offers empirical evidence to support her arguments for polycentrism in climate governance which shows that:

> Polycentric systems tend to enhance innovation, learning, adaptation, trustworthiness, levels of cooperation of participants, and the achievement of more effective, equitable, and sustainable outcomes at multiple scales, even though no institutional arrangement can totally eliminate opportunism with respect to the provision and production of collective goods. (Ostrom 2010)

To be clear, her claim is not that global-scale climate agreements are impotent. Rather, polycentrism argues for multiple sites of action on climate governance, many of which should inform what gets agreed by states at the highest level. On a polycentric approach it is a mistake to look for a silver bullet to fix climate change. On this view, silver buckshot is our best hope (Prins and Rayner 2007).

Does a polycentric approach to climate governance bring climate justice within our grasp? Polycentrism in climate policymaking is, in fact, the norm. A variety of community groups, cities, firms, churches, and regions are all engaging in a huge range of activities to tackle climate change (Umbers and Moss 2018). For example, a Global Covenant of Mayors for Climate and Energy convened in 2016, and represents over 10,000 cities;[4] numerous UK universities have declared a climate emergency; the Roman Catholic Church includes a Global Catholic Climate Movement.[5] And yet, if anything, we seem even further from achieving climate just outcomes. The world's poorest people remain most vulnerable to climate impacts, now and into the future. Have we just not 'done enough' polycentrism to achieve fair and effective climate policy? Or is there still something missing from the picture?

Readers of the last two sections might be struck by how technical the proposed 'solutions' to climate change are on Hardin's and Ostrom's models. These models present climate change as essentially a particularly hard and large-scale problem of social cooperation: what is sometimes referred to as a 'super wicked' problem (Levin et al. 2009). If this is true, then what we need are better ways to communicate, organise, and act together so as to achieve climate policy that is just and effective. These problems are external to us: the terms of our social cooperation must change, but we need not.

Many people think this misses an essential piece of the puzzle. We are in a climate crisis because we have delayed action that would have massively reduced the scale of the problem we face now. If we had taken radical action in 1992 to reduce emissions, then the reductions necessary now to stay below 2C by 2100 would be far lower. Our failure to start radical action in 1992 means that we, and those who will come after us, face a much more burdensome, and in many respects avoidable, set of climate challenges than might have been the case.

It is time to disaggregate the 'we' in these claims; by doing this we will start to see the deep moral failures missed by collective action approaches. Large-scale reductions in the emissions of the world's richest states and individuals, starting in 1992, would have significantly reduced the reductions necessary now. These reductions would have meant sacrifices in the luxuries enjoyed by citizens of these states, and rich individuals in other places. We knew enough in 1992 to see this, and we had enough by way of global and polycentric governance arrangements for rich states and individuals to take the necessary steps. And yet they did not, and still refuse to do so. At the same time most of these states engage in global negotiations over climate agreements and contain many sites and forms of action on climate change within their territories. What has gone wrong here, ethically speaking?

Is climate change an ethical failure?

Moral and political philosophers who have engaged with climate change have pulled no punches in their condemnation of our many ethical failures in the face of climate challenges.[6] For example, Henry Shue has remarked that: 'the economic/energy system in which [the rich] thrive and indulge in excess prevents [the global poor from] enjoying a decent life. The energy regime that makes life opulent for Belgians and Saudis makes it impossible for Rwandans and Haitians, who are helpless victims of a complex global social institution in which they have absolutely no voice' (Shue 2001: 452). And I have written that '[i]f we fail to make the cuts [to GHG emissions] required in the next couple of decades, it is no exaggeration to say that we, the particular cohort of people alive now, will have failed to do justice to the whole human race. For shame' (McKinnon 2011: 211) What is it about climate change that explains our ongoing failures to tackle it?

Stephen Gardiner takes on this question in his important book *A Perfect Moral Storm: The Ethical Tragedy of Climate Change*. He argues that the phenomenon of climate change whips up three 'storms' in the face of which the temptation to think and act in ways that are morally corrupt becomes almost irresistible to us. The storms created by climate change, which converge to create what he calls 'the perfect moral storm', are theoretical, global, and intergenerational.

Gardiner argues that the theoretical storm exists because the political philosophies and moral theories that inform our thinking about justice fail what he calls 'the global test' (Gardiner 2011: 217–18). What he means by this is that none of our major theories – such as utilitarianism, liberalism, socialism, and libertarianism – acknowledge that their failure to address the serious global threat of climate change is a potentially fatal criticism of them. Instead, advocates of these theories react by insisting that criticisms such as this fail to stick and that further refinements to the theory would enable it to pass the global test. Gardiner calls this the 'Teflon effect' (Gardiner 2011: 232–4). A dangerous consequence of the Teflon effect is that we lack a theoretical compass to navigate reliably through our temptations to moral corruption in the face of the other storms: at best, our major ethical theories remain silent on climate change but, at worst, they might guarantee failure to address it. I shall return to this question below in discussion of Dale Jamieson's views on the failures of political theory to address climate change.

The second storm is generated by the global nature of climate change. The causes of climate change (emissions and the destruction of carbon sinks) are spatially dispersed across the planet, as are its effects. There is no place on Earth that has not been a source of some GHGs and, once GHGs are emitted, they spread evenly throughout the atmosphere causing different climate impacts in different places. Another aspect of the global storm is the 'fragmentation of agency' in causing and addressing it, and the inadequacy of our existing institutions with respect to finding and implementing solutions. This gives the basic global storm of climate change the structure of a Tragedy of the Commons, as described by Hardin. But what Hardin and his followers have failed to register are some unusual features of the climate problem that show that the Tragedy of the Commons model masks ethical failure.

Gardiner argues that there are some special features of climate change that open the door to morally corrupt reasoning about action on climate policy. The moral corruption of people who could have taken, but have failed to take, serious action on climate change is what is missing from the Tragedy of the Commons analysis of the climate problem (and, by extension, also missing from Ostrom's polycentrism). These special features are as follows. First, scientific uncertainty about, for example, the severity and distribution of climate impacts, or climate sensitivity. These uncertainties can be exploited by ideologically motivated groups to scupper action on climate change (McKinnon 2016). Scientific uncertainty can also open the door to cognitive dissonance about climate change, whereby abstract knowledge of the reality of climate change is not connected to activities and events in everyday life (Norgaard 2011).

Second, the 'deep roots' of the problem in the infrastructures and ways of life of the global rich whose emissions have done most to cause climate change combine with scientific uncertainty to entrench inertia. The massive increases in GHG emissions we have seen over the last sixty to seventy years are the result of a transformation in the lives of those living in consumerist, highly industrialised countries. In the long term the transition to zero-carbon economies need not be damaging to the quality of life of people in these countries; indeed, there are many reasons to think this transition would have a very positive effect. But in the short term the changes necessary to reach net zero emissions by 2050 would have an impact, and it is naive to think that this would not be resisted by those who have to make sacrifices. Politicians who want to resist radical action on climate change know this. They push at open doors when they appeal to their constituents' settled expectations that they should not have to give up frequent air travel, fast fashion, meat-rich diets, and finely tuned indoor temperatures.[7] There are important questions here about whether voters' settled expectations should be challenged, and how to go about this. I address some of these issues in Chapter 6.

Finally, Gardiner highlights the 'skewed vulnerabilities' of people who will be worst affected by climate change. People in rich, industrialised countries are causing most of the climate problem and also have the power to tackle it. But, because they are wealthy and resilient, they are also best placed to adapt to climate impacts. Given the entrenchment of luxury in these societies these people have the least incentive to exercise that power to deliver just and effective climate policy. And their politicians – chasing the next short-term electoral win – echo this self-interest.

Taken together these facts about climate change as a global storm enable the global rich to justify their inaction on climate change to themselves and one another. The moral relevance of the historical emissions of people in rich, carbon-intensive industrialised countries are allowed to fall out of the picture on an 'essentially forward looking' (Gardiner 2011: 120) analysis of climate change as a tragedy of the commons. It is easier for people who contribute most to climate change to tell themselves that coordination challenges entirely explain their failure to take just action on climate change than to see themselves as selfishly clinging to luxury and advantage, and the world be damned. An analysis of climate change as a 'mere' Tragedy of the Commons opens up the possibility of what Gardiner calls 'shadow solutions' to climate change (such as the Kyoto Protocol (Gardiner 2011: 75–102) and the Paris Agreement (Gardiner 2021)). These are courses of action that give the appearance of effective action by aiming at coordination in the interests of all. Instead, shadow solutions actually enable the global rich to avoid the costly sacrifices that a clear-eyed acknowledgement of their moral obligations would require.

The third storm is intergenerational. This is a consequence of the fact that the causes and effects of climate change are dispersed across time, given the atmospheric life of GHGs (CO_2 in particular),[8] and the lag in the climate system (i.e. the fact that the climate system does not respond immediately to many emissions (Met Office 2019)). The emissions of any set of people alive at any given time make a causal contribution to climate change that will not be felt in full as climate impacts by that temporal cohort. Instead, future temporal cohorts will be affected. Gardiner is right to claim that the presentation of climate change as creating duties for members of the current generation to future people is the least visible of the three storms, because these duties are very demanding, and because those to whom they are owed can do nothing whatsoever to influence our performance of them: they are entirely at our mercy.

The key temptation to moral corruption in the face of this storm is intergenerational buck passing: ineffective action on climate change now (perhaps through shadow solutions) passes on to future people the costs of tackling climate change, which for them will be a bigger challenge than it was for us, given how climate change impacts caused by our emissions are 'substantially deferred'. A prominent instance of this form of moral corruption, according to Gardiner, is evident in the growing debate on geoengineering as a way of 'arming the future' against the climate change we will bequeath to them as a result of our focus on this, rather than on radically cutting our emissions: '[i]n essence, we'd be happy to spend a few million dollars on research our generation will probably not have to bear the risks of implementing, and we'd be even happier to think that in doing so we were making a morally serious choice in favour of protecting future generations. But thinking so hardly makes it the case' (Gardiner 2011: 364–5). I shall return to the question of geoengineering in Chapter 7.

The perfect moral storm of climate change enables rich and powerful members of the current generation to rationalise the pursuit of their own self-interest in making climate policy, at the expense of future generations and the global poor, by framing the climate problem (and proposed solutions) in ways that dilute the content, and relegate the status, of their moral obligations to the victims of climate change. For Gardiner, our failure to move towards just climate policy is best explained by our moral corruption in the face of climate change.

Gardiner's excavation of our moral corruption is unforgiving, but he does not conclude that, as an ethical problem, climate change is beyond us. This more frightening conclusion is drawn by Dale Jamieson in his book *Reason in a Dark Time: Why the Struggle Against Climate Change Failed – And What It Means for Our Future* (Jamieson 2014). Jamieson argues that we have now reached the point at which effective – let alone ethical – responses to climate change lie beyond our reach. Already, the consequences of our failure are suffering, death, and displacement for many vulnerable people, and extinction for many nonhuman species (Ceballos, Ehrlich, and Raven 2020). In Jamieson's view, our hopes for international, meaningful action on climate change died in Copenhagen at the UNFCCC Conference of the Parties meeting in 2009 (COP15) (Jamieson 2014: 237), and damaging climate impacts will shape the world in which human beings must live for as far ahead as we can see.

Why has this happened? There are questions to be raised about the adequacy of our political institutions and the contents of the climate-policy toolbox – and we will get stuck into many of these questions in subsequent chapters. For Jamieson, though, the bedrock of our failure to tackle climate change is our moral incapacity in the face of the climate problem, and this is a product of the world in which humans have evolved. Jamieson claims that understanding our failures involves facing up to some 'deep truths about our animal nature[s]' (Jamieson 2014: 103). Many of the psychological heuristics we have evolved in order to survive – and which may be hard wired into our brains – make it extremely difficult for us to handle climate change (Jamieson 2014: 103–4). For example, understanding climate change requires us to think probabilistically, and most of us are very bad at thinking in this way.

Jamieson thinks that the limits of our evolved frameworks for thinking about ethical questions show up particularly starkly when we try to figure out questions of responsibility for climate change at the individual level (Jamieson 2015). We are used to making accountability for a harm done to a person track the causal mechanisms by which the harm was done, thereby tracing a route back to an individual who can be held responsible for the harm from an ethical or legal point of view. Even when causal tracking does not pinpoint an individual, it signposts collectives of different kinds

– companies, state bureaucracies, or social institutions – within which we can identify individuals to be held accountable for the harm in virtue of their positions of responsibility within the collective. This practice of 'holding responsible' is fundamental to nearly all traditions in ethics. And yet, Jamieson argues, it is a very bad fit with the climate problem. He illustrates by starting with a case to which our traditional concept of responsibility applies very well. Imagine one individual, Jack, deliberately harms another individual, Jill, by stealing her bicycle. As Jamieson says, 'both the perpetrator and the victim are clearly identifiable, and they are closely related in time and space. This case is a clear candidate for moral evaluation, and most of us would say that what Jack did was wrong' (Jamieson 2015: 796). However, once we change certain features of the example in order to make it better resemble the case of climate change, our moral judgements – especially with respect to where responsibility lies – start to falter. Jamieson asks us to imagine the following case:

> Suppose that acting independently, Jack and a large number of unacquainted people set in motion a chain of events that cause a large number of future people who will live in another part of the world from ever having bicycles. In this case, most of what is typically at the center of a morally suspect act has disappeared. (Jamieson 2015: 797)

In the revised example, is it clear that any harm is done to anyone? If harm is done to future people who never get bicycles, is Jack to blame? Or should we hold responsible Jack and all the other people who caused the bicycle-less future to come about? Does the fact that all these people acted independently – and thus, presumably, in ignorance of the combined effect of their actions – undermine their responsibility, at the individual or the collective level?

The point Jamieson makes with this now well-known example is that our existing moral concepts and frameworks for thinking about responsibility and harm in ethical and legal contexts do not deliver clear verdicts in the climate case. Because our political efforts – insofar as they have had any ethical ambition at all – have been premised on these existing frameworks and concepts, they have not gained traction on the climate problem. This is not to let greedy politicians, malicious climate deniers, lazy leaders, and other climate delinquents off the hook. Rather, Jamieson's point is that even well-motivated, concerned citizens, who have aimed to act on climate change in ways that are fair and effective, have lacked the moral and ethical outlooks and codes adequate to the task. Part of Jamieson's purpose in *Reason in a Dark Time* is to turn our thoughts to the radical revisions to our worldviews and ethical codes that we will need in order to live with – perhaps flourish under – future climate change.

Jamieson does not advocate giving up on ethical approaches to climate change, or just ignoring the problem. Rather, he thinks that the focus of our efforts to act ethically in the face of climate change should shift away from accountability and towards the cultivation of:

> [C]haracter traits, dispositions, and what I shall call virtues. When faced with a global environmental change, our general policy should be to try to reduce our contribution regardless of the behaviour of others, and we are more likely to succeed in doing this by developing and inculcating the right virtues than by improving our calculative abilities. (Jamieson 2010: 318)

In the face of large-scale collective action towards problems like climate change, Jamieson thinks it would be 'madness or cynicism' (Jamieson 2010: 318) to try to calculate, as individuals, what we ought to do in order to do the most good. He thinks we should commit to bringing about the most good – i.e. maximum mitigation, just adaptation, protection for future generations – by crafting our characters to become virtuous. The 'green' virtues he has in mind conform to three types of strategy, all of which will be necessary to 'solve' climate change in ethically acceptable ways (Jamieson 2010: 325). First, we must aim at the preservation of what we already (rightly) value. Here, the virtue of humility in relation to the natural world could be important. Second, we must aim to rehabilitate valuable things we have lost: the virtue of temperance, leading to the reduction of consumption, could be a virtue that serves this strategy. Finally, we must aim to create new ways of valuing the natural world, and one another, that address the roots of the current climate problem. Jamieson identifies mindfulness as a potentially creative virtue in this category; for example, becoming aware of the environmental costs of hitherto mindless behaviour, 'taking on the moral weight of production and disposal when [purchasing] an item of clothing' (Jamieson 2010: 325). I shall return to accounts that focus on 'green' virtues in Chapter 6.

As we move through the chapters in this book, we will see which moral, ethical, and normative political concepts help us to move forward in thinking about climate change. We will also explore the sites of potential action on climate change – political, institutional, personal – which could be informed by these concepts, and consider how these sites of action would have to be reconfigured to enable real movement towards enduring climate justice. For now, let me turn to a worry about this focus that takes aim not at our moral concepts, but at the distance between what the world would have to be like for these concepts to be realised, and what the world is actually like.

Are (fair) climate solutions possible for us?

There are various ways of being sceptical about the prospect of fair, just, or ethical action on climate change. For example, one might think that judgements of what is fair, just, or ethical are nothing more than a matter of personal opinion; or that standards of fairness, justice, or ethics are entirely relative to particular cultures; or that these values and standards, albeit objective, cannot be known by human beings. These forms of scepticism can apply quite generally to moral and ethical values. I shall not engage with these views here beyond saying the following.[9] Even if one of these views is correct, it remains the case that we must make decisions about how to act in the climate crisis. This will involve assessing the quality of arguments for and against different courses of action at multiple levels. These three forms of scepticism address the foundations on which justifications for policy, political, and individual choices are built, but they do not undermine the need for, and possibility of, justifying our choices by reference to values such as fairness or justice. In this respect, scepticism about values leaves everything where it is in the debate about what justice and fairness require in the face of climate change.

A different way of being sceptical about the prospects for fair climate solutions focuses on two features of the current climate problem. First, its nature and scale. As we saw in the first chapter, the carbon budget for 2C is nearly spent, we are still burning fossil fuels, and there are many 'climate surprises' that could prompt the climate crisis to run away from our control. And as we saw earlier in this chapter, effective action on climate change will require political, economic, and social cooperation on a geographical and temporal scale never before seen in human history, in the face of severe temptations to moral corruption.

The second feature of the climate problem that might place fair solutions to it beyond our grasp relates to the limitations of our existing political, economic, and social institutions, and of human nature. Climate experts think that climate change has its origins in the Industrial Revolution, when fossil fuels were first dug up on a massive scale to support what was the biggest period of economic growth in history. In the countries in which the Industrial Revolution happened first, political and economic institutions of capitalism – enabling markets in goods, services, and labour – evolved in ways that enabled consumption of luxury and mass-produced goods. From cotton to cars, cheap beef to bananas, and iPhones to air travel, the last two hundred and fifty years of human history have been made possible by increasingly intense exploitation of fossil fuels in support of mass industrialisation to service the ever-changing desires of the world's most affluent people. In the same period, the global financial system grew, institutions of global governance emerged, and an international order based on the sovereignty of nation-states became entrenched. Perhaps connected with this, it is sometimes claimed, human beings (at least in the most developed countries) have become consumption-oriented, politically docile, and tribal in their political loyalties.

Putting together these two features can deliver grim conclusions: our political, economic, and legal institutions were not designed to deal effectively, let alone fairly, with a problem like climate change; the climate problem is proceeding at a pace that precludes making the necessary changes to these institutions; and people are anyway not motivated to commit to changes on the scale that would be needed even if the pace of climate change was slower. On this view, we are not doomed because there is no such thing as a fair solution to climate change, or because we cannot know what that is. We are doomed because those of us with the potential to make a difference are happy slaves of the institutions that are bringing about our end.

Consider, for example, the 'Manifesto' of The Dark Mountain Project, a UK-based group of artists and writers focused on our ecological crisis, and the social and cultural 'unravelling' that accompanies it. They call their Manifesto *Uncivilisation*:

> Today, humanity is up to its neck in denial about what it has built, what it has become – and what it is in for. Ecological and economic collapse unfold before us and, if we acknowledge them at all, we act as if this were a temporary problem, a technical glitch. Centuries of hubris block our ears like wax plugs; we cannot hear the message which reality is screaming at us. For all our doubts and discontents, we are still wired to an idea of history in which the future will be an upgraded version of the present. The assumption remains that things must continue in their current direction: the sense of crisis only smudges the meaning of that 'must'. No longer a natural inevitability, it becomes an urgent necessity: we must find a way to go on having supermarkets and superhighways. We cannot contemplate the alternative.
>
> And so we find ourselves, all of us together, poised trembling on the edge of a change so massive that we have no way of gauging it. None of us knows where to look, but all of us know not to look down. Secretly, we all think we are doomed: even the politicians think this; even the environmentalists.[10]

Or, consider James Lovelock's direct warning:

> We will do our best to survive, but sadly I cannot see the United States or the emerging economies of China and India cutting back in time, and they are the main source of emissions. The worst will happen, and survivors will have to adapt to a hell of a climate.[11]

If we and our institutions are deeply flawed, and if we are rapidly running out of time, why should we be interested in what political theory and ethics has to say about climate change? There are three reasons to value what political theory and ethics have to say about climate change, even if pessimism with respect to the prospects for fair and effective action on climate change is justified.

First, unless we think that the outcome of current climate change will inevitably be swift and result in total human extinction, the arc of climate pessimism will encompass ongoing efforts by vulnerable people to live with climate impacts.[12] Whatever these impacts might be, there will be better and worse ways of living with them. For example, imagine a world in which the resources necessary for human survival have become so scarce that not everyone can live, and in which there remain only a few thousand people huddled miserably on a ravaged island. Imagine that the most powerful group in what remains of humanity decides to sacrifice all remaining resources – food, medicines, potable water, textiles – to the gods of the climate, in the hope that they quickly reverse global warming. Perhaps the leaders make the biggest bonfire in human history, and dance around it naked. Is this outcome worse than one in which the resources are shared in some way that enables at least some of the remaining thousands to survive? I think most of us would agree that it is. And we would agree this even if we cannot agree on – or even have a clear conception of – the rules that ought to be used to share the resources. In other words, having very little idea of, or agreement on, the best outcome does not prevent us from seeing clearly and agreeing on what outcomes would be worse, or the worst.[13]

The second reason to value perspectives from ethics and political theory despite the enormity of the climate crisis relates to a particular type of pessimism about progress towards fair climate solutions. On this view, people are unable to act in the ways required for fair solutions to the climate crisis: our human nature means that we are doomed to end up in the worst-case climate outcomes.

A good way in which to understand the pessimism of this view is as a claim about the likely inefficacy of human action as a result of the limited motivational capacities of human beings with respect to taking action on climate change. The thought here is that humanity is doomed to climate catastrophe because people can't, or won't, do what is necessary to avoid it. David Estlund offers enlightening reflections on this type of view (Estlund 2011).

Estlund starts with a reasonable definition of what it means for a person to be able to do something:

> A person is able to (can) do something if and only if, were she to try and not give up, she would tend to succeed. (Estlund 2011: 212).

On Estlund's definition, it is possible that 'the inability to bring oneself to do something (to will to do it) might coexist with an ability to do that thing' (Estlund 2011: 213). If this is true then the fact (if it is one) that people cannot muster the will to take action on climate justice does not in itself establish that they cannot – that they are unable to – take that action. Instead, what must be assessed is whether *if people were to try and not give up*, they would tend to succeed with respect to the promotion of climate justice.

It is true that the difference any one person is able to make with respect to climate justice will not amount to much (although note that many of the superrich are able to make a relatively massive difference in comparison to those less rich than them (Tooze 2021)). But this fact (if it is one) has no bearing on the claim under consideration, which instead relates to what *people* could achieve if they tried without giving up. The claim is about the difference that the collective *humanity* could make to the pursuit of climate justice – or, at least, the avoidance of climate injustice – if we were to try and not give up. On this question, the most sceptical view that can be justified is that the jury is out. As a species, we have never before faced a problem like climate change, so we have no historical precedent to look towards. And because we have not really tried to tackle climate change in just ways – that is, persistently, without giving up, and facing the sacrifices needed head-on – we do not know whether we would tend to succeed if we really did try. In other words, we do not know whether we are able to promote climate justice.

At this point the pessimistic line could be pushed harder. For example, it could be objected that human beings are unable to live with sacrificial changes to their lifestyles, that we are unable to live without the various luxury goods that have appeared in the industrial age, or that – more generally – we are unable to act other than in pursuit of our own narrow self-interest. None of these objections stands up. Examples of sacrificial lifestyle change are not uncommon. Consider wartime rationing, or acceptance of Covid restrictions on social mixing. Indeed, many of the world's poorest people already live without luxury goods; and only unloved psychopaths always act in their own narrow self-interest.

However, even if it were a fact that all currently existing people are motivationally incapable of promoting climate justice, this does nothing to show that we are *unable* to promote climate justice. As Estlund nicely puts it:

> Suppose people line up to get your moral opinion on their behaviour. Bill is told that his selfishness is indeed a motivational incapacity, but that it does not exempt him from the requirement to be less selfish. Behind Bill comes Nina with the same query. Again, we dispatch her, on the same grounds as Bill. Behind Nina is Kim, and so on. Since each poses the same case, our judgement is the same. The line might contain all humans, but that fact adds nothing to any individual's case. (Estlund 2011: 220–1)

The third way in which political theory can help us to think about ways forward in the climate crisis relates to how we envision a world in which climate injustice is lessened, perhaps to the point of being entirely eradicated. Following G.A. Cohen, questions about the difficulty of getting from a state of extreme injustice to one of less (perhaps, no) injustice – what he calls questions of 'accessibility' – are not the only important questions to ask when evaluating a proposal for new institutions or forms of social and political organisation. We need to also consider the 'stability' of the proposal; that is, whether the proposal would be stable *if* we could get from here to there (Cohen 2009: 56–7). This means considering whether the institutions and new forms of organisation would themselves undermine, or shore up, the conditions for their own stability by eroding or encouraging the relevant commitments of people living with them. Our design of institutions fit to lessen climate injustice should be responsive to the requirement that these institutions should be stable, i.e. that they should endure and strengthen over time. For example, massive reductions in climate injustice might be accessible to us by abandoning democratic politics: a green dictatorship might be able to effect climate policy far more quickly, and with a higher degree of compliance, than the political institutions of democratic societies.[14] Taking Cohen's reflections on stability seriously means that this is not the end of the story: we must also think about whether nondemocratic institutions could generate forms of motivation, commitments, and a social ethos that would enable them to endure in ways effective for the purpose of climate justice. How far could we get with respect to the long-term project of securing climate justice if the people who have to see this project through are motivated by fear of disobedience, lack democratic solidarity with one another, and are dominated by an unaccountable political class?

Conclusion

This chapter has surveyed ways in which thinking about the nature of the climate crisis – and many other environmental problems – has evolved over recent decades. It is safe to say very few political theorists deny that climate change is a problem of justice – even when they disagree about the kind of justice that is at stake (Gardiner and Weisbach 2016; Posner and Weisbach 2010). At the same time, the worsening climate crisis – and the lack of ambition that is increasingly evident as entrenched in international climate politics – is leading some political theorists and ethicists to contemplate what justice requires (if anything) in scenarios of climate catastrophe creating extreme scarcity, political disintegration, and breakdown of international cooperation.

I shall return to these thoughts at the end of the book. For now, we should take heart: all is not yet lost. If we take climate change seriously as an ethical challenge, requiring the reduction of injustice, how should we tackle the climate crisis? The first step is to think about the victims of climate change.

3

Who are the Victims of Climate Injustice?

Climate change is often described as humanity's greatest challenge. In one respect, this is obviously correct: never before in human history has *Homo sapiens* imposed catastrophic risks on itself as a result of the unintended consequences of people simply going about their normal lives.[1] However, in a very important respect this framing is misleading. Human beings and their communities are not 'all in this together'. Some people are much better placed than others to adapt to climate impacts (perhaps even to benefit from them). Perhaps there are even a few of us who will be able to avoid climate impacts altogether if the techno-optimism of billionaires like Elon Musk allow the rich to escape from the planet.[2] Certainly, some communities and nations are more able than others to influence which climate scenarios for the future become history. This could be because their historical and/or present emissions make a large contribution to climate change (and so their mitigation efforts would be more impactful than those of groups with lower emissions), or because they have a more power to influence the political and economic direction of travel on climate change, or both.

The fact that vulnerability, resilience, power, and emissions flows are not evenly distributed across people, combined with the fact that climate change is being caused by human activity – and that its impacts on some people can be addressed by other people in positions of advantage – brings climate change into the domain of justice. Political theorists have rich, long, and diverse traditions of thinking about the nature, scope, and demands of justice. The recent upwelling of concern about climate justice in civil society raises questions about fair and equitable solutions to climate change that are the bread and butter of political theory. In this chapter I shall map some of the insights brought by political theory to climate justice by focusing on different groups of victims, and how the climate impacts they face – now and into the future – count as injustices. This is not to suggest that individual people and communities must fall into only one category. Some communities are sites of unjust disadvantage along multiple dimensions. Indeed, these are the communities that must take priority in action on climate change from the point of view of climate justice.

By using the words 'victim' and 'victimhood' I do not mean to suggest that those damaged by unjust climate impacts always lack agency of their own to find solutions, and are dependent on help from outsiders (as has sometimes been evident in the 'white saviour' response to famines in Africa). Bottom-up and homegrown solutions – making use of local knowledge, collective action, and skills embedded in communities – must be a central plank in any effort to translate NDCs into meaningful climate action. Instead, the language of victimhood indicates that the damage caused by climate impacts is not normatively neutral. Victims of climate change have their lives destroyed as a result of what other people do or fail to do, and justice tells us that victims should not have to bear the costs of such damages, despite the fact that strategies of adaptation and renewal are best devised by those who need them. In the cases of most damage, climate victims can be almost entirely robbed of agency by having their livelihoods, networks of support, and communities of meaning destroyed. Climate change creates climate victims. What does justice have to say about this?

There are two broad ways to think about the injustices suffered by climate victims. First, they could be conceived as freestanding and in need of address by principles and practices of justice specific to the climate domain. For example, Lukas Meyer and Dominic Roser argue for a per capita approach to the distribution of rights to greenhouse gas emissions by appealing to the importance of giving priority to those who have emitted least (Meyer and Roser 2006, 2010; Singer 2006). On this view, those who have emitted less than their equal per capita allocation have a right to emit more than those who have exceeded their equal per capita allocation. This type of approach is sometimes called 'isolationist' because it treats the injustices of climate change in isolation from broader sets of injustices and the principles that address them. In contrast, 'integrationist' approaches to climate justice embed arguments for principles and practices to reduce injustice in larger debates and histories. For example, Simon Caney argues that the unjust disadvantages suffered by victims of climate change – for example, loss of livelihood, illness, and displacement – are not new, and the distribution of these disadvantages by climate impacts is deeply intertwined with other injustices such as global poverty, histories of colonialism, health inequalities, injustice in trade, and corporate tax avoidance (Caney 2012b, 2020; Hayward 2007).

Should we be integrationists or isolationists about climate justice? For the large part we cannot answer this question in abstraction from analysis of the climate impacts that stand as prima facie climate injustices. For example, if we think that the depletion of the carbon budget by early-industrialising countries creates injustice for less developed countries only because their rightful share of the budget has been used up by early industrialisers, and that there is nothing more to the injustice than that, then an isolationist approach is vindicated. If, however, we think that what matters about being denied a rightful share of the carbon budget is that this will violate the basic rights of people in less developed countries, and has been made possible by historic abuses of power by early industrialisers – and that a failure to understand these things will generate mistakes about the nature, significance, and prevention of the injustice – then integrationism is the only option.

Beyond conceptual matters there also lie pragmatic considerations. For example, an isolationist might argue as follows. The urgency of the climate crisis and the depth of disagreement on ethical questions makes integrationism unrealistic: integrationism requires an understanding of the many dimensions of injustice made worse by climate change but we lack the time and capacity that would be needed for this. Integrationists offer a different perspective: by calling out climate injustice for what it is, viz. one of the many faces of global and intergenerational injustice, we have an opportunity to make radical progress to reduce injustice across multiple domains at the same time. In the remainder of this book I shall be mostly neutral about the isolationist/integrationist debate, leaving readers to form their own view on the status of the injustices created by climate change.

My discussion of the victims of climate injustice will be organised through a focus on the following groups, and the distinctive damages members of these groups stand to suffer as a result of climate change: people in the global South; indigenous people and displaced people; and future people. What these groups share is accentuated vulnerability to climate impacts, and (at most) a minor role in the human activity that is causing climate change.

How does climate change worsen injustice for the people of the global South?

It is clear that the impacts of climate change will be much worse for people in the global South than those in the global North. Many harmful climate impacts will also hit people in the global South sooner than in the global North. Stephen Gardiner calls this fact about climate change 'skewed vulnerabilities' (Gardiner 2011). Consider the following three sites of concern.

First, recent studies have projected increased extreme heat events for tropical regions in Africa and South Asia. Deadly heat-waves that combine sustained temperatures above 35C with >90% humidity for weeks on end are projected to become annual, rather than 25 yearly, events in these regions (Harrington and Otto 2020; Im, Pal, and Eltahir 2017). This combination of temperature and humidity (sometimes referred to as 'wet bulb' temperature) is the upper limit at which humans can survive (Sherwood and Huber 2010). By 2070, 1.5 billion people in Africa and South Asia will be at risk as deadly heatwaves multiply.

Second, the World Food Programme (WFP) reports that food security in the world's poorest places could be severely undermined if radical action is not taken to address a complex of climate-related impacts including availability of food, access to it, utilisation (e.g. for nutrition), and stability of supply. Drought, rainfall, temperature increase, sea-level rise, tropical storms, and existing levels of health and nutrition in a population affect food security. Climate change causes these impacts, or acts as a 'threat multiplier' for existing levels disadvantage (e.g. health-related).[3] These effects will fall disproportionately on people in the global South: especially sub-Saharan Africa, South and South East Asia.[4]

Third, rising temperatures in sub-Saharan Africa make plausible scenarios in which the disease burden is shifted from malaria (which peaks in transmission at 25C) to dengue fever (which peaks in transmission at 29C) and other arboviruses (such as Zika and West Nile fever). Experts worry that regions that could be affected lack the public health infrastructure of healthcare systems, disease control strategies, surveillance capability etc. to act quickly to prevent, or respond, to what could be an accelerating threat of increased arboviral disease spread (Mordecai et al. 2020).

Vulnerabilities are not only skewed across different places in the world. They are also skewed across sexes, with women suffering more than men in most domains of climate harm.[5] For example, 64% of studies find that women are more likely than men to suffer death and injury from extreme weather events; 79% find that women are more likely than men to suffer food insecurity; and 69% find that women are more likely than men to suffer poor mental health as a result of climate change.[6]

Why are vulnerabilities to climate impacts skewed across regions, and sexes? Part of the explanation is that existing meteorological conditions in many places in the global South make them particularly susceptible to the relatively large changes in temperature and precipitation patterns that climate change causes. For example, the high average temperatures and low-lying territory in Bangladesh make it imminently vulnerable to sea-level rise, flooding as a result of glacial melt in the Himalayas, and deadly heatwaves, in a way that Scotland is not.[7]

However, a moment's reflection lets us see that the topography and biophysical conditions in Bangladesh are only a part – and possibly a small part – of the story of its vulnerability to climate change. Bangladesh is one of the most densely populated countries in the world, with a growing population, which places increasing demands on land and water. Bangladesh is heavily dependent on rice cultivation, which could be severely impacted by rising sea levels and water shortages. 56% of households already report food insecurity during the year. Half a million people from rural and coastal areas are already moving to cities in Bangladesh each year, increasing pressures on resources in these places. Although Bangladesh has made significant improvements in recognising and implementing women's rights, it remains the case that women and girls are more vulnerable to climate impacts than men. This is a product of, for example, the fact that women are often excluded from decision-making processes, lack independent access to information about climate change, are less likely than men to relocate internally in the face of climate impacts, and have worse nutrition (as a result of only eating after men have finished). Poverty and a lack of resilience to climate impacts in Bangladesh have not come from nowhere. Bangladesh's turbulent political history, and lack of development, are intertwined with its origins in the rushed and reckless partition of India at the end of British colonial rule. Partition created East Pakistan, which became Bangladesh in 1971 after a war of independence backed by India. The colonial roots of Bangladesh's socioeconomic vulnerability to climate impacts matter for understanding responsibilities for addressing climate change.

A common way to understand the damage done to people in the global South by climate change is in terms of human rights. Human rights are legally enforceable protections and/or claims that correlate with obligations held by others. Rights are always held against other persons or groups: in principle, any person's human rights generate accountability for others who have a duty to respect these rights in their conduct. Human rights provide a prima facie attractive framework for thinking about climate injustice because they provide a focus on people, are action-guiding,[8] and already exist in multiple legal agreements in the international domain that reach within state borders (e.g. the European Convention on Human Rights).

Many political theorists have endorsed a human rights framework as morally appropriate for capturing the variety of harms inflicted on people in the global South by climate change. Existing legal conventions and declarations specify many different rights; for example, the UN Universal Declaration of Human Rights attributes to all people the right to life (Article 3), the right to own property (Article 17), the right to form and join labour unions (Article 23.4), and the right to rest and leisure (Article 24). One important advantage of using a human rights framework for thinking about climate justice is that it provides a currency for climate policymaking that specifies moral thresholds. But unless we have a way of ranking human rights in terms of their moral urgency we will be unable to guide policymaking in common cases in which climate change impacts on a variety of different people's rights, and we cannot act to prevent all rights violations. For example, if all human rights are of equal moral urgency, how should a national government act when an extreme weather event (caused by climate change) threatens the food security of one community, the property of a second community, and the access to rest and leisure of a third community?

Henry Shue's identification of a category of human rights of particular salience for climate injustice – basic rights – solves this problem. Basic rights are rights without which no other rights can be enjoyed, e.g. rights to life, physical security, means of subsistence, and freedom from torture and violence. Basic rights can specify side-constraints upon action (e.g. refraining from killing a rights-holder) and proactive conduct to satisfy the right (e.g. provision of food to a starving child). Basic rights are a guide to 'the morality of the depths. They specify the line below which no one is to be allowed to sink' (Shue 1996: 18; Shue 2020).[9] Basic rights take priority over other rights in climate policymaking. Although climate change threatens everyone's human rights, vulnerabilities are skewed because the people of the global South – women and girls in particular – face disproportionate threats to their basic rights.

Simon Caney argues that human rights are policy-guiding even if we adopt a minimally controversial interpretation of basic rights. On this interpretation, basic rights never compel us to act and only ever require us to refrain from acting (Caney 2010a): basic rights only ever correlate with so-called 'negative' duties,[10] and very few people would deny that the existence of universal duties not to actively do things that will violate the basic rights of others. Even on this minimalist view, the violation of the basic rights of people in the global South caused by climate change creates duties for more advantaged people to alter their conduct. On the minimalist view, the right to life is a right not to be arbitrarily deprived of life; climate change, caused by the disproportionate emissions of people in the global North, violates this right. The right to health is a right that others do not act so as to create serious risks to one's health, and the emissions of people in the global North cause this right to be violated. Finally, the right to subsistence is a right not to be deprived of the means of subsistence, and climate change, which is disproportionately caused by the emissions of people in the global North, is violating this right. The fundamental moral importance of basic rights, the ways in which climate change can violate them, and the uneven distribution of these violations affecting people in the global South worst and soonest, create an imperative to mitigate. I shall address questions of responsibility for climate change, and differential emissions, in Chapter 5.

In addition to the mitigation imperative, the skewed vulnerabilities of people in the global South are reflected in calls for sustainable development and/or green growth as core strategies of adaptation to climate change.[11] The moral force of these calls draws on the priority of basic rights over other rights. The ways in which climate change impacts on people in the global South – disproportionately violating rights without which no other rights can be enjoyed – makes support for sustainable development in these places a requirement of justice. As Henry Shue puts it:

[J]ustice requires that one not begin [to tackle climate change] by slowing the economic development of the countries in which considerable numbers of people are already close to the edge of starvation just so that the affluent can retain more of their affluence than they could if they contributed more and the poor contributed less. Poor nations, therefore, ought not to be required to make sacrifices in their sustainable development. Even in an emergency one pawns the jewellery before selling the blankets. (Shue 2014d: 46)

How does climate change wrong indigenous people and displaced people?

There is no official definition of 'indigenous', given the diversity of peoples that fall into this category; for example, the Maori people in New Zealand, the Saami people in northern Europe, the Potawatomi people of North America, the Inuit peoples of the circumpolar region, and the Aboriginal people of Australia.[12] Nevertheless, many indigenous peoples share characteristics. They are groups that retain social, cultural, economic, and political characteristics that are distinct from those of the dominant society in which they live. They often have historical continuity with pre-colonial and pre-settler societies, a distinct language and set of cultural beliefs, and are resolved to retain their distinctive identities and relationships with ancestral environments. There are 370 million indigenous people worldwide, spread across seventy countries.

Indigenous people are particularly vulnerable to climate change for six key reasons.[13] First, 70–80% of the world's indigenous people live in Asia and the Pacific, and this region is particularly at risk from climate change. Although indigenous people constitute around 5% of the global population they are 15% of the world's poor. Second, many indigenous people depend on the land and natural resources for their livelihoods, and so will be immediately damaged by climate impacts: for example, seventy million indigenous people depend on forests for their livelihoods. It is worth noting that although indigenous people are only 5% of the global population they are stewards of 80% of the world's remaining biodiversity. Third, indigenous people live in parts of the world already being transformed by climate change, such as polar regions, mountains, tropical forests, small islands, and coastal areas. The damage being done to these places by climate change makes it impossible for them to continue to live according to their traditions and values. In addition, measures adopted to mitigate climate change – such as large-scale renewable energy projects or conservation efforts – can often take place on indigenous territories, and indigenous peoples' rights to their lands are often not recognised. Fourth, indigenous people suffer disproportionately from forced climate displacement and resettlement, which destroys livelihoods, communities, and identity. Indigenous people who relocate to cities often struggle to find decent work and accommodation and are at heightened risk of exploitation and hazardous work in informal urban economies. Fifth, indigenous women are acutely at risk from climate change. They often face discrimination from outside and from within their communities, and bear the burden of generating income and performing unpaid domestic labour. When displaced to informal urban economies they are at greater risk of violence, abuse, and exploitation. Finally, although the human rights of indigenous people are recognised at the international level in the ILO Convention on Indigenous and Tribal Peoples 1989 (no. 169), only twenty-three countries have ratified the Treaty and implementation and accountability is weak.[14] Indigenous people are excluded from meaningful participation in decision-making on climate policy, and their voices are absent.

There is a growing recognition in political theory that mainstream approaches to climate justice and ethics are blind not only to the distinctive harms suffered by indigenous people as a result of climate change, but also to indigenous worldviews on climate change, which tell a very different story to the one that dominates debates. The dominant story is that climate change is a product of increasing GHG emissions from around 1750 onwards, when industrialisation began. On this story, the first best solution is to reduce emissions as quickly as possible in order to establish a global net-zero economy, which will eventually (ideally, if we are lucky) lead to the stabilisation of average global temperatures at under 2C. Some indigenous thinkers challenge this narrative. Kyle Powys Whyte argues that this story's focus on ecological tipping points – biophysical moments and processes we must avoid if we are to minimise risks of dangerous climate change – obscures the relational tipping points that matter for indigenous people:

> The relational tipping point concerns the inaction of societies to establish or maintain relational qualities connecting social institutions together for the sake of coordinated action. Such inaction eventually makes it impossible to carry out swift responses to urgent problems without perpetrating injustices . . . While many people are concerned about crossing the ecological tipping point, the relational tipping point got crossed long ago thanks to systems of colonialism, capitalism, and industrialisation. (Whyte 2020: 3)

The relationships necessary to create social and political institutions that deliver justice for all require trust, reciprocity, and respect if meaningful consent is to be possible. These relations do not exist between many – perhaps most (or all?) – indigenous peoples and dominant groups. The genocidal and shameful histories of colonialism, coupled with capitalism's treatment of the natural world as a resource for conversion into products and profits using industrial techniques, destroyed these relations. Whyte argues that restoring them, if it is possible at all, is the work of generations. This timescale does not superimpose onto the timescales for action to avoid ecological tipping points. This means that a commitment to climate justice forces us to face hard questions. Will we sacrifice justice for indigenous people by abandoning building relations of trust and respect, in favour of aggressive, whatever-it-takes action to avoid ecological tipping points? Or will we prioritise building 'kin' relationships with indigenous peoples, accepting that this will take decades if not longer, despite the escalating climate risks this will create? Or, Whyte asks us, '[a]re there additional possible futures, and ones that do not sacrifice indigenous consent, trust, accountability, and reciprocity? Can these qualities and relations be established at the pace of urgency?' (Whyte 2020: 5).

Turning to the distinctive harms suffered by indigenous people, the types of conditions necessary for many of their basic rights to be fulfilled are often sites of acute vulnerability to climate change. Consider the people of Kiribati in the Pacific Ocean. Kiribati is a nation-state comprised of 33 low-lying atolls that are on average only 2m above sea level. It is disappearing under the sea and is very unlikely to exist by 2100. Kiribati's political leaders have mooted ideas such as building sea walls, and creating floating islands to which people can migrate. The Kiribati government bought an island in Fiji to which a number of Kiribati people moved. Most recently, plans have been laid to dredge materials from a lagoon near the main island of Tarawa in order to raise the islands to avoid submersion.[15]

The people of Kiribati face an accelerating threat to their basic rights to subsistence, health, and life. They also face a loss of identity, culture, and self-determination given the nature of their homeland and the imminent existential threat posed to it by climate change (de Shalit 2011; Figueroa 2011; Heyward 2014; Zellentin 2015, 2010). These types of losses have been inflicted on indigenous peoples throughout history by settler colonists, and industrialist land grabs. For the people of Kiribati – tied to the sea, bound together in clans that share land, dancing to mimic birds, and meeting in the maneaba (meeting house) – the violation of their basic rights through the loss of their territory to the sea means being deprived of all these things.

The vectors of vulnerability for indigenous people make these losses incommensurable; that is, losses such as these cannot be compared to or ranked in value against other valuable goods. To illustrate, money has value for most people, but the value of a homeland cannot be given a monetary value. Money and homeland are incommensurably valuable. This means that a simple model of monetary compensation for the people of Kiribati, delivered by the international community or by high emitters, is inappropriate. Because homeland and money are incommensurable, no amount of money will enable the people of Kiribati to replace what they lose to the sea.[16] Instead of aiming to replace homeland as a means to the identity and self-determination of Kiribati people, we could instead focus on enabling them to form new ends and purposes, which are severed from their islands.[17]

Cara Nine's interpretation of this view of what is owed to indigenous peoples whose homelands are disappearing in the face of existential climate threats – she calls them 'ecological refugee states' – is that these people are owed sovereignty over a new territory to enable their continued self-determination. Other states might have to relinquish their territory to meet this obligation (Nine 2010). Her argument draws on a famous condition set on the acquisition of private property deployed by the political philosopher John Locke (1632–1704). Locke's 'as much and as good' proviso states that property rights are just and legitimate if and only if there is as much and as good left for others to acquire similar property rights.[18] One person's acquisition cannot deprive all others of the same opportunity to acquire. Applying this proviso to the case of ecological refugee states like Kiribati, Nine argues that:

> Currently there are 193 states in the world, each with its own territory. There is no inhabitable land that is not a territory. The self-determination of any group whose territory is destroyed, or made unusable, as is the case with ecological refugee states, is threatened with extinction because of the group's lack of access to the territories of others. States with territorial rights over viable lands have an obligation to allow reasonable access to their territory to the ecological refugee states. (Nine 2010: 366)

Locke's arguments for private property assume a baseline of original shared ownership of the Earth: on his view, 'God gave the world to men in common . . . and labour was to be his title to it' (Locke 1988: s34).[19] The idea that common or shared ownership of the Earth is the pre-political state of human beings in nature is disputed (Abizadeh 2014; Olsthoorn 2018; Stilz 2014). It is worth noting, however, that a version of Nine's argument for territorial rights for ecological refugees states could go through even if we abandon the assumption of original common ownership. Robert Nozick rejects the idea of common ownership and yet still makes the following claims about the limits of private property rights:

[A] person may not appropriate the only water hole in a desert and charge what he will. Nor may he charge what he will if he possesses one, and unfortunately it happens that all the water holes in the desert dry up, except for his. This unfortunate circumstance, admittedly no fault of his, brings into operation the Lockean proviso and limits his property rights. (Nozick 1974: 180)

On Nozick's view, no one can have rights over resources that are necessary for survival when those rights deliver a monopoly. Thinking about the plight of ecological refugees using this frame, it is clear that existing states have a monopoly over territory: there are no unowned places in the world. A key question is: what does 'survival' mean in this context? Does the survival of indigenous peoples depend on protection of their cultural identity? And, for people of ecological refugee states, does the connection between cultural identity and place make it a requirement of justice that they be granted a new territory (Bell 2004; de Shalit 2011; Zellentin 2015)? Does this requirement set limits on the types of territory that are suitable for this requirement to be met? For example, do the people of Kiribati need territory that enables fishing practices very similar to those they have traditionally pursued?

Some political theorists have advocated for remedies to the injustice of territorial dispossession that do not require provision of new territory, and so do not face these problems. For example, Clare Heyward and Jörgen Ödalen argue for a passport for territorially dispossessed people granting them freedom of movement, on the grounds that this is a 'second-best' response required by justice when full or perfect redress is not possible (Heyward and Ödalen 2016).[20] This passport would require states to grant citizenship to its holders, thus giving holders a free choice of where to relocate.

On both territorial and non-territorial approaches there are important questions about implementation to avoid exacerbating already existing injustices (climate-related and non-climate related). The places to which ecological refugee states and their peoples might want to relocate, or the citizenship they might most prefer, might be in the domain of states that are themselves suffering from climate damages, or which are otherwise unjustly disadvantaged. How can the injustices suffered by indigenous people as a result of climate change be addressed without worsening the injustices suffered by other people (Draper 2020)?

At this point, questions arise with respect to people displaced by climate change per se, regardless of whether they are indigenous (Draper and McKinnon 2018; Johnson 2012). Estimates vary widely, but it is expected that by 2050 between 25 million (roughly, the population of Australia) and one billion people will be displaced by climate change. The drivers of this displacement are multiple and many are already operating. They include sudden and slow onset extreme weather (e.g. Hurricane Katrina, or the shrinkage of Lake Chad);[21] impacts on crops and water (e.g. the disruption of monsoons in Asia);[22] rising sea levels (e.g. the submersion of Isle de Jean Charles in Louisiana);[23] conflict (e.g. in Syria (Kelley et al. 2015));[24] and, displacement induced by development aimed at tackling climate change (e.g. the Sami people of Norway).[25]

There are two broad categories of climate-displaced persons: those who cross state borders, and internally displaced people. In both categories numbers are hard to estimate beyond top-line figures such as those given in the previous paragraph. This is in part because it can be hard to attribute specific events that displace people to climate change: floods, droughts, and hurricanes happen naturally as well as being manifestations of a changing climate.[26] That said, the World Bank gives the following estimates for internal displacement by climate change by 2050: 86 million in sub-Saharan Africa; 40 million in South Asia; and 17 million in Latin America.[27]

Figures for cross-border forced displacement by climate change are even harder to come by. This is in part because existing international refugee law only recognises as refugees people forced from their home countries as a result of persecution based on race, religion, ethnicity, or political opinion. The legal status of refugee does not at present apply to people displaced across borders by climate change (or other environmental disasters). A number of political theorists have argued that the category of refugee should be expanded to include such people (Bell 2004; Eckersley 2015; McEldowney and Drolet 2021; de Shalit 2011; Wilcox 2021). An alternative approach advocates for new international governance specifically to deal with cross-border climate refugees: for example, Frank Biermann and Ingrid Boas argue for a Protocol on the Recognition, Protection, and Resettlement of Climate Refugees to be housed in the UNFCC, and accompanied by a Climate Refugee Protection and Resettlement Fund (Biermann and Boas 2008).[28]

A different perspective for both cross-border and internally displaced people involves a 'bottom–up' approach. With Alex Arnall and Christopher Hilson, I have argued the capacities of affected people themselves to develop and formulate their own justice-based solutions to the problems of climate-induced displacement require much more attention (Arnall, Hilson, and McKinnon 2019). Such 'bottom–up' processes of claims-making could put new and potentially powerful forms of pressure on local and national governments, and international bodies, as they attempt to manage displaced communities. Moreover, the pervasiveness of climate change means that it is highly likely that communities will need to play a central role in organising themselves and advancing their own claims in the face of displacement and resettlement rather than relying solely on central governments and authorities. In these cases, communities will benefit from knowledge of what has and has not worked best in prior community-based claims-making processes.

Bottom–up claims-making involves communities exerting agency to mobilise for a desired outcome in relation to climate displacement and resettlement. For some, the desired outcome will be for their whole community to be physically moved to a new location and for financial support to be provided to enable this; for others, it will be to prevent an unwanted resettlement from taking place. Where resettlement of a community as a whole is not possible, claims might be made for alternative forms of redress, such as individual compensation to relocate.

Although claims-making can progress in different ways, it is our contention that unpacking the constituent parts of the process involved provides a useful lens through which to view climate displacement and resettlement. To this end, we draw on Felstiner et al. (Felstiner, Abel, and Sarat 1980), who identify three steps in the claims-making process: naming, blaming and claiming, to which we would add one more: framing.

Naming requires affected communities to identify and designate climate change as the main driver behind their displacement. This matters for future empirical research in this area. We need to know when communities name, or deliberately do not name, climate change as the underlying cause of their move. In some cases, communities might, for strategic reasons, decide to emphasise climate change as the cause of their grievance; in other cases, the role of climate change might be downplayed or contested. It might be downplayed because a community does not want the 'baggage' that can come with describing their move in these terms: they could, for example, be suspicious of the international non-governmental organisation involvement that it is likely to attract, or be wary of government interest due to a history of past exploitation (Maldonado et al. 2013). It might be contested because the community is resisting forced relocation, which is driven by other motives but where the state is using climate change as a convenient cloak (Kothari 2014).

Next, blaming is a matter of establishing which party or parties are responsible for the climate displacement and thus who could in theory be the object of the claim (i.e. relational grievance). This raises the issue of the geographical scale at which claims-making takes place: in principle, claims might be made at one or more of local, regional or national government, or even at international levels. Equally, the objects of claims could be private-sector corporates, states or sub-state public-sector bodies.

Claiming is the final stage wherein communities make demands using the range of different mobilisation strategies referred to above, including protest, litigation, and political lobbying. Thus, for example, the Guna people on the Panamanian island of Gardi Sugdub, faced with rising sea-levels, have engaged in political lobbying to secure government funding for the infrastructure and house-building costs associated with a move to a new village at La

Barriada on the mainland. They have also protested over continued delays to the opening of the new village school promised by the Panamanian government. Claims-making in the form of climate displacement litigation, which forms a sub-genre of 'climate change litigation', has been less common. Thus far, the only obvious example of community-based litigation known to us is the Kivalina case, in which an Alaskan Native American community faced with inundation of its coastal village sued ExxonMobil for damages to pay for relocation (Johnson 2013). The case ultimately failed. However, if the mushrooming of other forms of climate litigation is instructive, this is likely to be a growing area.

The final component of claims-making, on our view, is framing. Framing describes the way in which 'actors define the issue for their audience . . . A frame highlights some aspects of a perceived reality and enhances a certain interpretation or evalua-tion of reality' (Hänggli and Kriesi 2012: 266). Of course, naming, considered above, is itself a form of initial framing. However, framing plays an even more important role later in the claims-making process. Regardless of how claiming is channelled (e.g. the streets – when claiming coincides with protest – the courts, or political institutions), communities are likely to seek to frame their claims in a language that emphasises what matters for them. Ideally, this framing should also resonate with the wider public and policymakers who are the object of their claims. Frames may be legal in nature (such as human rights) and may be deployed in non-court settings as well as court-based ones. Frames may, equally, be non-legal in nature, drawing on alternative normative justifications such as justice, security, and humanitarianism.

Bottom-up claims-making is not a panacea. Some communities might be reluctant to advance claims, or be unsure of how to do so, particularly those with long experience of oppression. Other communities might expend considerable energy on making claims that go nowhere. Some claims-making might provoke backlash against a community and change the ways in which similarly situ-ated communities pursue claims in the future. This is a reason why people often engage in 'hidden' forms of resistance rather than pursue open protest (Scott 1985). These points emphasise the

importance of the wider structural conditions within which communities are located and the political and legal opportunities for,
and barriers to, claims-making that result from these.

What do we owe to future people in the climate crisis?

People who will come into existence in the future are particularly
vulnerable to climate impacts. Time's arrow travels in just one
direction which means that any temporal cohort of people cannot
be held directly accountable by the majority of future people for any
harm they often inflict on them. Furthermore, any set of people
in the present will not see most of the risk they impose ripen into
harm, which makes it tempting for present people to ignore the
moral salience of these risks in their decision-making. Vulnerability
is especially acute for future people in groups discussed in the
previous sections: poor people, indigenous people, and those at
risk of displacement. And within these groups, women, children,
and people with disabilities are the most vulnerable.

There has been an explosion of philosophical interest in intergenerational ethics and justice in the last few decades, which reflects
the growing recognition in academia and in the public imagination
that what we, the people of the early Anthropocene, are doing
and failing to do will have consequences for generations many
hundreds, if not thousands and tens of thousands, of years from
now. A number of compelling theories of intergenerational ethics,
telling us what present people owe to future people, and why they
owe this, have evolved in the literature. Key approaches include:

- *Intergenerational duties as indirect reciprocity*: any current generation
  has an obligation to deliver at least equivalent benefits to the
  next generation as it received from the generation preceding it
  (Barry 1977).
- *Intergenerational duties as community bonds*: generations are bound
  together in forms of political community with one another

that generate duties for each generation to sustain environmental and other conditions necessary for continued community through time (de Shalit 1994; Thompson 2009).

- *Intergenerational duties as a requirement of justice as fairness*: John Rawls' theory of justice contains a principle of justice to protect future people – the 'just savings' principle. This principle directs any generation to conserve resources that will enable future generations to achieve and sustain a just society (McKinnon 2012; Rawls 2001).

- *Intergenerational duties to leave enough for future people*: Independent of the relations that present people have, or ought to have, with future people, present people have a duty to ensure that future people are bequeathed sufficient resources per se, or to deliver sufficient levels of well-being (Gosseries 2016; Page 2007).

- *Intergenerational duties that correlate with the rights of future people*: If future people will have the basic rights that Henry Shue argues give us 'the morality of the depths' (e.g. rights to subsistence, health, life, etc.), then present people have duties to ensure these rights are not violated. The fact that these rights do not yet exist does not undermine the duties they impose on us in the present (Caney 2008; Meyer 2003).[29]

- *Intergenerational duties to maximise the well-being of future people*: This approach draws on a rich history of utilitarian thinking which is not always straightforward to translate into intergenerational duties, especially towards people in the far future. Dale Jamieson develops a version of this view that emphasises the cultivation of certain virtues and character traits such as humility that are likely to promote the well-being of future people (Jamieson 2010). Tim Mulgan's version of this view casts it in terms of the adoption and intergenerational transmission of a moral code fit to bring about the maximisation of collective well-being in circumstances of great uncertainty about the future (Mulgan 2017).

The philosophical debates between advocates of different approaches to intergenerational ethics lie beyond the scope of this book (Gardiner 2021). This is especially the case given that, with respect to the duties of the present generation to future people in the climate crisis, all roads lead to Rome. What I mean by this is that there is agreement between theorists on the following points despite their multiple and more fundamental philosophical disagreements:

a. Present people have duties to future people – including those not yet born – to take action on climate change.
b. This action will require radical change – for example, to institutions, forms of social cooperation, cultural norms and practices, global economic structures, visions of what makes a life good – that will be costly to present people.
c. This action is not being taken.
d. The longer present people delay taking action, the harder it will be to achieve change, and the greater the risks to future people.

We are failing to act on climate change so comprehensively that the fine distinctions between different theoretical approaches to what we owe to future people have few implications for what we ought to do now: all roads lead to Rome. Imagine a different present in which people take aggressive and immediate action on climate change so as to: remain within the carbon budget for 2C; properly support and resource adaptation to the climate change we cannot now avoid; raise up women and people with disabilities; build trust with indigenous peoples; and enable a swift and fair transition to a zero-carbon global economy by 2050. The achievement of these things could mean that, for example, the debate about whether we owe future people sufficient resources for a decent life or resources fit to maximise their well-being could become live, and make a difference to the policy pathways we choose en route out of the climate crisis. In comparison to the reality of our situation in the present, we would be blessed to be in that scenario.[30]

Theories of intergenerational justice converge on the view that the point in time at which a person is born does not, in itself, have relevance to their moral status – their 'considerability' in ethically informed action. What difference does this make to climate policymaking and politics? There are two key areas I shall discuss.

The first relates to presently dominant methods in policymaking that deny moral status to some or most people in the future, and the second relates to the presentist bias that is built in to most of our political institutions across the board.

When trying to set policy that could have impacts down the generations to come, how much can be expected of any set of people in the present? Given that we do not know how many people there will be in the future (potentially, there could be far more than have ever lived to date), how much should people in the present sacrifice in order to make good on what they owe to people in the future?

A first thought might be: 'whatever it takes'. However, this suggests that sets of people coming in and out of existence might be required to make everlasting, and potentially large, sacrifices in order to fulfil their duties to future people. This is especially the case with respect to some utilitarian approaches that require advantaged people in the present to reduce themselves and their families to the 'point of marginal utility' in an effort to improve the position of much less advantaged people elsewhere in the world (Singer 1972). The point of marginal utility is the point at which any further sacrifice on the part of an individual would be detrimental to maximising the overall utility of the collective. If we extend this approach to intergenerational obligations, our deep uncertainty about the number of people who will come into existence in the future, and the conditions in which they will live, seems to require generations of humanity to make extremely demanding sacrifices for the sake of the future.[31]

One reply here is to deny that this is a problem at all. Obligations can be demanding, and this is especially so in the Anthropocene, given how our technologies and interventions in the natural world have the potential to change things forever for all future people. With great power comes great responsibility, and this responsibility creates burdens that present people cannot justify evading.

There are some deep waters here. For example, is it reasonable to expect any set of people in the present to bear burdens that are heavier than they would have been had all people in the past fulfilled their duties to future people? If the Boomers lived high on fossil fuels despite knowing enough about climate change to realise the consequences, is it unfair that Millennials face climate challenges that will require sacrifices far greater than would have been necessary had the Boomers acted responsibly?[32] A different set of questions relates to what people can and cannot do in the face of demanding moral obligations: is it realistic to think that people in the present can make potentially very large sacrifices for the sake of non-existent distant strangers in the future?[33]

Climate policymakers have taken an entirely different approach to this problem. They have employed a 'social discount rate' to assign monetary value to damages (and benefits) to people in the future.[34] The social discount rate discounts future harms and benefits to a present value which, advocates argue, enables us to make rational climate policy using 'cost-benefit analysis' techniques in a way that takes proper account of the long-term impacts of these policy choices. I address cost-benefit analysis in climate policymaking in the next chapter. For now, an easy way to think about the social discount rate is as the inverse of an interest rate on savings: just as the value of £100 in the present will increase in the future under different interest rates, so the value of £100 of damages in the future will decrease in the present under different social discount rates. Economists have recommended discount rates for climate policymaking that range from 1.4% (Stern 2006) to 3–5% (Nordhaus 2007).

The difference between a discount rate of 1.4% and 3% or 5% might seem inconsequential. It would be a mistake to think this. Consider the difference in what we should pay to avoid £100 of harm in 100 years using different social discount rates:

- 5%: spend £0.76 now to avoid £100 harm 100 years
- 3%: spend £5.20 now to avoid £100 harm in 100 years
- 1%: spend £36.97 now to avoid £100 harm in 100 years

Setting the social discount rate at 5% creates costs for present people that are far lower than those created if the rate is set at 1%. Importantly: at any rate higher than 0% there will be a point in the future at which the present value of damages happening at that

point in time, and thereafter forever, falls to zero. This means that
for any positive discount rate, at some point in the future we ought
to ignore entirely any harms caused by our choices to people living
then, and all those who will come into existence beyond that point
in time. In this way any positive social discount rate sets limits on
the demandingness of burdens created by our intergenerational
obligations.[35]

The social discount rate is not (at least, not explicitly) advocated on the ad hoc grounds that it relieves present people of
unwelcome burdens created by their intergenerational obligations.
Instead, it has been argued that: (1) the discount rate is justified
because future people will be more wealthy than we are (and
thus that the monetary value of damages to them is lower than
the monetary value of those damages were we to suffer them); (2)
democratic policymaking should reflect people's preferences in
the present (which prioritise present and near-term benefits over
postponed benefits); and (3) the point in time at which a person
exists affects their moral considerability such that future people are
not as morally considerable as present people.

Many moral and political philosophers are highly critical of the
social discount rate as a way of circumscribing the policy implications of what we owe to future people on ethically unjustified
grounds. Tyler Cowen and Derek Parfit capture this scepticism
nicely:

> Why should costs and benefits receive less weight, simply because they
> are further in the future? When the future comes, these benefits and
> costs will be no less real. Imagine finding out that you, having just
> reached your twenty-first birthday, must soon die of cancer because
> one evening Cleopatra wanted an extra helping of dessert. How could
> this be justified? (Cowen and Parfit 1992: 145)

Let us address the three buckets of justifications described above.
John Rawls calls the claim in (3) a 'pure time preference' and
argues that it should not inform our thinking about principles of
intergenerational justice because 'the different temporal position
of persons and generations does not in itself justify treating them

differently' (Rawls 1999: 259). For Rawls, position in time is just as morally irrelevant as sex, religious belief, skin colour, IQ etc. in thinking about what justice as fairness requires (Rawls 1999: 118–23).

I shall return to the claim in (2) in discussion of cost-benefit analysis in the next chapter. Suffice to say here that even if is the case that people prefer temporally near benefits over those that are distant (and so prefer to avoid damages that are temporally near over those that are distant), it does not follow (a) people's preferences for how damages are valued in their own lives ought to govern how public policy is made, and (b) that respect for people's preferences has any role to play at all in democratic decision-making. Furthermore, recent empirical work suggests that discounting in fact plays very little role in people's attitudes towards future-oriented policies related to climate change (Fairbrother et al. 2021)

With respect to (1), critics have argued that in the climate crisis we are not safe to assume that people in the future will be more wealthy than people in the present; runaway climate change has the potential to make humanity extinct (Bostrom 2013; Finneron-Burns 2017; McKinnon 2017). Furthermore, even if people in the future are more wealthy than us it does not follow that climate damages we inflict upon them as a result of our decisions are permissible because (a) wealth cannot compensate future people for an irreversibly trashed planet (Ackerman and Heinzerling 2004), and (b) if we are the cause of future damages then we have duties of corrective justice to make good (as far as possible) on this damage, regardless of how wealthy future people turn out to be (McKinnon 2012).

Is there an alternative to the social discount rate in climate policymaking that makes all future people morally considerable? Turning back to non-utilitarian, justice-based accounts of intergenerational duties could provide a start. If the content of the duties that generate burdens for individuals relate to intergenerational *justice* rather than intergenerational ethics, does this make a difference to the type, spread, and demandingness of burdens created by the duties of present people to future people?

If justice is a property of political institutions then what is owed to future people are institutions that can secure their basic rights (Caney 2008, 2014; Shue 2014b), keep them above a threshold of harm, or maximise their utility. People have duties of justice to create and sustain these institutions, but this does not necessarily generate heavily demanding duties on all individuals as envisaged in the everlasting sacrifice objection (McKinnon 2012).[36] It is an open question on whom the burdens created by these duties of intergenerational justice fall most heavily, and soonest. For example, perhaps those who have benefited most from past injustice have a duty to make the greatest efforts to create less unjust institutions for the benefit of future people. Or perhaps these burdens should fall most heavily, and soonest, on those who are most able to bear them. I address these questions of responsibility in Chapter 5.

Stephen Gardiner points to this 'institutional gap' (Gardiner 2014: 304) as a major driver of our failure so far to address climate change (and other challenges of the Anthropocene) as crises of intergenerational justice. This gap reflects a presentism that pervades contemporary politics, political culture, and citizens' engagement with it (MacKenzie 2016). From the incentives created for politicians by short electoral cycles, to an almost complete lack of representation of the interests of future people in political decision-making bodies, to cultures of consumption that encourage us to see the good life in terms of repeating cycles of short-term preference-satisfaction fulfilled by shopping, our political, economic, and social lives are governed by very short-term horizons. And yet, when we reflect upon what we care about, it is clear that we value people who will come after us, and that we want to be remembered as a generation that did well by them (Scheffler 2013; Shue 2021). Furthermore, new institutions to reduce intergenerational injustice could have the potential to improve lives in the present, especially those of the most vulnerable people. For example, fair and long-term measures to address locked-in climate impacts on indigenous people in Greenland into the future could, at the very least, help to reduce the sense of loss and grief that present-day islanders feel for their children.[37]

Some of the most innovative and ambitious work on intergen-erational justice being done by political theorists today addresses this 'institutional gap'. Examples include the following:

- Stephen Gardiner's call for a 'global constitutional convention' as a procedural framework for advancing towards intergenera-tional justice in the climate crisis and beyond (Gardiner 2014, 2019);
- Simon Caney's 'fivefold package' for political institutions for the future, which includes a requirement on all incoming gov-ernments to produce a manifesto for the future, a Committee for the Future to be included in all legislatures to evaluate and scrutinise policies,[38] and a regular 'Visions for the Future' day during which the Government's manifesto and record can be scrutinised in public deliberative forums (Caney 2016b).
- Ludvig Beckman's and Fredrik Uggla's proposal for an Ombudsman for Future Generations, to hold states to account on decisions and actions as they affect future people (Beckman and Uggla 2016).
- My argument that International Criminal Law ought to be extended to incorporate a new criminal offence of 'postericide', which is committed by conduct fit to bring about the extinc-tion of humanity (McKinnon 2017, 2021).

Conclusion

The range of victims of climate change, and the nature of the damage that is and will be done to them by climate impacts, makes aggressive mitigation, and support for wide-ranging and meaningful adaptation, urgent imperatives. Aggressive mitigation will require cuts in GHG emissions far greater than current efforts. The UN Emissions Gap Report 2020 states that current emissions put the world on track for a 3C average temperature increase by 2100, and that emissions reductions pledged under the Paris Agreement must be increased roughly threefold for a good chance of staying below 2C, and fivefold for staying below 1.5C (UNEP 2020).

This raises numerous questions. With the window for action to achieve aggressive mitigation to achieve the goals of the Paris Agreement closing month by month, and given the implications for the severity and spread of climate injustice across victims, what are countries, corporations, and individuals required to do? Which agents should act soonest, and bear the greatest share of the burdens created by this action? I shall address these questions in Chapter 5. Before that, we need to know what principles for decision-making should guide policymakers and political decision-makers in the climate crisis, understood as a series of events, processes, and impacts fit to violate the basic rights of millions of us, now and into the far future.

4

Risk, Uncertainty, and Ignorance: Challenges for Climate Policymaking?

Public policy ought to be evidence-based. Policymakers cannot be experts on all the sites of action for which public policy is required, and must call on relevant experts to inform and advise them. The scope of expertise relevant for policymaking should be understood in broad terms. The specialised knowledge that is the hallmark of expertise is found not only in the science-oriented disciplines, but also in the social sciences, arts, and humanities. Expertise can also be practice-based: experts can inform policymaking by having specialised knowledge generated by their experience of doing something, rather than (or in addition to) more theoretical knowledge. Expertise can also be understood as local, place-based, or cultural.

Experts provide input into evidence-based policymaking in at least the following ways:

1. Framing: experts offer a way of seeing the nature of the problem in hand; for example, by appeal to data, precedents, past experience, cultural understanding, and values.
2. Options: experts can lay out the pros and cons of various options for tackling the problem; for example, by appeal to practicability, costs, risks, moral principles, and legal constraints.

3. Solutions: experts can advise on the design of any new institutions, procedures, or agreements necessary for a policy choice
   to succeed; for example, by indicating different ways to divide
   the labour involved, or working through the risks of unwanted
   unintended consequences.

Experts rightly input into the policymaking process from beginning to end. There are many important questions about the role
of experts in policymaking (Christensen 2020), how to identify experts in various domains (Anderson 2011), how to settle
disagreement between sets of experts, and how to improve communication between experts and those they advise (Keohane, Lane,
and Oppenheimer 2014). Climate policymaking with input from
experts is at the sharp end of many of these questions. In particular,
because climate change could have globally catastrophic impacts,
policymakers need to know how to navigate the permanent lack
of certainty in climate science. The science of climate change is
ever evolving and never certain. In this respect, scientific enquiry
into climate change is no different to any other type of scientific
enquiry. Science never delivers 100% certainty on anything, and
does not aspire to do so. This is an important point, especially
given how some ideologically motivated right-wing think-tanks
have used the lack of certainty in climate science to cast doubt on
the veracity of the whole field (McKinnon 2016).

There are three dimensions of uncertainty in our knowledge
of climate futures, related to the following areas: (a) what these
futures could be; (b) how likely these futures are to come about;
and (c) how confident experts take themselves to be with respect
to (a) and (b). Dimensions (a) and (b) map what experts know,
whereas (c) maps their own judgements of how well they know
things in dimensions (a) and (b).

When policymakers have confidence in their knowledge of the
outcomes that could be brought about by a policy choice, and are
also confident in assigning probabilities to these outcomes, the
scenario is one of policy choice under risk.[1] Given that all policy
choice is future-oriented, and that the future is never certain,
scenarios of risk are in fact the best that policymakers can hope for.

Well-established methods of risk assessment direct policymakers in these scenarios to evaluate the costs created under the various outcomes, establish the risk these outcomes represent by multiplying the probability of each outcome by policy by its costs, and then choose the least risky policy. This approach can work well in contexts of choice calling for policies to govern short-term risks. For example, public policy decisions about road safety have this character. Experts have enough data showing how accident and fatality rates decline under different speed limits in different areas to be confident in assigning probabilities along these dimensions to proposed speed limits in new housing developments. Although probability is itself a way of expressing uncertainty about the future – any event with a probability of more than 0 and less than 1 might, or might not, happen – there can be good grounds on which any particular probability can be assigned to any particular event.

When experts lack confidence in their knowledge of outcomes that could be brought about by policy choice, and/or their knowledge of the probabilities of these outcomes, policymakers are in *scenarios of uncertainty*. The most common scenarios of uncertainty are those in which experts have some, but not much, confidence in their judgements about the possible outcomes of different types of policy (in)action, and either (a) cannot assign any probabilities to these outcomes or (b) have some, but not much, confidence in the probabilities they assign to the outcomes. These policy scenarios can involve unprecedented events, new technologies, and catastrophic futures.

In the most uncertain scenarios, experts lack any knowledge of outcomes that could be brought about by different policy choices, and so are unable to assign any probabilities to these outcomes. Call these *scenarios of ignorance*. For example, it could be the case that an attack by an aggressive alien species with unimagined weapons technology is imminent. Scenarios of ignorance, involving 'unknown unknowns', present particular challenges for policymakers, for reasons I shall discuss later on.

The distinction between scenarios of risk and of uncertainty can be seen in the treatment of climate impacts in the IPCC's Fifth Assessment Report. Each key climate impact, outcome, or process reviewed in the report is assigned a numerical score for probability, and a separate score for the level of confidence experts have in that assessment of probability. The probability score indicates how likely it is that the outcome, impact, or process will occur. The level of confidence score indicates the epistemic warrant experts take themselves to have with respect to the probability assessment. Levels of confidence can rely on a range of facts; for example, the amount and quality of evidence available to support the probability assessment, or the extent to which the methods used to generate the probability are well established. Levels of confidence are never 100% (which would indicate certainty) or 0% (which would indicate no confidence at all), and probability assessments are never 1 (which would indicate that the outcome etc. will happen) or zero (which would indicate that the outcome will not happen). For some impacts identified by the IPCC, levels of confidence in estimates of probability are very low. These impacts are uncertain. One criticism of the IPCC reports is that they do not address, or even acknowledge, scenarios of ignorance: the 'unknown unknowns' of climate change. In particular, that they do not address the 'unknown unknowns' of passing tipping points beyond which climate change could run away from human control. This is a worry given the authority of IPCC reports in climate policymaking. Some critics have argued that the absence of discussion of tipping points in these reports has meant that these potentially catastrophic 'unknown unknowns' have not been addressed by climate policymakers.

The question for this chapter is: when climate experts advising policymakers are in scenarios of risk, uncertainty, or ignorance, how should climate policy be made? I shall consider two fundamentally opposed answers to these questions. The first answer is that climate policymaking should be driven a technique called 'cost-benefit analysis', whereby the costs and benefits of each policy option are assessed, and the option with the highest net benefits is the optimal policy. The second answer is that climate policymaking should be driven by a precautionary approach. This approach applies when policymakers face risks of catastrophic outcomes, and have good reason to believe that pathways to these outcomes are live.

Should we 'do the maths' to get just climate policy?

The core idea of cost-benefit analysis is simple and prima facie compelling. When faced with a policy choice, policymakers should assess the beneficial and detrimental impacts of different available policy pathways, and choose the one that has the greatest net benefits. Cost-benefit analysis techniques exhibit consequentialism with respect to the question of what policymakers ought to do. These techniques point attention to the anticipated consequences of policy choices as the measure of which choices are better than others. The goodness (or badness) of a policy choice inheres in the state of affairs it is likely (or unlikely) to bring about. A further attraction of cost-benefit analysis is that it delivers clear guidance. In the realm of public policy, where issues are always complex, disputed, and knotty, a technique that can consistently provide a way forward has been very attractive to policymakers (Sunstein 2002, 2004a).

Cost-benefit analysis is a form of consequentialism. According to consequentialism, what morally required action and/or the virtuous character aim at is bringing about good outcomes. What makes an action morally required and /or a character virtuous is that it will, or is likely to, bring about good states of affairs as a consequence of the action being performed, or the nature of the character. The most well-known consequentialist ethical theory is utilitarianism, of which there are many varieties (Egglestone and Miller 2014). What they all have in common is a view of what makes states of affairs good, and a commitment to maximising that good. For utilitarians, goodness consists of utility, and utility is generally understood in subjective terms; that is, in terms derived exclusively from the nature of the subject to which moral duties are owed. Utilitarian conceptions of goodness have ranged across: hedonic happiness (Bentham 1784), 'higher pleasures' involving the intellect (Mill 1998), and preference satisfaction (Singer 2011). The second unifying feature of a utilitarian moral theories is the view that this good ought to be maximised, either as a sum total

or as an average. For example, taking Bentham's hedonic view of
utility as the presence of pleasure and the absence of pain, either
we are required to act so as to bring about states of affairs that
maximise the total net amount of pleasure (Bentham's view), or
which maximise the average amount of pleasure.[2]

For Bentham, and many other utilitarians, utilitarian standards
apply to both the private and the political realm. One of the most
forceful criticisms of utilitarianism in the political realm is famously
made by John Rawls. Rawls argued that because utilitarianism
aims to maximise the goodness inherent in states of affairs, it fails
to respect the separateness of persons (Rawls 1999: 24). From the
point of view of each of us as an individual person, there are things
we reasonably want as conditions for our pursuit of a life we think
of as worth living. In the political realm, these goods – Rawls calls
them 'primary goods' – include basic rights and liberties, opportunities, income and wealth, and the social bases of self-respect.
According to Rawls, what utilitarianism fails to recognise is the
political requirement to secure for each individual a certain provision of these goods before considerations of maximising utility
become appropriate (if they ever do). Making the maximisation of
utility the starting point for thinking about how to structure society's fundamental institutions, and the goods they distribute, risks
treating individual citizens merely as conduits of utility feeding
into a total or average utility, which must be maximised in the outcomes of policy choices. Utilitarianism's focus on bringing about
good states of affairs as the focus of public policy is misplaced. For
Rawls, these considerations are always subordinate to a focus on
what individual citizens are owed as a matter of justice. Hence,
Bentham's defence of utilitarianism on the grounds that 'everyone
counts for one, and no one counts for more than one' in utilitarian
calculations is inadequate: a real commitment to respect for the
individual requires recognising the separateness of persons.

Cost–benefit analysis shares utilitarianism's subjective conception
of goodness. It also sometimes shares utilitarianism's commitment
to maximising the goodness in states of affairs, but this is not,
strictly speaking, built into the techniques of cost–benefit analysis.
Cost–benefit analysis in public policy is always consequentialist,

but not always utilitarian. There are three features of cost-benefit analysis on which I shall focus for the remainder of this section, as follows: (1) Measurement and comparison: how does cost-benefit analysis measure and compare the goodness of states of affairs?; (2) Value: what conception of value is operative in cost-benefit analysis? (3) Uncertainty: how does cost-benefit analysis register and respond to uncertainty? On each of these dimensions, I shall argue that cost-benefit analysis struggles to be plausible as a tool for climate policymaking.

How is the goodness of states of affairs to be measured using cost-benefit analysis? At present, the dominant technique is 'contingent valuation'. This involves establishing how well different scenarios (at which public policy could aim) would satisfy the preferences of people affected by the policy under consideration. This is determined experimentally: people are presented with different outcomes and asked how much they would be willing to pay to avoid these outcomes. Willingness to pay (WTP) is supposed to measure how well different scenarios would satisfy people's preferences: if a person is willing to pay a lot to avoid an outcome this shows that she has a strong preference that the outcome should not come about. Policies can be ranked according to how much people would be willing to pay to avoid states of affairs likely to be produced by these policies. Policies attached to outcomes that people would be willing to pay the least to avoid will rank higher than those that people would be willing to pay the most to avoid. The metric used in contingent valuation is money. Willingness to pay different amounts of money to avoid an outcome is taken to be a good enough proxy for people's preferences with respect to those outcomes.

There are reasons to worry about WTP as a measure of the goodness of states of affairs. First, WTP expresses an entirely subjective view of value: the value of states of affairs in the world is entirely a product of the relationship between the human subject and the world. For many thinkers in green traditions of political thought, this 'anthropocentric' view of value is wrongheaded, and is the root of our present ecological and environmental crises. On an opposing 'ecocentric' view of value, human beings are not the measure of all things: there are things of value in the world that would have had value if humanity had never been, or if we disappear from the universe. For example, the mountain gorillas of Rwanda are valuable regardless of how much we are willing to pay to avoid their extinction: their value is intrinsic. On an ecocentric approach, the damage that climate change causes to the nonhuman world should be addressed by public policy for reasons that have nothing to do with any value that human beings project on to it, and everything to do with the intrinsic value of nature itself.

Second, using WTP to evaluate the impact of environmental policy choices appears to be a remarkably egoistic approach that allows too much room for human greed, shortsightedness, and arrogance. WTP makes preference satisfaction the measure of the value of the impacts of policy choices on the nonhuman world, but it places no restrictions on the nature and content of those preferences. This criticism is sometimes expressed by reference to the idea that some parts of the nonhuman world have 'existence value'. For example, regardless of whether any human being had been willing to pay a large amount to avoid the Bramble Cay melomys (a small brown rodent) going extinct, the existence of this species had value, and its extinction due to climate change made the world a less valuable place.[3] This value could be construed in eco-centric terms, but it is also possible to understand existence value within an anthropocentric frame. On this view, the Bramble Cay melomys had existence value because well-informed and reasonable human beings would recognise it as valuable. Some of the most sophisticated advocates of cost-benefit analysis present WTP as tool of valuation that has this counterfactual aspect. Here, what matters is not what people were actually willing to pay to avoid the Bramble Cay melomys going extinct, but what they would have been willing to if they had been well informed. If being well informed had involved grasping the existence value of the Bramble Cay melomys, then cost-benefit analysis could accommodate such cases by excluding malformed and uninformed preferences from contingent valuation. Of course, this will not satisfy those who have an ecocentric view of value.

Third, these reflections are related to a broader debate about whether preference satisfaction – however well informed – should ever be the object of public policy. Do racist and sexist preferences qualify for measurement by contingent valuation methods? How about envious preferences? Or extremely strong preferences for outcomes that would require diverting a large amount of resource to a particular person or community (Dworkin 1981)? With respect to the environment, and climate in particular, there is a specific reason to worry about the priority given to preference-satisfaction under cost-benefit analysis. As we saw in Chapter 1, climate change presents us with a perfect moral storm (Gardiner 2011). The costs of actions adequate to mitigate it will fall hardest on present people for the sake of benefits for future people, and this dynamic could intensify over time as climate change worsens. The causes and effects of climate change are dispersed in time and space. This skews vulnerability to climate impacts, and makes it difficult to attribute responsibility for these impacts on direct causal grounds. The agency necessary for effective action on climate change is similarly fragmented across time and space: any real political solutions will require unprecedented levels of international and intergenerational cooperation. Our existing ethical and political theories provide inadequate guidance in the face of all of this.

The perfect moral storm of climate change opens doors to morally corrupt reasoning. This is a process by which we tell ourselves stories about the choices we make that obscure the sometimes deeply immoral self-interested reality of those choices. Using WTP to assess climate-policy choice fits this profile. Consider Cass Sunstein's argument that contingent valuation is a good way of protecting individuals from state incursions on their autonomy:

> [P]eople should be sovereign over their own lives, and this principle means that government should respect personal choices about how to use limited resources (. . . so long as those choices are adequately informed). . . If regulators reject people's actual judgements then they are insulting their dignity. (Sunstein 2005b: 371)

Here, as was the case with respect to malformed and uninformed preferences, the qualifier that preferences must be 'adequately informed' is doing some heavy lifting. I shall shortly return to the question of what it means for choices to be adequately informed. For now, focus on the move from a commitment to protection for personal autonomy ('people should be sovereign over their own lives') to a claim about what that commitment means for policy choice ('government should respect personal choices about how to use limited resources'). In what ways might this move exhibit moral corruption?

The first thing to note is that WTP only narrowly models ways of valuing goods and outcomes. WTP excludes common and important ways of valuing that people often apply to environmental goods. The metric used by contingent valuation is money. The problem with this metric is not related to money per se, but rather to what money is for. Money is a medium of exchange: we use it to mark the value of things in ways that make possible exchange with one another. We could have used pretty shells instead, or we could exchange goods for labour (as in barter systems). WTP in contingent valuation could work with any of these metrics; it just so happens that in our large-scale, fast moving, global economy, we use money as a marker of value in exchange. What cost-benefit analysis measures with WTP is this dimension of value only: that is, the exchange value of goods, outcomes, and states of affairs.

But this is not the only way in which human beings value things. There are other goods and states of affairs that have great value to us in virtue of the beneficial uses to which we put these goods. The 'use-value' of goods, states of affairs, and outcomes should not be read in a narrowly instrumental way: 'use' incorporates both things that are necessary for survival, and things that make life worth living for a person. Examples include clean air, potable water, networks of friendship, music, sunshine after the rain, memories of childhood captured in old photo albums, or the companionship of a loving dog. Things such as these are extremely important to many people, but this is not captured by their exchange value, which is minimal or non-existent. As Wolff and Haubrich put it:

[T]he things which have the greatest value in use (water) have frequently little or no value in exchange; and, conversely, those that have the greatest value in exchange (diamonds) have frequently little or no value in use. Exchange value bears no necessary connection to value in use. Yet, while the latter produces the benefit to individuals and thus augments society's well-being, it is the former that is used to impute values into economic valuations such as cost-benefit analysis (CBA). (Wolff and Haubrich 2008: 9)

At best, WTP models exchange value only.[4] In asserting that autonomy requires respect for personal choices as modelled by WTP, Sunstein implicitly limits the domain of value that matters for autonomy to exchange value. But there is no reason at all to think that respect for personal autonomy requires protecting only those goods and states of affairs on which people put a price (Ackerman and Heinzerling 2004). Personal autonomy requires clean air and water, a stable climate, social networks, and the love and respect of others (MacKenzie and Stoljar 2002). The use of WTP in policymaking makes these considerations invisible. Given that climate policy as informed by contingent valuation has enabled states to continue business as usual, more or less, there is good reason to see cost-benefit analysis approaches to climate policy as sites of moral corruption.

Building out from these reflections, some critics have argued that the exclusive focus on exchange value found in contingent valuation is a symptom of a deeper problem. This is that the comparisons and rankings made possible by WTP are at best illusory, and at worst pernicious. Regardless of whether value is ecocentric or anthropocentric, there many valuable states of affairs which ought not to be compared or ranked at all. On this view, many values are 'incommensurable'. Consider the value of friendship and the value of money (Raz 1988: 321–66). We think it is good to have friends: a life without friendship is less valuable than one with friendship, all else being equal. We also think it is a good thing to have money: a life of scrabbling by and debt is less valuable than one above a threshold of financial security, all else being equal. But we think that a person who is willing to assign a monetary value to friendship, or a person who is willing without regret to give up her friends for a lump sum payment, fails to understand the value of friendship. Friendship and money cannot be traded off against one another because there is no common measure of their value: each is valuable, but their value cannot be compared.

The criticism of contingent valuation is that WTP is an exceptionally crude and inappropriate measure of the value of many things that cannot be measured against one another, and so cannot be ranked. For many people, this criticism is particularly sharp with respect to how contingent valuation applies to risks to human life. Using WTP as a measure, the 'value of a statistical life' (VSL) is often set at $6m, in the US context. This prima facie reduction of what is for many people priceless to a cash value reveals the moral bankruptcy of cost-benefit analysis. From human life, to ecosystems, a stable climate, and cultural artefacts, the incommensurability of value is whitewashed by WTP.

We must be careful with criticisms of cost-benefit analysis focused on incommensurability. While, all else being equal, it may be true that some things are valuable in ways that makes it inappropriate to compare and rank them, all else is not equal in the domain of policymaking. It is of the essence of policy choice under conditions of moderate scarcity that hard choices involving comparisons and rankings must be made. When faced with policy choices that force comparisons between valuable outcomes, it would be irresponsible to refuse to make any choice at all. Furthermore, VSL should not be understood to express the true or metaphysical value of a human life. Instead, VSL expresses what, on average, people would have to be paid to avoid a (typically, low-level) risk (Sunstein 2002). This enables policymakers to factor into their decision-making the true costs of risks to people who could be subject to them in different policy outcomes.

A better criticism of VSL is that it does not capture the use-value that each person's life has for them. But then, given that policy choice is often hard choice, there may be no way to make any choice that does not override this use-value for some people and not others. Here, again, we should worry about the influence of moral corruption. When the VSL of an American life is $6m and the VSL of an Indian life is $1.2m, are policymakers encouraged to think that the loss of American lives is of higher priority than the loss of Indian lives (Broome 2000)? Advocates of cost-benefit analysis are adamant that this is not an implication of the differential VSLs delivered by contingent valuation (Sunstein 2004b). However, once we are on the lookout for invitations to morally corrupt reasoning, reassurances by those who theorise about cost-benefit analysis may be hollow, given that decision-makers are working within presentist institutions and answerable to voters with parochial interests.

None of this is to say that we cannot make any choices in the domain of environmental policymaking using cost-benefit analysis. Nor is it to say that goods and states of affairs with high use-value must always be prioritised in environmental policy choices. Instead, we should land on the conclusion that policymakers must make use of tools to inform their thinking on these matters that map use-value as well as – and, depending on the case, perhaps instead of – exchange value. There are such tools available: for example, deliberative fora, multi-criteria mapping, and scenario planning have the flexibility to reflect the use-value people attribute to goods, outcomes, and states of affairs. These tools have the additional benefit of delivering information that respects the autonomy of people whose valuations are consulted, because no *ex ante* restrictions are placed on the way in which people value the things registered by these techniques.

Let me return now to the question of what it means for people's preferences to be well informed in the domain of climate change. Putting aside questions raised by malformed preferences, the exchange-value/use-value distinction, and incommensurability, what do people have to know in order to be adequately informed in a way that means we should take seriously any price they report themselves willing to pay to avoid an outcome? First, they have to know what the outcome is; and second, they have to know the likelihood of that outcome coming to pass. When people know neither of these things, or know about the relevant outcome without knowing how likely it is to come about, they will either be unable to determine what they are willing to pay to avoid the outcome, or their willingness to pay tracks something other than the value they give to avoiding the outcome (Richardson 2000).

Climate policy – especially that which aims to bring about long-term changes – is riddled with these uncertainties. As discussed earlier on, experts can sometimes sketch scenarios of risk for policy choice. These are scenarios involving reasonably well-specified outcomes to which probabilities can be assigned with a good degree of confidence. At most, and ignoring all the criticisms already canvassed here, cost-benefit analysis can be used in this policy domain. What is distinctive about this domain is that the policies in it have short time horizons. It is this fact that partly explains why experts are able to assign probabilities to outcomes with confidence in this domain of policy choice: we are much more confident in our judgements about what will happen tomorrow or next week than we are in judgements about a decade or century from now.

However, a proper appreciation of the climate crisis requires facing head-on the many scenarios of uncertainty, and of ignorance, to which climate policy must speak. Climate change is a temporally extended, intergenerational phenomenon. The impacts of climate change are mediated by numerous complex natural and human systems. Many of these systems are not well understood, and neither are the points at which they do – or could – interact as a result of climate change. Although some domains of climate policymaking involve scenarios of risk, the multiplicity and centrality of scenarios of climate uncertainty and climate ignorance must not be ignored. Arguably, the hegemony of cost-benefit analysis in policymaking has hidden from view the deep uncertainty and pervasive ignorance that is, and always will be, a fundamental characteristic of the climate policymaking domain. Even if people were immune from moral corruption, and all things of value could be given a price within a framework of exchange, this makes cost-benefit analysis deeply unsuited for making climate policy.[5]

What gambles are we willing to take in the climate crisis?

Policy adequate to address climate damages in ways that are fair cannot be made using cost-benefit analysis, given the multiple uncertainties of the climate crisis. Many political theorists advocate a precautionary approach as an ethically adequate alternative.

One simple way to understand precaution is in terms of an action-guiding commitment to the slogan 'better safe than sorry'. This is a poor version of a precautionary approach. Because it does not specify from what we must be kept safe, it offers self-defeating guidance both to policymakers and to individual persons. As Cass Sunstein puts it, '[t]he regulation that the principle requires always gives rise to risks of its own . . . hence the principle bans what it simultaneously mandates' (Sunstein 2005a: 14). Under 'better safe than sorry' we are required to protect against all possible risks, regardless of their nature or likelihood. This is incoherent: each course of action required of policymakers is simultaneously prohibited. We would never adopt such a precautionary approach in our individual lives, because, '[t]he likely result would be paralysis, because so many courses of action would be forbidden. (Even doing nothing might be prohibited; human beings who do nothing . . . will probably end up pretty unhealthy. Will they even eat? What will they eat?)' (Sunstein 2009: 14).

No advocates of precautionary approaches have the view that Sunstein attacks. Precautionary approaches do not aim to provide guidance in scenarios of ignorance. Instead, these approaches aim to be action-guiding in scenarios of uncertainty. In the domain of climate policy, precautionary approaches provide a framework for decision-making for policymakers when experts have limited knowledge of climate impacts and their probability, and/or have low confidence in the judgements they are able to offer to policy-makers. Precautionary approaches are best understood as ruling out sets of policy choices rather than specifying one particular choice over another. Very often, the policy choices that precaution rules out involve inaction in the face of uncertainty.

Precaution is central to the UN Framework Convention on Climate Change (UNFCCC) (1992), which states that:

> The Parties should take precautionary measures to anticipate, prevent, or minimise the causes of climate change and mitigate its adverse effects. Where there are threats of serious or irreversible damage, *lack of full scientific certainty* should not be used as a reason for postponing such measures, taking into account that policies and measures to deal with climate change should be cost-effective so as to ensure global benefits at the lowest possible cost.[6]

The UNFCCC requires cost-effective precautionary action to address threats of 'serious or irreversible damage' about which there is a lack of 'full scientific certainty'. What does this mean? There are many things about which we lack full scientific certainty, not least because the domain of human ignorance is vast. Does the precautionary approach in the UNFCCC imply a requirement to act to 'anticipate, prevent, or minimise' all the possible serious or irreversible impacts of climate change, including unknown unknowns? And, if we commit to this requirement in the domain of climate policy, should we not also commit to it in all policy domains so as to protect against all possible but unknown threats of serious or irreversible damage? For example, should we be anticipating and protecting ourselves against imminent attack from aggressive aliens, even we have no evidence at all for this threat? But what if these precautionary preparations themselves create a new unknown threat? What if, by preparing for an imminent attack by one aggressive alien species, we spook another, better armed, alien species who turn their fleet towards Earth at warp speed? How can we possibly know what to do, if we must take precautions against all possible threats?

Most precautionary approaches do not fall foul of this criticism because not only do they (a) apply only to outcomes that are sufficiently serious (as we saw in discussion of the 'better safe than sorry' interpretation), but also (b) they apply only to these dangers when they lie above a threshold of probability.[7] When these thresholds are met, decision-makers are in a scenario of uncertainty rather than ignorance. This is how the precautionary approach is specified in the UNFCCC. The 'lack of full scientific certainty' specified in the agreement maps on to partial knowledge of climate impacts, and limited confidence in expert judgement about the future speed, severity, spread, and longevity of these impacts.

Daniel Steel's 'tripod' analysis of precautionary approaches aims to capture their shared structure. He argues that all precautionary approaches depend on some level of evidence that an activity may lead to some harm, which activates the demand for a precautionary action. Steel calls the three legs of the tripod the 'knowledge condition', the 'harm condition' and the 'recommended precaution'. The knowledge and harm conditions set thresholds for evidence and harm: when both thresholds are met, precautionary action is required (Steel 2014).

Now we face a new puzzle. If experts are able to assert with reasonable confidence that the relevant threshold for sufficiently serious damage has been met, then why are they not, *ipso facto*, in a scenario of risk? Doesn't reasonable confidence in knowledge of the nature and probability of damaging outcomes mean that experts are not uncertain about these things? And when policymakers are informed by experts that the probability of a damaging outcome is above an important threshold, surely policymakers are then in a scenario of risk, in which the techniques of cost-benefit analysis apply? On this line of thought, there is no space for the scenarios of uncertainty in which precautionary approaches apply. Policymakers are either ignorant of the probabilities of unwanted outcomes, in which case policymakers cannot (and, arguably, should not) act; or, they know enough about the probability of unwanted outcomes to undertake risk assessment using cost-benefit analysis.

This line of thought is unclear about the space that exists for precautionary policymaking. First, remember that there are two dimensions of scenarios of risk, uncertainty, and ignorance. The first relates to what experts know about outcomes and their probabilities, whereas the second relates to the confidence experts have in their judgements on these matters. Scenarios of uncertainty are those in which experts either have little knowledge of outcomes and their probabilities, and/or have low confidence in this knowledge. Experts are in this scenario when the following things are true. First, they have reasonable confidence in their judgement that a threshold of probability for an unwanted outcome has been reached (or is likely to be reached without policy intervention). Second, they lack detailed knowledge of the outcome, but know enough to identify it as unwanted (according to ethically acceptable criteria).[8] And third, they either lack knowledge of, or have low confidence in their judgements of, the exact probability that attaches to the unwanted outcome on pathways either side of the threshold. Policymakers informed by experts in this position lack the epistemic warrant to use cost–benefit analysis, but are not in a position of ignorance. This is the domain of precautionary approaches.

If experts do not know the exact probabilities of unwanted outcomes, how can they know whether they are above any threshold of probability? The right approach here is to make a distinction between exactitude in our judgements of the probability of uncertain outcomes and accuracy in our judgements about whether these outcomes are above some threshold of probability: judgements of the latter type can be well founded when judgements of the former type are not. Henry Shue defends this approach in his articulation of a precautionary approach fit to protect future people from damaging impacts of climate change. Shue asserts that 'one can reasonably, and indeed ought to, ignore entirely questions of probability beyond a certain minimal level of likelihood' (Shue 2014d, 263). In threshold-meeting cases, Shue argues we are required to take precautionary action to minimise the danger of damages.

Shue describes the conditions in which precautionary action is required as follows:

Massive loss: the magnitude of the possible losses is massive;
Threshold likelihood: the likelihood of the losses is significant, even if no precise probability can be specified, because the mechanism by which the losses would occur is well understood, and the conditions for the functioning of the mechanism are accumulating.

Non-excessive costs: the costs of prevention are not excessive (a) in light of the magnitude of the possible losses and (b) even considering other important demands on our resources. (Shue 2014d: 263)

Massive loss (which fulfils Steel's harm condition) limits the domain of precautionary action so as to avoid Sunstein's 'paralysis' objection: precautionary approaches are only warranted in the face of sufficiently damaging losses. The UNFCCC specifies these losses as 'serious and irreversible'. Shue's own account of what makes climate losses massive puts basic rights at its core. Basic rights are rights without which no other rights can be enjoyed; for example, rights to physical integrity, food, shelter, and water.

Threshold likelihood (which fulfils Steel's knowledge condition) avoids the 'aggressive aliens' objection. It also shows why it is not the case that experts able to confidently assert the threshold for likelihood of massive losses, and the conditions under which it has been met, are therefore positioned to confidently assert the risk of the massive losses. *Threshold likelihood* is specified by Shue in a way that reflects expert uncertainty and secures the domain of precautionary approaches. Threshold likelihood has two components. First, the mechanisms through which massive losses could occur must be well understood by experts. These mechanisms could be physical, social, or even cultural. With respect to climate change, there is a clear, core consensus between climate experts on a number of mechanisms that cause climate change. We know how and why climate change happens, we know that our continued greenhouse gas emissions and massive land-use changes are exacerbating climate change, we know with very high levels of confidence how climate change causes devastating impacts, and we know that these impacts are getting worse. Our knowledge of the mechanisms by which warming happens, and the mechanisms by which it impacts on human beings, is not complete, and never will be; but what we do know is 'well understood'. As Shue puts it, '[t]he specification of a clear mechanism is the central contributor to our conviction that the probability [of an outcome] is significant in spite of our not being able to calculate it' (Shue 2014d: 267).

The second part of threshold likelihood relates to our observations of whether the conditions for the mechanisms we understand well are present, and accumulating. In the case of climate impacts, we know the mechanisms by which increases in the atmospheric concentration of greenhouse gases cause warming that could lead to massive loss. If we also observe that things are happening in the world that could increase the atmospheric concentration of GHGs – such as emissions from the manufacture of concrete, or the clearing of the Amazon rainforest – then we know enough to take action to address these conditions. Policymakers do not need to know by precisely how much a particular type of conduct will increase warming to be justified in taking action to minimise the impact of the conduct, or prevent it altogether. Indeed, when the possible losses are massive, policymakers are required to take action.

The third condition for precautionary action identified by Shue is *non-excessive costs*. This condition prevents all, or a disproportionate amount, of society's resources being dedicated to precautionary action. There will inevitably be many pressing problems in need of resourced policies, and wise policymaking will always involve making decisions about how to distribute resources across important policy domains. The proportionality of resource allocation is to be determined by the scale of the possible losses, and how quickly conditions are accumulating for the functioning of the mechanisms that we know are fit to cause these losses. All political theorists of climate change agree that the resources dedicated to taking precautionary action on climate change have been completely inadequate to date.

So far, I have focused on showing that precautionary approaches can provide cogent and coherent guidance to policymakers in scenarios of uncertainty, in which cost-benefit analysis has no place. Now I shall turn to the question of whether policymakers ought to take a precautionary approach in the face of climate change. I shall argue that the nature of the climate problem creates a precautionary imperative for policymakers, given the intergenerational nature of the climate problem.

Is there a precautionary imperative for climate change?

A good place to start in understanding precaution as a requirement of justice is with Stephen Gardiner's Rawlsian defence of the conditions in which precaution is required.[9] These are when (a) decision-makers are in a state of uncertainty with respect to the probability of the events in question; (b) decision-makers are indifferent to gains above the minimum that would be guaranteed by a strategy to make the worst-off people in any policy pathway as well off as possible, i.e. their concern is focused solely on improving the position of the group with least; (c) the alternative strategies of distribution, wherein (b) above is not the priority, are unacceptable.[10]

The condition to focus on here is (b), which forces policymakers to prioritise those who would be made worst off by any policy pathway and, within the limits of uncertainty, to enact a pathway fit to make this group better off than they would be on any other pathway. What is ruled out by condition (b) is, for example, a focus on maximising average utility, or the sacrifice of the worst off to achieve large gains for the best off. Condition (b) is inspired by John Rawls' account of equality. Famously, Rawls argues that to treat people as equals means (among other things)[11] to ensure a distribution of (dis)advantage among them that makes the worst-off group as well off as possible. Rawls calls his principle of egalitarian distributive justice 'the difference principle'. Additionally, Rawls conceives of justice as intergenerational in scope, governing relations across generations as well as within them. He argues that each generation is required to conserve and transfer resources (understood broadly) to the next and future generations according to a rate of saving that any generation would choose if they did not know at which point in human history they exist. He calls this the 'just savings' principle (Rawls 1999: 251–9).

We can see how Rawls' difference principle and his just savings principle work to direct the focus of any precautionary approach, as indicated in condition (b) of Gardiner's account, as follows. Imagine that global climate policymakers must decide whether to include 'blue carbon' initiatives in the suite of measures to be pursued under a mitigation pathway. These initiatives include protecting existing carbon sinks provided by mangroves and coastal seagrass, but also possibly scaling up newer potential carbon sinks such as seaweed aquaculture (Duarte et al. 2017). Blue carbon initiatives alone will not provide adequate mitigation and, unless a suite of mitigation measures are enacted in parallel, blue carbon measures might do nothing to mitigate climate change. Global policymakers are in a scenario of uncertainty about many of the other measures in the mitigation suite, about whether the suite will be rolled out, and about the possible damage that could be caused by some blue carbon measures themselves (Campbell et al. 2019). But they know enough about the underlying mechanisms of climate change to know that blue carbon could act as an important mitigation tool, and we also know that climate change is accelerating. Taking a Rawlsian precautionary approach, how should the policymakers proceed?

They should start by asking the following questions:

1. What are the reasonably unavoidable impacts on people made worst off by rolling out blue carbon initiatives?
2. What are the reasonably unavoidable impacts on people made worst off by *not* rolling out blue carbon initiatives?

There are three important things to note about these questions. First, the impacts should be understood as lying above Shue's 'threshold likelihood'. That is, the impacts that matter for a precautionary approach are not those that are merely imaginable, but those that we have good reason to take seriously (Gardiner calls these 'realistic outcomes'). Second, the worst-off affected people to be given consideration are both people currently in existence and people not yet born. (We saw in the previous chapter how some economistic climate policymakers have sought to limit the temporal scope of this concern just to present people, and people in the relatively near future.) Let us assume that because all people in the future, whoever they may be, will be people, they are owed justice for exactly the same reasons that people who actually exist in the here and now are owed justice. Third, the qualifier 'reasonably unavoidable' indicates that there will be costs created by whatever policy decision is made, and that some of these costs can be imposed legitimately. The qualifier 'reasonably unavoidable' directs policymakers to focus on the ways of delivering these policies that avoid gratuitous or unnecessary damaging impacts on people worst affected, while allowing for some costs to be imposed consistent with an egalitarian version of the precautionary approach.

It is important to be critical and forensic in an assessment of whether costs are really reasonably unavoidable. In political discourse, we are familiar with claims that policy options are strictly limited by various political, economic, and social constraints. The feasibility of policy pathways are often judged against confident assertions about the lack of resources available (for example, in the UK context Prime Minister Theresa May's claims that there is 'no magic money tree' to fund food banks (Dearden 2017)), collective capacity for coordination (for example, PM Margaret Thatcher's notorious statement that 'there is no such thing as society' (Keay 1987)), and institutional realities. We should treat these assertions about constraints on what is unavoidable with caution, if not scepticism. What is reasonably unavoidable is not fixed by current political and economic realities, nor by the ambitions of politicians in short electoral cycles. Assessing whether costs are reasonably unavoidable involves ethical analysis and, if necessary, institutional imagination. In the domain of climate policy, treating a commitment to ever-increasing gross domestic product (GDP) is a good example. The fact that a suite of mitigation policies would slow economic growth is not in itself a good enough reason not to enact these policies. There are good ethical reasons to question whether GDP measures what really matters in human life, and if it does whether continued growth in GDP ought to be the goal of public policy (Alkire 2016).

Once questions 1 and 2 are addressed in the right way, the next step in applying a Rawlsian precautionary approach is to assess which sets of impacts are worst. In other words, we need to judge whether the worst consequences of not taking precautionary action are worse than the worst consequences of taking precautionary action. And then choose a policy (or policy suite) that has the least bad impacts on people worst affected by the policy pathway. Making these judgements in specific cases, given uncertainty, will require garnering input from a wide range of experts and perspectives. But there are general things we can say about the power of the precautionary rationale for the implementation of suites of aggressive mitigation policies immediately, despite the costs these policy pathways could impose on people in the present and the near future.

The worst consequences of precautionary aggressive mitigation are that the costs of adapting to climate change turn out to be lower than the costs of taking precautions. This could be the case if climate sensitivity turns out to be at the lowest end of expert estimates and climate impacts may turn out not to be as dire as experts' worst fears.[12] Perhaps future climate change will happen much more slowly than experts' worst fears, giving us more opportunity for cheaper precautionary action at a later date. In this scenario, we spend a lot of money and time, with all the associated opportunity costs this creates, in implementing precautionary aggressive mitigation now when in fact this action is not necessary, or not necessary yet. Estimates of how much it would cost to implement adequate precautions vary widely: for example, Bjorn Lomborg puts the figure at $37.632 trillion, whereas the European Commission (working with a generous stabilisation target of 550ppm to be met by 2100) chooses between $1 trillion and $8 trillion,[13] and the Stern Review estimates the cost at one per cent of world GDP in 2050, or $1 trillion.[14] These figures are hotly disputed but, to make the case against precautions as powerful as possible, let us adopt the Lomborg estimate. So, the worst outcome of taking precautions now is 'Unnecessary Expenditure'.

Now we must think about the worst outcome of *not* taking precautions through aggressive mitigation now. This is that the worst predictions of the IPCC turn out to be very conservative,[15] that climate sensitivity is at the top of the range of expert estimates, that climate change will not always happen gradually, and that we are on the verge of various tipping points, with everything this entails.

The worst outcome of not undertaking aggressive mitigation now is 'Climate Catastrophe'.

With these outcomes identified, a Rawlsian precautionary approach directs policymakers towards choosing a pathway that has the least bad impacts on those worst affected. Assuming that the interests of future people have the same moral significance as the interests of present people, and given how terrible the impacts on those worst affected under Climate Catastrophe would be, most political theorists have concluded that we ought to take aggressive mitigation measures now. Remembering the condition that costs imposed must be reasonably unavoidable, this commitment to precautionary aggressive mitigation carries with it a requirement to address the impacts of this policy pathway on those worst affected by it. This will involve addressing questions of transitional justice; for example, how to compensate those who lose their livelihoods as a result of aggressive mitigation, or how to deal equitably with 'stranded assets' created by mitigation efforts (e.g. reserves of coal that must be left in the ground (Caney 2016a)). It will also involve thinking about global distributive justice: how can precautionary aggressive mitigation be undertaken in ways that ensure the costs do not fall on the world's poorest people (Moellendorf 2013)?

At the heart of a Rawlsian precautionary approach is the thought that it is impermissible to gamble with the interests of the worst-off people when making policy choices in scenarios of uncertainty. Acting as if the worst consequences of taking precautions are more probable than the worst consequences of not taking precautions is ruled out because the damage that would be caused to present and future people by policy made on this assumption, if it turns out to be false, is much greater than the damage that would be caused by policy made on the first assumption, if this turns out to be false. If we are to treat all people, present and future, as equals we ought not to take a bet on the probability of the worst consequences of no precautions being lower than the probability of the worst consequences of precautions, given the nature of these consequences.

Conclusion

This chapter has explored two competing approaches to climate policymaking. Advocates of cost-benefit analysis claim that these methods provide policymakers with clear practical guidance, and that the techniques express respect for the autonomy of persons by treating their preferences about outcomes as binding the hands of policymakers choosing pathways to manage risk. Advocates of precautionary approaches do not deny that there may be some place for cost-benefit analysis, but they claim that it has at best a very limited role to play in the domain of climate policy. In the scenarios of uncertainty that characterise this domain, treating future and present people as equals requires precautionary action; and this is justified despite the lack of knowledge that is a permanent characteristic of this domain. Although these approaches are often in direct opposition to one another, there are points at which they can come together.

First, cost-benefit analysis can be an approach that provides useful guidance as to which particular precautionary policy to adopt, once an overall precautionary approach has been decided upon for reasons not delivered by a cost-benefit analysis itself. Commitment to a precautionary approach does not *ipso facto* rule out the use of cost-benefit analysis as a tool that can be used to assess the details of different policy proposals, when all the proposals serve the precautionary rationale. Indeed, some have claimed that the precautionary approach is delivered by a cost-benefit analysis that '[places] a thumb on the cost side of the cost-benefit analysis' (Posner 2006: 148).

Second, it may be that cost-benefit analysis itself recommends a precautionary approach for a limited class of cases in which the possible damages in question are catastrophic. Although opposed to the precautionary approach in general, Sunstein takes just this view with respect to some specific cases; notably with respect to climate change. He argues for a 'Catastrophic Harm Precautionary Principle', 'designed to provide guidance for dealing with extremely serious risks' (Sunstein 2009: 14). This principle is heavily qualified and, as Sunstein admits, does not stand as a 'decision rule' for policymakers (Sunstein 2009: 168). It guides policymakers facing uncertainty with respect to the worst-case scenario outcome of their decisions to weigh these scenarios against one another in terms of the losses involved in each scenario, and whether precautionary action to avoid each scenario is 'extraordinarily burdensome'. If an uncertain outcome A would impose losses far greater than an uncertain outcome B and, if the costs of precautionary action to prevent A are not extraordinarily burdensome, then policymakers should take this action. However, if precautionary action to avoid A is very costly, and/or A is not much worse than B, then B ought to be addressed through precautionary action, unless the costs of this action are extraordinarily burdensome and/or there is another worst-case scenario C only slightly less bad than B . . . etc. (Sunstein 2009: 167–8).

These points of confluence between cost-benefit analysis and precautionary approaches should be exploited by policymakers: if there are clear climate-policy pathways to which all roads lead, then taking those pathways is a no-brainer. However, we should not be too optimistic about this eventuality, given a fundamental difference between how advocates of precautionary approaches, and of cost-benefit analysis, treat damages to future people. Unless advocates of cost-benefit analysis can offer more ethically persuasive arguments for the employment of a social discount rate, or unless they abandon commitment to the discount rate, there will remain a fundamental and unbridgeable divide between cost-benefit analysis and precautionary approaches as primary tools for climate policymakers.

5

Who is Responsible for Climate Injustice?

This chapter addresses dimensions of responsibility for climate injustice. When we ask of an injustice 'who is responsible?' we could mean a number of things. We could be asking who perpetrated the injustice, that is, who is causally responsible for it. We could be asking who ought to address the injustice, that is, who has a duty to bear the burden of action to make good on the injustice, and perhaps prevent it from happening again. Or, we could be asking about the site of responsibility or duty: for example, do individuals, communities, states, or multinational corporations have duties to take action on climate change? These domains of enquiry are entangled with the nature of the injustice itself: when we understand the nature of the wrong at the heart of the injustice we will be better guided towards identifying causal responsibility, duties to address the injustice, and the agents to whom or to which these responsibilities attach.

Consider a straightforward case from everyday life. I rear-end your car because I am checking my phone in slow-moving traffic. Here, I have wronged you by damaging your property as a result of my negligence. I am causally responsible for the damage to your car because I had control over the conduct that caused it. Because of this I ought to compensate you for the damage I have caused to your car. This responsibility falls to me as an individual person. The nature of the wrong I do to you (negligently damaging your car) makes compensation the appropriate response (as opposed to, for example, hanging). And the fact that the damage was a result of my negligence means that the injustice ought to be addressed by civil law (which legally requires me, qua individual, to pay you compensation). If I had intentionally rear-ended your car, criminal law (and its attendant sanctions) would be appropriate. In this straightforward case we can determine who ought to bear the burden of addressing the injustice by understanding how the injustice was caused, which also enables us to see which agents are responsible for seeing justice is done (in this example, the negligent driver, and the small-claims court). In paradigmatic cases like this, moral responsibility tracks causal responsibility, and both are attached to individuals.

Responsibility questions under climate change also address causal responsibility, duties to address injustice, and the agents to which these duties attach. Unlike the paradigmatic case, the answers to these questions in the climate case are far from straightforward. This is in part because climate change is, as we saw in Chapter 2, arguably a 'perfect moral storm': its causes and impacts are geographically and temporally splintered and dispersed; agency fit to tackle it is fragmented; and the nature of the wrongs at the heart of climate injustice are disputed (Gardiner 2011).

In this chapter I shall untangle some of these questions about responsibility for climate injustice. In doing this I will make the greenhouse gas (GHG) budget central. Grasping the ethical significance of the GHG budget will give us insight into the nature of the wrongs suffered by victims of climate injustice. As illustrated above, this will guide us in thinking about who is responsible for addressing climate injustices (those who are causing them? Or some other agents?), and the site(s) of agency at which these responsibilities take root.

To begin, remember the idea of the GHG budget. The GHG budget is the amount of GHGs we can 'safely' release into the atmosphere for any given temperature threshold. The GHG budget for a given temperature threshold captures what remains of the absorptive capacity of the atmosphere if we are to have a reasonable chance of staying below that threshold. The higher the threshold, the greater the budget.[1] And, as we saw in Chapter 1, the higher the value of climate sensitivity, the less budget there is remaining for any given temperature threshold. Making the GHG budget central to thinking about responsibility for climate injustice allows us to identify three climate-specific questions. First, we can ask about the fair distribution of what remains of the budget, and what conditions, if any, attach to its use. Call this the 'budget question'. Second, there is the question of how the burdens of action to achieve this fair distribution, including any conditions that attach to it, should be shared. Call this the 'burdens question'. And third, there is the question of the agents to whom these responsibilities attach. Call this the 'agents question'. The following sections will discuss each of these questions.

What are the implications of the carbon budget for responsibility?

A focus on the GHG budget helps to reveal the wrongs at the heart of climate injustice, but perhaps not in the most obvious ways. The GHG budget is a way of thinking about the remainder of the Earth's absorptive capacity for different temperature thresholds. This makes it tempting to think that questions of justice it raises are straightforwardly about how to distribute fairly what remains of the budget between us. Some political theorists have put this question front and centre in their thinking about climate injustice. For example, Peter Singer has argued that the fairest (and most pragmatic) way to distribute the remainder of the GHG budget is to allocate an equal per capita share to all people (Singer 2004; Vanderheiden 2008).[2] The emissions allowances of countries can then be calculated by summing the allowances of all nationals.

Equal per capita approaches to the budget question face challenges. First, prima facie, they make no provision for transition to non-carbon energy sources within the lifetimes of presently existing people; effectively, they permit people in any current time slice to blow the GHG budget entirely, leaving them with no means by which to satisfy their own future energy needs. (Of course, in this scenario, people would just continue to use GHG-based energy and blow the budget even more.) Second, these approaches take no account of the claims that future people have to the GHG budget. Consider how emissions allocations within a carbon budget would look if (1) a very large number of people will exist in the future and (2) all those future people's energy needs will require carbon intensive energy in order to be satisfied. If (1) and (2) are true, then the fixed amount of carbon remaining in the budget has to be divided by a much larger number of people than if we attended only to the carbon-based energy needs of present people. And this generates highly negative emissions allocations for present people.

Recalling the discussion in Chapter 1, Simon Caney calls the equal per capita approach 'isolationist' because it treats questions about the fair distribution of emissions in isolation from other questions of distributive justice (Caney 2012b). People in more developed countries will have a 'head start' under this approach, as they have already benefited from their country's past use of the GHG budget. These problems are avoided if we take (what Caney calls) an 'integrationist' approach to emissions. On this approach, we determine a fair distribution of what remains of the GHG budget by reference to what is required by a just distribution of goods per se. This more holistic approach starts with a vision of what distributive justice requires and works back to an account of what allocation of emissions is necessary to achieve this. On this view, a fair distribution of the atmosphere's remaining absorptive capacity does not matter for its own sake. Emissions per se have no special moral significance. Rather, like money, they enhance access to other goods that matter for human flourishing.

At present, access to emissions matters because emissions are, as Henry Shue puts it, an 'avoidable necessity' in a global economy powered by fossil fuels (Shue 2014a). Emissions are 'avoidable' because a global carbon economy is not the only way in which we could organise our activities on the planet. Yet they are a 'necessity' because, at present, there is no other way for most people to access basic goods other than by doing things that create emissions. But emissions themselves have instrumental value only: they are means to the ends of human survival and flourishing. And emissions have this instrumental status only contingently. If we transition to a zero-carbon economy the ends of human survival and flourishing will be served by access to energy that does not create emissions (Shue 2013). In this scenario, the GHG budget will no longer be governed by principles of distributive justice because emissions will no longer be necessary for human survival and flourishing.

We should note a worrying possibility at this point. What if what remains of the GHG budget is so limited that, were every person presently alive to be granted an entitlement to subsistence emissions, the budget would be blown (McLaughlin 2019)? This is far from a mere bad dream. If climate sensitivity is above 5C, if countries do not massively ratchet up their ambition under the Paris Agreement, and/or if we are on the verge of a climate tipping point, subsistence emissions for all will not be possible. This raises hard questions about who should, and who should not, get subsistence emissions: tantamount to the question, 'who should live and who should die?' (McKinnon 2012). It raises questions about the permissibility of any non-subsistence emissions in the service of securing access to non-fossil-fuel-based energy for all in the future: should we use part of the GHG budget to build ocean wind farms if this means that some people in the present and near future will be denied emissions necessary for their survival? And it raises questions about the place, if any, for justice in a world in which the good of atmospheric absorptive capacity is extremely scarce. As we shall see in Chapter 7, some people have argued that the awfulness of this extreme scarcity scenario can justify the use of geoengineering.

Putting scenarios of extreme scarcity to one side for now, what is it that emissions do for people, given the nature of the global economy? Emissions are necessary for most people to access goods necessary for survival and flourishing: all people must create subsistence emissions if they are to access basic survival goods such as food, water, shelter, and medical care. Access to goods beyond this that are necessary for human flourishing – such as education, cultural goods, stable and rich community life, or enjoyment of nature – also requires emissions, given the 'avoidable necessity' of the global carbon economy. By not fetishising emissions we can remain clear-eyed about the nature of the prize of distributive justice under climate change. Importantly, we are also then positioned to make judgements about the relative priority of claims to a share of the remaining GHG budget. Prima facie, claims that do not service survival or flourishing will have the lowest priority from the point of view of distributive justice. A British Boomer's desire for a holiday home in Marbella will not compete with a Somalian mother's need for reliable access to clean water, or with a Rio favela community's need for affordable energy to sustain a fragile school.

Given that there is not enough left in the GHG budget for all people now and forever into the future to have emissions sufficient for survival, what does distributive justice require with respect to the budget question? Does this fact mean that the budget question is redundant, given how profligate we, and our ancestors, have been with the budget? Remembering that emissions have instrumental importance only allows us to see that the budget question is still live. We can see this by starting with the worst-case scenario in which presently living people entirely use up what remains of the budget. Henry Shue offers a revealing analogy for this scenario:

> [S]uppose that a picnic table is set with enough food for one dozen people, and one dozen eventually come. I arrive early and, being a glutton, eat enough for two or three people, as usual. The last one or two people to come have nothing to eat because I have eaten their share. I have harmed them because I have deprived them of what they were entitled to, unless we make some heroically implausible assumption such as that they had no right to be there or that I am so special that I have a right to double the share of ordinary folks. If we add the assumption that the meal was part of the minimum those deprived needed for their survival, which would make the picnic more analogous to GHG emissions, then I have injured them severely – arguably, I have killed them. (Shue 2001: 453–4)

In the worst-case scenario, people in the present and the near future who use up the GHG budget and make no alternative provision for those who will come after them cause impermissible harm to future people. The stronger case that present people kill future people in this scenario is not that hard to make. If every person is entitled not to be deprived of what is necessary for her survival by any other person's avoidable conduct, then when someone in the present uses the GHG budget for anything other than subsistence, the present person kills the future person (Nell and O'Neill 1975; Nolt 2011a). The fact that the present person did not mean to do this is no excuse (we do not excuse a dangerous driver who kills a child on the grounds that the driver did not mean to do it).

We might object here that if, as seems to be the case for most people in the present global carbon economy, present people cannot avoid emissions in order to survive then their conduct is not impermissible even if it does cause the death of someone in the future. If it is my survival or yours, I cannot be faulted for prioritising my own life.

If this were in fact the nature of the worst-case scenario we are considering then the budget question and, indeed, other questions of justice would have no place. However, this is not the nature of the worst-case scenario, or any scenario in which present people find themselves. It is true that present and near-future people might be committed to using up all of the remaining GHG budget in order just to survive. But the nature of the global economy that makes this an inevitability for present and near-future people is not fixed. What matters for survival and flourishing is access to energy, and there are multiple effective, cheap, scalable ways in which access to energy can be secured for future people without emissions. If distributive justice permits present and near-future people to use up the remainder of the GHG budget, it also requires them to secure access to renewable energy for future people. If people in the present and the near future do not aggressively mitigate *and* quickly scale up renewable energy, they behave like people who come first to the picnic and leave no food for those who come later. If people in the present are to have justified entitlements to emissions they must commit to the rapid and effective development of non-GHG-based energy technologies that will ensure that future people's energy needs are as well satisfied as those of present people (Shue 2013).[3] This is why aggressive mitigation, teamed with transition to a zero-carbon global economy, is imperative in the name of distributive justice across generations.

So far, we have explored different approaches to the allocation of whatever remains of the GHG budget. Wherever we land on this question, it opens up a second set of questions about where the burdens of reducing injustice ought to fall. I turn to these responsibility questions next.

Where do responsibilities to reduce climate injustice lie?

Reducing climate injustice will create burdens for some and benefits for others. It will require people in more developed countries to wean themselves off fossil fuels so as to enable people in less developed countries, now and into the future, to satisfy their basic rights. Because emissions are not presently being claimed in ways aligned with a fair distribution of the GHG budget, reducing climate injustice is likely to require substantial changes to the status quo. For example, some agents are likely to be required to: reduce emissions so as to enable others to emit more; support the adaptation efforts of those who will be, and are being, hit hardest by climate impacts; invest in effective, scalable, renewable energy that provides a fast route to a zero-carbon global economy. On whom should these burdens fall? Who ought to do most, soonest, to absorb these burdens? Call this the 'primary duties' question. Furthermore, when agents with primary duties to shoulder these burdens refuse to do so, which agents, if any, should take them on? Call this the 'remedial duties' question.

Starting with primary duties, there are three types of answer in the literature. First, that those who have caused (and are causing) climate change bear primary responsibility (the 'polluter pays' approach). Second, that those who benefit from activities that cause climate change bear primary responsibility (the 'beneficiaries pay' approach). And third, that those who can afford to take on primary responsibilities for reducing climate injustice bear primary responsibility (the 'ability-to-pay' approach).

The polluter-pays approach has intuitive force: those who have contributed most to the problem are those who have a primary duty to resolve it. The approach is an example of a powerful general principle that those who have caused harm ought to make good. We apply this general principle all the time in everyday life: for example, we think that those who have done us wrong owe us an apology. It is also embedded in many civil law jurisdictions: for example, in the UK the law of torts assigns liability for compensation to those who have caused damage to innocent others.[4]

With respect to the primary responsibility question, the polluter pays principle would allocate higher absolute emissions reductions targets to countries in a more advanced state of development in virtue of their historically disproportionate emissions. More developed countries have achieved their gains as a result of using up more than their fair share of the GHG budget. Their historical emissions have caused climate change, and continue to do so. Because of this, they are required to immediately and aggressively reduce their emissions so as to limit the size of the unfair share of the carbon budget they have consumed.

However, primary responsibility under a polluter pays principle requires more than mitigation. Countries with high historical emissions have a negative emissions allowance. This means that their net emissions must increase the GHG budget: their activities must 'give back' to the budget so that those less developed countries, whose shares have been unfairly used by more developed countries, can access the budget. This has two implications for countries with high historical emissions. First, they must invest heavily in the research and development and scale-up of non-GHG based energy technologies and infrastructures for use within their own borders. This will prevent any further unfair consumption of the budget by them. However, a domestic scale-up of renewables is very unlikely to be sufficient for countries with high historical emissions (especially those that industrialised early) to 'give back' to the budget in ways that make a dent on what they have unfairly taken from the budget. For this, the polluter pays approach requires that they enable the global scale-up of renewables, with a particular focus on less developed countries.

Finally, the polluter pays approach requires countries with high historical emissions to compensate those who have been damaged by climate change, as part of their adaptation efforts. Again, there is an asymmetry between more developed and less developed countries, and there are a variety of specific duties this could generate for countries with primary responsibility.

The polluter pays approach faces problems. Any temporal cohort located within a more developed country responsible for the burdens mentioned above might object that they are being required to bear heavy burdens as a result of conduct not their own. The polluter pays principle tells us that those who have caused damage are responsible for action to address it. The majority of any country's use of an unfair share of the GHG budget is a result of what previous nationals did, and they are now dead. To hold existing members of historically high-emitting countries responsible for the conduct of their ancestors would be deeply unfair because these people had no control over that conduct.

In response, defenders of the polluter pays principle could point out that primary responsibility is assigned to countries under this approach rather than to individuals. While we might think it is unfair for individuals to be held responsible for the sins of their ancestors, the case is not so clear with respect to countries. It could be claimed that countries have an identity over time that enables us to make sense of the claim that, for example, the present-day UK is responsible for the atrocities of the British Empire, and ought to take action to make good on this. Even if this is true, the burdens that come with an assignment of primary responsibility to a country will, ultimately, be passed on to its citizens. In which case the worry about making individuals bear the burdens of the sins of their ancestors remains.

A different way forward is to deny that all polluters are dead. Causal contribution to climate change is ongoing and so the polluter pays principle can distribute primary responsibilities for climate injustice without relying on any principle of liability-emitting inheritance. In response, it could be argued that the current emissions of any country are only causes of climate change in combination with the historical emissions of others: if emissions had been at pre-industrial levels in 1992 then we would not be in a climate crisis today. At most, this response suggests that primary responsibility for climate injustice should be assigned in ways proportionate to causal contribution, which would support some primary responsibility for present people. In fact, if we accept that primary responsibility is appropriate only when an agent could reasonably be expected to foresee that their conduct would be harmful, and the conduct is avoidable, we might be justified in assigning much more – perhaps all – primary responsibility to people from 1992 onwards. If 1992 – the year of the Rio Declaration – is the latest point in time at which reasonable ignorance of the climate-changing effect of emissions could be claimed as an excuse fit to defeat responsibility, then perhaps any avoidable emissions after that point create liability for the emitter. In which case assigning primary responsibility to present emitters using the polluter pays principle does not face the problem of dead polluters.

We have now moved some distance from the original intuition that made a polluter pays approach attractive, viz. that those who make an (avoidable) mess should clean it up. The version now on the table is: those who make an (avoidable) mess should clean it up if they can reasonably be expected to know they are making a mess. On this version, given its cumulative CO_2 emissions 1992–2019 China will bear similar levels of primary responsibility for reducing climate injustice as America, because China has emitted 143.11 billion tonnes of CO_2 in this time period and the USA has emitted 137.1 billion tonnes.[5] This is despite the fact that the USA has emitted 399.53 billion tonnes of CO_2 (1751–2017), whereas China has emitted 199.85 billion tonnes of CO_2 in the same period;[6] the USA's CO_2 emissions account for 24.82% of total emissions since 1751, compared to China's 13.3%;[7] and China's CO_2 emissions per capita in 2017 were 6.86 tonnes compared to per capita emissions in the USA of 16.16 tonnes.[8] And the UK will have much less primary responsibility than either China or America, despite its status as a turbo-charged first mover in early days of the Industrial Revolution.[9] These outcomes overlook the majority of historical usage of the GHG budget.

One way to push back at this is to argue against 1992 as the right baseline for judging reasonable ignorance. If countries can reasonably be expected to have known about the effects of their GHGs in, say, the mid 1880s when Eunice Foote was doing her pioneering experiments, then the distribution of responsibility will look very different and fall almost exclusively on early industrialising countries.[10]

Another attractive approach to primary responsibility for bearing the burdens of reducing climate injustice is the 'beneficiary pays' approach (Barry and Kirby 2017; Butt 2014; Page 2012). On this approach, those who have benefited from conduct causing the problem are those who ought to bear the costs of solving the problem. This holds even when beneficiaries could not have had any control over the conduct of those who caused the problem. On this view, people in more developed countries who have benefited massively from their predecessors' emissions are required to bear the largest burdens (soonest) of action to reduce climate injustice across the spectrum of mitigation, support for adaptation, and rapid research and development of renewables.

The beneficiary pays approach requires a reliable method for identifying and measuring present benefits generated by past emissions. It requires the identification of clear chains of causation linking benefits enjoyed by present people to past emissions. And it requires a normative account of what makes a change in a person's, or group's, conditions qualify as a benefit. A promising approach to the normative question draws on Sen and Nussbaum's 'capabilities' approach (Nussbaum 2000; Sen 2001). On this view, what matters from a political point of view for the assessment of advantage is not levels of welfare enjoyed, or amounts of resources owned or controlled, but rather the extent to which people are free to achieve well-being, understood in terms of objective opportunities to do, and become, what they have reason to value.

Objections to the beneficiary pays approach have, as with objections to the polluter pays approach, focused on the fairness of requiring people who have not caused a problem to bear the burdens associated with tackling it. Variations of the 'benefit foisting' objection abound in the literature (Nozick 1974: 95). Here is mine. Imagine that you go away on a three-month trip, and when you return you find that an uninvited skilful gardener has cultivated a flourishing vegetable patch in an unused bed in your garden, and that she died shortly thereafter, and before your return. You enjoy eating the vegetables and your health is benefited. In cultivating the patch the gardener made liberal use of the village fertiliser stored in the barn, without realising that the supply is limited. Your neighbours, who have also been away on a three-month trip, are now trying to get their vegetable patches established. On seeing your abundant crop, and learning of how it came about, they might make the following demands of you: (i) that you stop using any more of the limited supply of fertiliser; (ii) that you share your vegetable bounty with them, given that its existence is entirely dependent on the mystery gardener having used a disproportionate share of the fertiliser; and (iii) that you work hard to find new vegetable growing techniques that do not rely on fertiliser which you must share with the village, given that traditional fertiliser is fast running out. Advocates of the beneficiary pays principle must explain why your unrequested, but welcome, receipt of the vegetables generates an enforceable and non-voluntary requirement for you to comply with some or all of demands (i)–(iii).[11] And they must unpack the analogy in a convincing way. Eating freshly grown vegetables has clear, measurable benefits for health. How do the products of carbon intensive development benefit people?[12]

One problem with this approach is that the climate case is far more complex than the mystery gardener case. In the mystery gardener case it is clear what you could do to refuse the juicy vegetables: don't eat them and redistribute them to the other villagers. But how can a person born into a more developed country with high historical emissions refuse those benefits? By the time a beneficiary has reached adulthood they will have already accrued many benefits which they cannot divest: for example, an education, a nutritious childhood diet, and freedom from child labour. If beneficiaries cannot refuse some of their benefits, then in what sense do they have control over them? And if they do not have control over them then, why does enjoyment of these benefits generate primary responsibility?

The point is well put by David Hume in criticism of John Locke's claim that individuals give their tacit consent to political authority simply by 'possession, or enjoyment, of any part of the dominions of any government' (Second Treatise on Civil Government, Chapter VIII, s. 9). In criticism, Hume says:

> Can we seriously say, that a poor peasant or artisan has a free choice to leave his country, when he knows no foreign language or manners, and lives from day to day, by the small wages which he acquires? We may as well assert, that a man, by remaining in a vessel, freely consents to the dominion of the master; though he was carried on board while asleep, and must leap into the ocean, and perish, the moment he leaves her. (Hume 1987: 475)

There are at least three ways forward here. First, we could argue that only benefits received during adulthood generate primary responsibility for climate injustice. However, this will not do much to address the worry. In more developed countries, for example, many of the benefits accrue to people as citizens of that state, for example, clean drinking water, sanitation, and clean air. These benefits cannot be rejected without renouncing citizenship and moving out of the territory. The costs involved in doing these things make it deeply questionable whether the majority of people in receipt of such benefits can really be said to make a choice to accept them.

Second, we could argue that this approach should not be used to assign primary responsibility to individuals, but rather to countries: it does not follow from the fact that individuals cannot divest themselves of the benefits of historical emissions that countries cannot do so. For example, an international climate agreement to reduce injustice could require beneficiary countries to divert almost all their GDP to support less developed countries whose share of the GHG budget they have used. However, it is not clear that this reply avoids having burdens fall ultimately on individuals:

the effect of countries complying with a climate agreement like this will be to burden individual citizens, which takes us back to Hume's objection above.

Third, we might abandon the beneficiary pays approach in favour of an alternative, the 'ability-to-pay' approach. This approach to primary responsibility abandons the thought that it must be justified by reference to causal responsibility, or receipt of benefits. On this view, those most able to bear the burdens of reducing climate injustice are those with primary responsibility for doing this. The 'ability-to-pay' approach appeals to many people because it is a clean, forward-looking way of assigning responsibilities when we need urgent action on climate change. The ability-to-pay approach is integrationist; that is, it places the damaging impacts of climate change under the remit of a more general theory of distributive justice that governs the distribution of advantage across different scales. Most advocates of the ability-to-pay approach view distributive justice in global terms. For example, Darrel Moellendorf argues that an 'anti-poverty principle' should guide all efforts to reduce climate injustice. He describes this principle as follows:

> Policies and institutions should not impose any costs of climate change or climate change policy (such as mitigation and adaptation) on the global poor, of the present or future generations, when those costs make the prospects for poverty eradication worse than they would be absent them, if there are alternative policies that would prevent the poor from assuming those costs. (Moellendorf 2013: 22)

On Moellendorf's view, if our overriding priority is poverty reduction we should assign primary responsibility for climate injustice to agents most capable of taking the most effective action, soonest. Regardless of their historical emissions, or the benefits that have accrued as a result of these, more developed countries are best placed to reduce climate injustice in line with the anti-poverty principle.

The ability-to-pay approach has implications for intergenerational justice that worry many advocates of climate justice. First, the emphasis in its application is on fast action to alleviate present poverty. Taking this seriously could have damaging unintended consequences for future people. For example, if alleviating present poverty creates new pockets of disposable income could emissions rise in ways that will damage future people in poverty? This suggests that applications of the ability-to-pay approach must commit to net zero GHG measures to reduce climate injustice.

Second, if ability-to-pay on its own guides where primary responsibility falls, then present people might have very limited responsibilities to reduce climate injustice. If people in the future will be more advantaged than present people (as we saw in Chapter 4 this is often assumed in justification of the social discount rate) then, qua more able-to-pay than present people, they will bear primary responsibility for addressing climate injustice. This does not necessarily mean that present people should do nothing on mitigation, adaptation, and renewables: to do nothing knowing that this will cause damage to future people would show reckless disregard for the interests of future people, and this is impermissible regardless of how advantaged future people will be. Instead, the position that becomes defensible on the ability-to-pay approach is making future people pay for present efforts to reduce climate injustice. For example, we could divert various types of investment away from programs that will benefit future people and towards climate injustice reduction efforts in the present. On this view, we take the action but future people bear the burdens (Broome 2012a).

The polluter pays, beneficiary pays, and ability-to-pay approaches to assigning primary responsibility for reducing climate injustice remain in dialogue in the literature. The point of identifying bearers of primary responsibility is to justify requirements that they take swift, effective action to reduce climate injustice. Imagine that the debate between these approaches is settled, and we are justified in singling out some agents as required to take this action. These agents do not take action. What next? We do not really need imagination to envisage this scenario: we are already in it. In the world as it is, the polluter pays, beneficiary pays, and ability-to-pay approaches will largely converge to identify the same sets of agents: rich, more developed, early industrialising countries. In the world as it is, all roads lead to Rome when it comes to primary responsibility. And in the world as it is, these countries fail to act. How does political theory guide us on questions of remedial responsibility in our deeply non-ideal climate crisis?

Moral philosophers have paid attention to the general question of who, if anyone, ought to act when others fail to discharge their responsibilities, and what is required of these agents. For example, Liam Murphy defends a 'compliance condition', which sets limits on the extent to which the demands made on any agent by a moral principle can increase when other agents do not discharge their duties under that principle (Murphy 2000). The question has also received attention in the literature on climate justice, in ways that illuminate the contribution that political theory can make to thinking about climate justice in the real world.

For example, Simon Caney's 'hybrid approach' addresses both primary and remedial responsibility for climate justice. He argues that some version of the polluter pays principle should be used to assign primary responsibility,[13] but that this principle is not fit to provide guidance on the question of remedial responsibility. To satisfy this dimension of the burdens question, Caney suggests that those most able to pay should bear remedial responsibility to act on climate injustice to address the emissions of dead polluters, the emissions of people excusably ignorant about the effects of their emissions, and noncompliant polluters (who bear primary responsibility). Not only do the most advantaged have responsibility for 'taking up the slack' of inaction on climate injustice created by noncompliant, dead, and excused emitters, they also have a duty to 'construct institutions that discourage future noncompliance' (Caney 2006: 746). This helps to discharge intergenerational justice by ensuring that future people who do their bit on climate justice are not always having to do more in order to take up the slack of future noncompliers. Caney's argument for the hybrid approach is that, 'if the choice is of either ascribing duties to the poor and needy or allowing serious harms to befall people (many of whom are also poor and needy) or ascribing duties to the most advantaged, it would seem plausible to go for the third option' (Caney 2006: 748). If we are to do anything to reduce climate injustice, the burdens of action will fall somewhere. When not everyone does what they ought to do, we can either let avoidable climate injustices accumulate (on the heads of the poor and needy), or we can seek a way to maximise the reduction of climate injustice by allocating the burdens of action to those most able to bear them. If this is unfair to the most advantaged then the unfairness is far outweighed by the gains made on the front of climate justice.[14]

But is it unfair to allocate the burdens of remedial responsibility to more advantaged agents? Daniel Butt's approach to rectifying international injustice asserts that it is not. He argues that beneficiaries of historical emissions have remedial responsibility for reducing climate injustice because they have not rejected unrequested benefits to them that were created as a result of historically unjust usage of the GHG budget. The fact that many (perhaps most) of these agents cannot divest themselves of these benefits is beside the point when we are assigning remedial duties. If there is to be action on climate injustice, and those who bear primary responsibility cannot (or will not) take on the burdens of this action, the buck has to stop somewhere, or we give up on reducing climate injustice altogether. People in more developed countries who benefit from high historical emissions, and/or early industrialisation, ought to bear these burdens because they have willingly accepted benefits that make them best placed to act on climate injustice. Butt adds to Caney's approach by identifying receipt of benefits, even those that cannot be divested, as morally sufficient to justify remedial responsibility (Butt 2008).[15]

A question for Caney, Butt, and other defenders of the fairness (rather than, for example, the expediency) of remedial responsibility is whether the distinction between primary and remedial responsibility can be upheld at all, on their views. If it is fair to allocate the slack-taking burdens of action to reduce climate injustice to the more advantaged, or to beneficiaries, then why shouldn't we assign primary responsibility to them too? Will the answer call on differences between the burdens of primary and remedial responsibility? For example, is primary responsibility more burdensome than remedial responsibility?

To sum up, different approaches to primary and remedial responsibility ultimately all point in the same policy direction, given our past and ongoing failures to get climate change under control. The Rome that all roads lead to is this: more developed countries should bear primary and remedial responsibility for rapid and aggressive emissions reductions, extensive support for adaptation programmes, and scale-up of effective renewables. This is not to say that the costs of rapid action on climate change should be distributed equally across all people in more developed countries: considerations of distributive and climate justice will apply here too. If people one day find themselves in a world in which each road points in a different policy direction, that will be cause for celebration because the world will have moved closer to the ideal state in which these approaches disaggregate different sets of primary and remedial responsibility bearers.

Who – or what – has duties to act on climate change?

A full account of responsibility for action on climate injustice requires an answer to the following question: which agents have duties to take action on climate change? Some candidate answers are: individual people, households, municipalities, states, regions, multi-national corporations (MNCs), religious organisations, non-governmental organisations (NGOs), the planet's (or rich countries') most wealthy ten per cent, or meat-eaters. The answer to the 'duties question' will make an enormous difference to climate policy that aims for just solutions. For example, the Paris Agreement assigns responsibilities to states and lets them decide how to discharge their legal duties under the Agreement.[16] This is part of what gets reported in states' NDCs. But, for example, if we think that justice requires directly assigning duties to fossil-fuel intensive MNCs to transition to clean energy at speed, then the Paris Agreement's flexibility with respect to how states discharge their duties might not deliver on the demands of climate justice.

Regardless of the grounds on which we think responsibility for taking action on climate change ought to be assigned, as explored in the last section, we need to know which agents have duties to discharge these responsibilities. We can make headway on this question by, first, thinking about what it means to be an agent and second, considering what it means to be an agent with moral responsibility for actions (i.e. with duties).

To be an agent is to be capable of pursuing purposes according to representations of the world that are responsive to the ways in which circumstances change.[17] Agents do things, whereas non-agents (like volcanoes, wind, or viruses) merely cause things to happen. Dogs, Boris Johnson, and dolphins have agency; peat bogs and meteors do not. Agency is necessary but not sufficient for moral responsibility. My dog acts according to his purposes of devouring delicious human food and takes his opportunity to steal a sausage roll from my plate when I am not looking. But we do not really think that my dog has a moral duty not to steal from my plate, or that he has done something morally wrong when he does (despite what his supplicant eyes and cowering stance suggest when I catch him in the act). Dogs and dolphins are agents but are not morally accountable for their actions: they are 'moral patients'.

Most adult human agents are not moral patients. Most adult human agents pursue their purposes by forming intentions to act, which they execute in bodily movements, and which are informed and directed by their ever-changing beliefs about how the world is and their desires about how it should be (that is, their representational mental states). Our legal and political structures, religions, friendship groups, families, and economies all reflect these facts about human agents.

Following Philip Pettit, what distinguishes most human agents from most animal agents is the property of 'conversibility', in virtue of which they are persons (Teichmann n.d.).[18] Persons are able to (a) identify their own beliefs and desires, which enables them to act as 'spokespersons' for themselves, and thus (b) commit themselves to others. It is because human persons can know what they believe, want, and mean to do, and how this relates to what they owe to others, that we legitimately hold them accountable for not delivering on what they owe to others, and assign duties to them on the basis of this. Much of what we owe to one another is governed by morality and, as such, has the force of moral duty.[19] This is certainly true of duties to reduce climate injustice with which we are concerned here. These are duties either to avoid action that causes climate change and/or to take remedial action to address the damage done to the victims of climate change. Which agents have these duties?

We can make an initial distinction between individual and group duty-bearers.[20] We are at ease with the idea of individuals as duty-bearers; individuals can acquire duties through exercising their agency (e.g. by making a promise), or they can have duties that are independent of any particular act they have undertaken. All individual persons (i.e. conversible agents) have a duty not to kill innocent children just for fun. This is not a duty any individual person can cast off by an act of will, or by striking a deal with a child she would like to kill for fun. We treat such people as dangerous psychopaths. The idea that there are some 'strict' – i.e. nonvoluntary and universally binding – duties owed by each person to all others is fundamental to our idea of ourselves.[21]

However, we also appear to be at ease with the idea of certain types of groups as moral agents: we speak commonly about how an MNC is responsible for cleaning up an oil spill and can rightfully be held accountable for not taking precautions to avoid another spill in the future. In the domain of climate justice, do these ways of talking suggest that we can, and should, assign primary and/or remedial climate duties both to individual persons and to group agents? If so, do they have the same duties?

Let us start with individual persons. There are two ways in which to make the case that individual persons have climate duties, and each of these approaches helps to delineate the content of these duties.

On the first – 'difference-making' – approach, individual persons have duties to reduce their GHG emissions if these emissions make climate change worse and thereby cause climate impacts that harm innocent people. We are all very familiar with calls to reduce our personal or household carbon footprints in the name of this duty by doing things such as consuming less and locally, offsetting, reconsidering transport options, or limiting family size.[22] The force of the difference-making approach lies in its appeal to a Harm Principle as the source of individual duties, and its implicit claim that duties not to harm are to be assigned on the basis of causal contribution to the harm in question. There are many ways in which 'the' Harm Principle can be understood, each of which appeals to a different underlying set of values. Most philosophers accept that harm extends beyond physical impacts on a person to which they do not consent. For example, harm is often thought to include damage to a person's capabilities, cultural losses, or the imposition of serious risk (Finkelstein 2002; Wolff and de Shalit 2007). We do not need to settle these questions in order to get a grip on what the difference-making approach could mean for the climate duties of individual persons.

Consider John Nolt's claim that the emissions of the average American will kill one or two people in the future (Nolt 2011a). If Nolt's analysis is correct, we can reason as follows. If future people have a right not to be killed, then all people – present and future – have a duty not to kill them. Any individual person in the present with emissions equal to or higher than that of an average American *ipso facto* breaches this duty because they are causally responsible for their emissions. They are climate killers. The fundamental nature of the right not to be killed (if anything qualifies as a basic right in Shue's sense, this does) means that ignorance is not a defence here. Just as the person who does not intend to kill a child with their avoidable dangerous driving is still morally responsible for the death, so the fact that the average American does not mean to kill future people as a result of their avoidable emissions does not get them off the hook, morally speaking. (Nell and O'Neill 1975). The fundamental nature of the duty not to kill and other duties that correlate with basic rights violated by present and future climate impacts directs individual persons, as a matter of moral imperative, to reduce their emissions.

One qualification to this approach (as evidenced in Nolt's focus on the average *American's* emissions) is that not all persons are similarly situated with respect to the avoidability of their emissions. As Shue reminds us, for many of the world's poorest people, emissions are an 'avoidable necessity': they are necessary for survival because the global economy is carbon-intensive, but the global economy could be otherwise. If your emissions are necessary for your survival, morality cannot ask of you that you reduce them in order to save someone else (McKinnon 2012: 107–27), just as you cannot be asked to avoid killing in a self-defence scenario in which your own life is threatened. For the world's luxury emitters, however, the demands of the difference-making approach are not a matter of life or death. If your family holiday to the Caribbean will create emissions that kill innocent people, you have a duty not to take the holiday (Singer 1972).

There are three ways to attack the difference-making approach: (1) question the Harm Principle as a generator of duties for individuals; (2) argue that climate impacts are not harmful; or (3) engage with claims about the difference that individual emissions make to climate impacts. I shall dismiss (2) and return to (1) shortly.

Focusing on (3), Walter Sinnott-Armstrong argues that individual emissions cause no harm and so individuals do not have duties to reduce their emissions (Sinnott-Armstrong 2010). At the core of his argument are two claims: (a) that individual acts creating emissions are not necessary for climate change to happen and (b) that these acts are not sufficient for climate change to happen. With respect to (a), he argues that for any individual emissions-creating act, climate change will happen whether or not that act is performed. Cancelling your Caribbean holiday will not stop climate change getting worse. If we think that what it is for A to cause B is for A to be something without which B would not have happened (the so-called 'counterfactual' account of causation), then no act creating individual emissions causes climate change, and so no individual has a duty to reduce their emissions according to a Harm Principle.

On a different account of causation, what it is for A to cause B is for A to be a part of a collection of things without which B would not have happened (the so-called 'necessary element of a sufficient set', or NESS, account of causation (Moore 2019)). Prima facie, it is more compelling to think of individual emissions-creating acts as causes of climate change in this sense because my emissions could only ever cause climate change in combination with the emissions of many others. Sinnott-Armstrong argues against this that any particular emissions-creating act performed by me is not a necessary part of the set of all emissions causing climate change. Climate change is causally overdetermined by anthropogenic emissions, and so we cannot assert that my act creating emissions is the one that makes a difference to the causal powers of the set of all emissions with respect to climate change.

Sinnott-Armstrong does not have the final word on the difference-making account: there are a number of ways to counter his arguments (e.g. Hiller 2011; Lawford Smith 2016; McKinnon 2014). For now, it is important to be very clear that his argument is not that individuals have no climate duties, but that they have no climate duties to reduce their emissions. Instead, and in relation to his core example of driving an SUV on a sunny Sunday just for fun, he says: '[i]t is better to enjoy your Sunday driving while working to change the law so as to make it illegal for you to enjoy your Sunday driving' (Sinnott-Armstrong 2010: 344).

This takes us to the second way to think about individual climate duties, viz. that because climate impacts will not be mitigated or avoided without collective action, individuals have duties to bring about effective collective action on climate change. Elizabeth Cripps calls this the 'Cooperative Promotional Model' of individual climate duties. She describes these duties in general terms as follows:

> Act with motivated others, insofar as possible at reasonable cost to oneself, so as best to promote effective progress on global level climate change mitigation and adaptation as fairly and efficiently as feasible. (Cripps 2020: 113)

Cripps argues that individuals already motivated to act on climate change have a duty to connect with other similarly motivated people to promote coordinated, effective, and fair collective action on climate change. What this means for any particular individual will depend on their circumstances, skills, and talents. For a gregarious, charming, talented public speaker from a well-heeled background with no dependants, cooperative promotional duties might involve spearheading a PR campaign for action on climate change, or offering services for free as a speaker at large climate protests and rallies. In contrast, a single parent with three pre-school children and heavy debts might have cooperative pro-motional duties limited to bringing up her children to care about climate change. The flexibility built in to the cooperative promo-tional model means that it might be the case, for some people, that reducing their emissions is in fact the best way for them to promote the right kind of collective action on climate change: the influence of a high-profile rock star or political leader giving up air travel could make that reduction in emissions a very effective way to promote collective action. It should be noted, too, that this model generates duties for the motivated to strive to bring unmotivated people within the scope of the model: the cooperative promo-tional model does not let unmotivated people off the hook or treat them as beyond reach.

If motivated people succeed in the performance of their climate duties and cooperative collectives of various sorts – political, eco-nomic, religious, and social – form, does it make sense to assign climate duties directly to these groups? Does it make sense to assign climate duties to any groups? This question matters because, regardless of the contributions that individual emissions make to climate change, we know that emissions that can be legitimately attached to the activities of certain types of groups make a large contribution to climate change. For example, just twenty firms (many of them state-owned and/or heavily state subsidised) are responsible for one third of all the GHG emissions since 1965 (Taylor and Watts 2019). And, the Paris Agreement assigns legal duties to states as parties to the Agreement. If states and MNCs can have agency in ways similar to human agents, then perhaps some of them can also be duty-bearers and be subject to the ethical requirements of climate justice.

Broadly speaking, there are three positions on the question of whether groups can be duty-bearers. First, that groups qua groups can be literal duty-bearers; second, that groups can be duty-bearers but that group duties resolve without remainder into the duties of individual members. And third, that groups cannot be duty-bearers but certain individuals within groups have moral responsibility for what the group does.

The first position is defended by List and Pettit (List and Pettit 2011). They argue that what matters for agency is how parts of a system are related so as to: represent the world in ways that are sensitive to changes; have motivational states (e.g. intentions or purposes); and, do things as directed by these motivational and representational states. Group agents are, they say, 'organised so as to seek the realisation of certain motivations in the world and to do so on the basis of certain representations about what the world is like' (List and Pettit 2011: 32). This way of thinking about agency is known in the literature as 'functionalist'; that is, agency is a matter of any system being organised so as to function in a certain way, regardless of what the system is made of, its size, complexity etc. Importantly, List and Pettit do not argue that group agents have existence that is independent of the individual members of the group: there is no group agent that can exist apart from its members, and it is in virtue of what members do (e.g. promote the purposes of the group) that the group is able to do anything.[23]

As we saw in discussion of individual duties, agency is a necessary but not a sufficient condition for bearing duties. Dogs are agents but have no duties. Pettit's idea that 'conversibility' is the mark of agents fit to have duties – i.e. persons who can know their representational and motivational states in ways that enable them to commit to others – is described by List and Pettit as a 'performative' conception of personhood. What matters for whether an agent is a person is not what the agent is made of, but whether 'they can call on one another as parties to a shared system of expectation and obligation and expect that call to be heard' (List and Pettit 2011: 174). Many group agents – MNCs, states, families, religious communities – have exactly this property: they can commit themselves to others (e.g. through contracts) and expect others to deliver on their commitments. List and Pettit argue that it follows that such groups have rights. For example, states as group persons might have a right to self-determination, religious communities might have a right to freedom of worship, and MNCs might have a right to trade in a variety of markets. However, they argue that the rights of group persons are always subordinate to the rights of individual persons, and the power differences that often exist between group persons and individual persons justifies pursuing special checks – e.g. legal, constitutional, regulatory – on the conduct of group persons.[24]

If List and Pettit are right,[25] what might this mean for climate justice and the duties it generates? Here, we could apply the same reasoning we used with respect to individuals, viz. that a group has climate duties either in virtue of the harm caused by its emissions, or in virtue of its capacity to promote meaningful action to reduce climate injustice. For many group agents, especially large MNCs and states, a difference-making approach is likely to generate significant and clear duties. If Nolt is right that the emissions of the average American will kill one or two people, then the emissions of Exxon will be responsible for a very large number of deaths and mean that Exxon has duties to cut its emissions immediately and drastically and offset what cannot be cut right away. On the cooperative promotional model applied to groups, influential groups with standing on regional and international platforms are likely to have duties to push for legal and trade agreements that move the global economy quickly towards zero carbon. In the case of fossil fuel MNCs this is very likely to require them to cut emissions too, in order to have any moral authority.

What can be done if group agents fail to act on their climate duties? There are interesting questions here about whether group agents such as states can meaningfully be punished (Wringe 2012), whether punitive fines are ineffective insofar as they are likely just to be built into the business model of any MNC subject to them, and what sorts of global political institutions we would need to hold group persons truly accountable for their failure to perform their climate duties.

A different way of thinking about group climate duties takes group agency seriously but rejects personhood for groups. Stephanie Collins argues for a version of this view by focusing on corporations (Collins 2020). For her, the duties of a corporation are performed when the members of that corporation perform their 'membership duties': the performance of the latter by individual members constitutes the performance of the former by the group. Membership duties are not to be confused with duties that members might have qua individual persons. Rather, membership duties relate to the role held by an individual in the corporation. For example, we might (or might not) think that a cleaner employed by Exxon has duties to vote Green and engage in climate protests. If these duties attach to him as a private individual then they remain constant regardless of the job he does. However, his membership duties are indexed directly to the role he has, if any, in a corporation. As a cleaner at Exxon HQ perhaps he has duties to lobby to use more climate-friendly cleaning products. If he changes employment to become a delivery driver for Amazon perhaps his membership duties shift focus to pressing for a move to electric delivery vans.

Collins' approach seeks to deliver requirements at the individual level that, taken together, deliver on the duties of the group. She recognises that most individual members of corporations will play a role in them that generates relatively limited duties, and that the circumstances of people's lives must play a role in assessing what membership duties they have. If the Exxon cleaner's lobbying for climate-friendly products jeopardises his job, meaning he can no longer support his children, then that is too high a price to pay.

At this point we might wonder whether a focus on membership duties can take us far enough. As noted, most members have very limited influence or control over what their corporations do. That said, at the top of all corporations is a limited number of people – CEO, board members, major shareholders, owners – who have a disproportionately large amount of influence on what the corporation does. If we want corporations to stop killing the planet shouldn't we focus on those who actually direct what corporations do? Furthermore, a focus on the duties of corporate leaders, and here I mean to include political leaders of states understood as group agents, makes it very clear who is to be held accountable should these duties not be performed. It also enables us to leverage existing legal and political accountability mechanisms that already apply to individuals.

But there is a problem here. By holding leaders of groups accountable for what the group does have we severed the connection between causing a wrong and being responsible for the wrong in a way that is problematical? Most of the time, in legal contexts, individuals are punished for harm only when the harm has been caused by their conduct. In the case of corporations, a CEO is not the cause of what the corporation does: Rex Tillerson is not causally responsible for Exxon's emissions during the period 2006–17. This is even more the case once we recognise that corporations can exist over long periods of time with multiple successive leaders. By holding corporate leaders accountable for the harms caused by corporations, when these harms are not caused directly by anything the leader has done, do we violate a fundamental moral principle?

Arguably, we do not. As Doug Husak argues, '[p]ersons are responsible and deserve punishment only for those states of affairs over which they exercise control . . . the absence of control, not the absence of action, establishes the outer boundary of deserved punishment and responsibility' (Husak 2010: 34). According to the 'control requirement' for liability what matters is not whether an outcome is caused by what an individual did per se, but whether that individual had control over the coming about of the outcome. In many cases, individuals are morally responsible for a harm caused by their actions because, qua persons, they have the capacity to understand what they are required to do and not do, foresee (at least some) of the outcomes of their conduct, and regulate that conduct. But individuals in positions of power and authority in systems that count as group agents can also satisfy the control requirement, independently of any direct causal connection between their conduct qua individuals and the harms caused by the group agent. This opens up space for a third approach to group agency and responsibility for climate harms, in which groups cause harm and the leaders of the groups are liable for that harm.[26]

Conclusion

We have covered a lot of ground in this chapter, much of it contentious. Although perhaps not apparent on the surface, much of the knottiest points of friction in climate agreements and policymaking relate to questions of responsibility: which agents have it and why, and the duties it generates for those agents. Debates in political theory and philosophy about these issues matter. In the present moment, and in the face of any significant progress towards reducing climate injustice, all roads led to Rome. Regardless of whether the bases of responsibility are best captured by the polluter pays, beneficiaries pay, or ability-to-pay principles, we can identify a core group of state actors that have primary responsibilities to take action on climate change but are not meeting these responsibilities: Australia, the US, Canada, and the EU (at least).[27] Realities about the fast-disappearing carbon budget deliver very clear imperatives that give substance to these responsibilities: this core group must slash their emissions immediately in order that people in less developed countries can meet their basic rights as we transition to a zero-carbon global economy, and the core group make every effort possible to speed up this transition. And those of us with any influence in these core groups have at least individual duties to do whatever we can, given our circumstances, to force those who can bring about a transition to do this at speed and with justice. That all theoretical roads lead to Rome means that there is no place to hide for those who could create a zero-carbon world in which the basic rights of all people are met. There are no excuses.

6

What are our Options in the Face of Climate Failure?

Much of this book has addressed arguments that assume that we can get ahead of the climate crisis if agents of various types do what they ought to do. This assumption is (still) warranted. If states act together, with courage, to take strong precautionary action to move away rapidly from a fossil fuel global economy (for example, by no longer subsidising the fossil fuel industry at a rate of $11m a minute (Carrington 2021; Parry, Black, and Vernon 2021)), we could achieve a just transition to a zero carbon global economy. Or, if the 10% of the planet's ultra-rich were to forswear their grossly disproportionate appropriation of the carbon budget (this group is responsible for 50% of CO_2 emissions and produces 175 times more than the poorest 10% of people (Chancel 2021; Gore 2020)) it would enable the remaining 90% to take action on climate change secure in the knowledge that the richest people on the planet will not scupper their efforts.[1]

But what if we know enough about the agents who have these duties to be confident that, in fact, they will not do what they ought to do in the climate crisis? There is ample evidence here. Climate Action Tracker reported in 2021 that real-world policies and action are putting us on track for warming of 2.7C by 2100 (with a high end estimate of 3.6C).[2] And Climate Action Tracker also tells us that most countries are very far from delivering on the promises they made in their NDCs.[3] The world's richest people show no signs of voluntarily restraining their emissions and consumption in ways that are meaningful for tackling climate change, and the very richest among them are often fantastically clever at managing their financial affairs so as to avoid and evade tax (Collins 2021). When agents with duties to take immediate action in the climate crisis fail to do what they ought to do, what does that mean for everyone else?[4]

Some political theorists have called for so-called 'non-ideal' theory to answer questions like this (which, of course, arise in many scenarios as well as climate change).[5] As laid out in Chapter 1, on this approach we can think of political theory as being done against two contrasting sets of background assumptions, each of which describes 'ideal' and 'non-ideal' circumstances. 'Ideal theory' works on the assumption that all parties are willing and able to do what is required or recommended by the ideal theory: it assumes 'full compliance'. In contrast, 'non-ideal theory' assumes that some parties are unwilling and/or unable to do what is required or recommended by the ideal theory: it assumes 'partial compliance'. Non-ideal theory asks what ought to be done in these conditions, when we cannot expect to realise the ideal outcome. For example, if some states are not willing to do what they ought to with respect to cutting emissions – the so-called 'climate laggard' states[6] – are non-laggard states required to do more to 'take up the slack' created by climate laggards?[7]

Political theorists have tackled these and other normative questions, which arise in the non-ideal circumstances of climate failure. Overwhelmingly, they have done so by articulating forms of political action that are justified in our current climate crisis: the focus, by and large, has not been on 'guilt-tripping' ordinary people about their 'carbon footprints'.[8] Instead, political theorists have taken aim at those who are failing the most and putting all of us, including future people, in peril. If our circumstances in the climate crisis are radically non-ideal, in part because we in more developed countries are a society of 'altruists governed by psychopaths' (Monbiot 2019), what can and ought we to do force our political and economic leaders to act differently?

Some of the most exciting work by political theorists working on climate change is being done in this area. Proposals fall roughly into three categories. First, those that deploy democratic arguments for radical institutional reform. Second, those that call for revitalised 'ecological citizenship', and other forms of political mobilisation, as a win–win way to get ahead of the climate crisis. And third, those that challenge the thought that 'it is easier to imagine the end of the world than the end of capitalism' by plotting routes out of the climate crisis that would also mark the end of our global capitalist economy.

Can democracy get us out of the climate crisis?

In an earlier wave of environmental philosophy, democratic routes out of ecological crisis were not held in favour by many influential thinkers. As we saw in Chapter 2, Garrett Hardin saw the ecological crises of the 1960s and 1970s as collectively irrational, and a product of humanity's overuse and despoilation of the planet's natural resources. The solution he recommended was 'mutual coercion, mutually agreed upon' (Hardin 1968). While not necessarily anti-democratic,[9] Hardin's solution has been gathered up with those of other environmental thinkers of the time who questioned the fitness of democratic politics in an ecological crisis and foretold the rise of authoritarianism as environmental conditions collapse (Heilbroner 1974; Meadows et al. 1972; Ophuls 1977).

This deep scepticism about democratic solutions to ecological crises is not the flavour of much of the more recent work on political action in a time of climate failure.[10] Instead, democratic theorists have acknowledged the ways in which liberal democratic politics has enabled, or even encouraged, the climate crisis. They have argued that reformed, or transformed, democratic politics has the power to make good on our climate failures: that by preserving (or enhancing) the democratic legitimacy of political institutions we can turn around the climate crisis.

There are at least two clear points in the 'democracy–environment nexus' (Schlosberg, Backstrand, and Pickering 2019) at which arguments for the power of democracy to address the climate crisis cluster: reformist and radical. Broadly speaking, reformist approaches advocate the improvement of existing liberal democratic institutions and processes (Hailwood 2004; Shutkin 2001; Wissenburg 2013) whereas radical approaches focus on deep critique of existing liberal democratic institutions and propose foundational transformation of these institutions and associated processes (Christoff 1996; Eckersley 2004). These different points generate different types of political action. Reformists, for example Green political parties in the UK or Germany, are likely to work within existing democratic institutions in order to improve them, whereas radicals, for example Extinction Rebellion, more often stand outside these institutions and call for them to be gutted or abolished.

One key difference between reformist and radical approaches to 'green democracy' can relate to the type of value they assign to nonhuman nature. Many radical approaches allow for nonhuman nature – systems, entities, landscapes, species etc. – to have intrinsic value independently of the value (if any) assigned to them by human beings (Leopold 1989; Naess 1990). This is known as an 'ecocentric' theory of value. In contrast, most reformist approaches often operate with an 'anthropocentric' theory of value whereby the value of nonhuman nature is to be determined only by the way in which human beings value it.[11]

A classic illustration of the distinction between ecocentric and anthropocentric approaches to the value of nature can be found in Richard Sylvan's [Routley's] example of the Last Person on Earth (Routley 1973). Sylvan asks us to imagine a scenario in which all but one human being have died, and in which there will be no more people in the future. If the last person on Earth goes on a destructive rampage – cutting down ancient redwood trees, finishing off the orangutans of Sumatra, and dynamiting the Dolomites – do they do anything wrong? If you think they do, that cannot be because of the way in which these wonders of nature are valued by human beings, because there is only one left and (by stipulation) she does not value them. In that case, you hold an ecocentric theory of value. The alternative response is that the last person on Earth does nothing wrong in her destructive rampage because the absence of humans who value the things she destroys means that they have no value. In this case, you hold an anthropocentric theory of value.

A related difference between reformist and radical approaches can be the weight they have given to changing people's consciousness in making democracy work for the environment (Dryzek 2021). For radical democratic thinkers who make room for the ecocentric value of nonhuman nature it is often a natural next step to argue that people in democratic polities ought to embed these values in their worldviews and change their behaviour accordingly. The changes in consciousness that have been proposed by radical environmental thinkers have taken many different forms. Some would involve a significant set of transformations in our conception of our place in the world; for example, quasi-spiritual claims about self-realisation through immersion in the natural world (Naess 1990), or identification with all the elements of nature in a 'transpersonal ecology' (Fox 1995). Others would require less deep changes; for example making conscious planet-friendly consumer or reproductive choices (Cripps 2015).

Beyond changing hearts and minds, radical democratic approaches have also focused on creating new democratic institutions, processes, and cultures that are both much more democratic than those that currently exist and are (for this reason, it is argued) fit for purpose in our ecological crises. In particular, political theorists working on 'deliberative democracy' have argued that our ecological crises can be addressed far better in democratic politics by improving the quality of our deliberation within this form of politics.

Deliberative democracy is often understood in contrast to aggregative democracy. In aggregative systems, an outcome is democratic if it has been chosen by the majority. Aggregative systems do not scrutinise the reasons voters have for voting as they do, and do not require any special interactions between voters prior to the casting of their vote. Deliberative democracy requires more of voters, and of those charged with acting on decisions that have been made democratically. Under deliberative democracy, citizens engage together on the question in hand in advance of making a decision and are guided by experts where necessary to gain understanding of specialist topics. The processes of deliberative democracy are inclusive and aim at consensus. There are various ways in which this might be done on the ground, for example, through deliberative polling (Fishkin 2018) or a 'Deliberation Day' (Ackerman and Fishkin 2004).

Why think that deliberative democracy is more friendly to environmental problem-solving than aggregative forms? Advocates have argued that this form of democratic decision-making is inclusive and enables local knowledge to influence policymaking (which can matter for finding solutions that will work on the ground), and that it can serve the ends of environmental justice by ensuring that the perspectives and stories of victims of injustice influence future pathways (Baber and Bartlett 2018; Schlosberg and Collins 2014). Advocates have also argued that outcomes are better – for people, and for the environment – when deliberative methods are used, because when citizens engage with experts in these processes they become resilient against the manipulation of their attention by vested interests (such as in cases of climate denial) (Dryzek and Pickering 2018).

Political theorists have made proposals for climate-friendly institutional reform that exploit these features of deliberative democracy. For example, Simon Caney proposes a regular 'Vision for the Future Day' of democratic deliberation about a government's manifesto promises to deliver on intergenerational justice and its action on them (Caney 2016c). At the global scale, Stephen Gardiner argues for a Global Constitutional Convention to address the 'institutional gap' in our present political systems with respect to protecting future people from the wrongdoing of their ancestors (Gardiner 2014). This Convention is envisaged as a discursive, open process leading to agreement on a Global Constitution in which the interests of future people are properly represented.

Democratic proposals for reducing climate injustices in conditions of failure focus on how we can improve the structures, processes and deliberations leading to action in the policy and political domain. Some political theorists have argued that, in addition, we must work to change the norms and values of the people who engage in these structures; that is, that we must work towards a revitalised conception of citizenship as ecological.

Can we make good our climate failures through ecological citizenship?

There are many ways we could incentivise people to engage in pro-climate behaviour. For example, we could pay them to participate in Caney's Vision for the Future Day. Or, we could tax carbon intensive goods (such as out-of-season imported food) or require the purchase of carbon offsets for carbon intensive services (such as taking long-haul flights). The most prominent existing market-based approaches are emissions trading schemes whereby agents purchase emissions allowances: the number of allowances (or 'permits') available is set by a cap reflecting mitigation ambition. Countries or firms with excess permits can sell to those with a deficit. The idea is that emissions-trading ensures the internalisation of the true costs of emissions without a loss of efficiency (Grantham Research Institute 2018; Page 2013). 'Market-based solutions' exploit existing economic structures and financial instruments in order to influence choices made by individuals and households so as to make them more climate-friendly.

There are some arguments that say market-based approaches can be designed so as to contribute to climate justice but that existing incarnations of these approaches do not meet the bar defended in these arguments (Caney 2010b; Sayegh 2019). In general, advocates for existing market-based approaches argue that they avoid restrictions on individual freedom, which can be anti-democratic and illiberal. To take consumer carbon offsetting as an example, the argument would be that requiring the purchase of offsets for long-haul flights that reflect the true cost to the climate of the emissions created by this form of travel is not tantamount to banning these flights or forcing anyone not to take them. If you, sitting in the gloom of a Devon January, really want that winter sun in Grenada, the means to get you there are still available. All that has changed is the price, which reflects the full cost to the environment of such flights.

An immediate worry about the 'freedom-protecting' argument for market-based approaches is that it takes freedom to be a matter only of the absence of legal restrictions, whereas freedom arguably requires far more than this. In particular, some political theorists have argued, a lack of resources to act in the space created by an absence of legal restrictions diminishes freedom: a lack of money is a lack of freedom (Cohen 2015). On this view, it is not the case that all are equally free to escape to the winter sun of Grenada by taking long-haul flights: Richard Branson can do this at the drop of a hat and without making sacrifices elsewhere, whereas a single mother of a disabled child who is dependent on welfare benefits will never be in a position to afford this. Critics have argued that it is an affront to claim that Branson and the mother are equally free to fly to Grenada, and that market-based solutions have the potential to worsen climate injustice (Anderson 2012; Goodin 2010; Hyams and Fawcett 2013).

Another claimed advantage of market-based solutions is that they are relatively easy to enact. This is because the necessary structures and processes already exist, and because they leverage the ways in which people are already motivated. This second claimed advantage depends on conceiving of human agents as *Homo economicus*: (perfectly) rational decision-makers motivated at all times to optimally satisfy their subjectively defined interests. Given these (neoclassical economic) assumptions about what will move people to act, and given that money is an all-purpose means ultimately necessary for the pursuit of any individual's interests, market-based solutions to the climate crisis aim to bring about behaviour change by making climate-unfriendly conduct more expensive, and thus less aligned to the purposes of *Homo economicus*.[12]

It is this claimed advantage of market-based solutions that is the launchpad for arguments for ecological citizenship. An obvious reaction to the line of thinking in the previous paragraph is that modelling human decision-making using *Homo economicus* as an ideal creates a false picture of the reasons for which real people act. People are neither perfectly rational, nor uniformly motivated to pursue their subjectively defined interests.[13] Furthermore, the focus on manipulating the means available to people to pursue their subjectively defined interests is misplaced and at odds with the claimed pragmatic benefits of market-based solutions. If the aim is, as it has to be, permanent, embedded, reliable pro-climate behaviour change, then the focus should be on influencing people's subjectively defined interests directly, so as to make them more pro-climate. Without this focus, market-based solutions are always at the mercy of political winds that we know often stall progress out of the climate crisis. Taking economic structures and financial instruments as they are means that any incoming government can reverse market-based solutions. If the only incentives people have to act in ways that are pro-climate reside in these solutions, then pro-climate behaviour change will remain vulnerable to the failures of political will that created and sustains the climate crisis.

Advocates for ecological citizenship have argued that what we need is behaviour change that is delivered by changes in attitude, values, and orientation to the natural world. Pro-climate behaviour change that has these roots can persist in the face of political intransigence and makes it less likely that political leaders will fail on climate change. Ecological citizens will be motivated to vote pro-climate, and to live, work, and think in ways that open up routes out of the climate crisis. The ecological citizen is motivated in this way because she sees these ways of being as in her subjectively defined interests, rather than being motivated by economic reward (Dobson 2006, 2007).

The 'ecological citizen' is sometimes contrasted with the 'environmental citizen' (MacGregor 2014). This distinction maps well on to reformist and radical positions in the environment–democracy nexus, as described in the previous section. Environmental citizens work to improve existing political institutions and processes so as to make them, inter alia, more pro-climate. Advocates for environmental citizenship often retain a focus on liberal rights, and are mindful of the liberal requirement for the just state to remain neutral between different visions of the good life (including those that do not prioritise nature or assign particular value to the environment) (Bell 2005, 2006). Advocates for ecological citizenship propose norms of citizenship that are more demanding, and that require the abandonment of liberal political neutrality. The ecological citizen is motivated to act in ways that put nature first because her worldview assigns value to nature and includes commitment to limiting damaging human impacts on as well as making good past damage. There are many so-called 'conceptions of the good'; that is, evaluative standpoints on the world, other people, and how one stands in relation to them (Rawls 1999: 347–86) that are ruled out by ecological citizenship (for example, consumerist, technophile, and colonial conceptions of the good).

Ecological citizenship involves deep behaviour change for more environment-positive outcomes as a result of citizens adopting an ethical standpoint. The ecological citizen acts in pro-climate ways because she believes it is the right thing to do – that she has a duty to act in this way – or because her character makes pro-environment behaviour habitual or part of her identity. Many advocates of ecological citizenship have focused their attention on the latter dimension of ecological citizenship by describing the virtues of the model ecological citizen. For example, Peter Christoff has argued for the cultivation of an 'ethic of stewardship' (Christoff 1996) as the mark of ecological citizenship; Andrew Dobson has argued for the importance of solidarity and care (Dobson 2006); and Tim Hayward identifies resourcefulness as a virtue of this kind of citizenship (Hayward 2006). And others who do not align themselves so closely with the 'ecological citizenship' literature have identified virtues that nevertheless play the same role. For example, Jedediah Purdy argues for self-restraint (Purdy 2015), and Dale Jamieson argues for categories of virtue – preservation, rehabilitation, and creation (Jamieson 2014: 186) – that he believes we will need in order to live with our climate failures.

What does ecological citizenship mean in practice? Advocates point out that ecological citizenship is an activity not a status (Dobson 2003): one becomes an ecological citizen by doing certain things rather than by acquiring a legal or political status. The things that ecological citizens do as a result of the virtues they cultivate or the norms to which they adhere transgress the traditional liberal boundaries between public and private domains. Mainstream conceptions of citizenship relate to what people do in the public realm: these conceptions treat citizenship as a political persona which can be set aside once one is acting as a private person (say, with family or friends). Ecological citizenship blurs these lines. Because everything a person does potentially has an effect on the environment, there are few (perhaps no) domains in which an ecological citizen can shed this identity. What one eats, how one travels to work, one's reproductive choices, where and how one's children are schooled, what one wears, one's banking choices, one's interment preferences: all these and more are potential sites of activity required by ecological citizenship. On an ecological citizenship approach these hitherto personal matters become political.

Beyond the personal, some political theorists have argued that ecological citizenship should drive large-scale changes in the 'basic structure' of society: that is, 'the major social institutions [which] distribute fundamental rights and duties and determine the division of advantages from social cooperation' (Rawls 1999: 6). For example, John Barry argues for a 'green republican' version of ecological citizenship, which generates a case for compulsory (i.e. enforced by the state) 'civic sustainability service'. This service would impact on the liberty of citizens. He says:

> This service could take the form of all citizens having to give up some proportion of their time to engage in a range of sustainability services [which] could include cleaning up a polluted beach or river, working in community-based recycling schemes [or] working on community wind-farms . . . The amount of time given up to sustainability service could range from one year (post-education) in the service of the common good, to a couple of hours each week over a longer period. (Barry 2012: 260).

Some people might find it hard to imagine willing acceptance of measures such as those described by Barry. Here, the discussion in Chapter 2 of feasibility based objections to the pursuit of climate justice has resonance. Even if it were the case that people did not accept civic sustainability service schemes this would do nothing to show that they are unable to, or cannot, accept this and similar schemes. What people can find a will to do does not delimit what they are in fact capable of doing (Estlund 2011). In any case it is far from obvious that people will not in fact accept and, indeed, support and promote requirements imposed in the name of the greater good. For example, wartime rationing of food, military conscription, or requirements for physical distancing and masking in the Covid 19 global pandemic. Furthermore, many examples of large-scale, relatively swift, radical social and political change have been bottom-up and driven by changes in people's fundamental attitudes which have accelerated change as a result of 'norm cascades'. In England, examples include female suffrage (1928), and the legalisation of homosexuality (1967).

Advocates of ecological citizenship argue that the political participation that can lead to the reduction of injustice in society can be a 'win–win': active and participatory citizenship can not only promote justice but also benefit individual citizens. Civic participation to address climate failures can foster bonds of solidarity, community, and mutual aid between citizens, thus making their lives go better (Barry 1999, 2006). On this view, it is a mistake to see the activities of ecological citizenship as burdensome. Instead, they are opportunities to enrich social relations, exercise virtue, and live a life more meaningful than would be possible under nature-destroying consumer capitalism.

One important line of criticism of this approach starts by asking who, in the real world, is likely to have to answer the call to action of ecological citizenship. As discussed earlier, ecological citizenship blurs the line between the public and private spheres by requiring significant change in domestic practices. As Sherilyn MacGregor argues, work in this sphere is disproportionately done by women (Charmes 2019). If ecological citizenship is blind to the unjust distribution of essential work in this sphere that meets social needs

– i.e. work that ensures citizens are fed, clothed, and cared for – then it risks worsening these injustices by imposing even more burdens on women already at the sharp end of patriarchal injustice (Chiro 2008; Latta 2007; MacGregor 2006a, 2006b). As she puts it:

> [W]henever and wherever the private or domestic sphere is impli- cated in strategies for social or ecological change, consideration must be given to the unequal and deeply gendered division of labour and responsibility . . . [t]aking for granted that duties will be shared and the necessary work will get done is tantamount to making 'more work for the mother'. (MacGregor 2006a: 112)

This line of criticism has also been made by reference to other victims of injustice: poor and ethnically marginalised people. For example, Julian Agyeman argues that ecological citizenship must focus on 'just sustainability' (Agyeman 2013). This means both casting our gaze beyond ecological goals to consider how the demands of this citizenship could exacerbate already existing injus- tices and inequalities, and ensuring the perspectives and voices of people suffering environmental injustices are central in finding environmentally sustainable ways to alleviate the unjust harm they suffer (Schlosberg and Craven 2019). Arguably, the emphasis on justice and fairness here loops the debate back into more 'ideal theory' type analyses of what justice requires in the climate crisis.

Spheres of citizenship are not the only domain in which politi- cal theorists have proposed action to combat our climate failures. Citizenship traditionally involves working within existing politi- cal, social, and economic structures in order to make them less unjust. In the next section I consider proposals for action under climate failure that recommend law-breaking, mass mobilisation, and revolution as routes out of the climate crisis.

Is climate change the 'cancer stage of capitalism'?

Consider the extent of our failure in the climate crisis. For at least the last three decades, we have had ample evidence for anthropogenic global warming. We have a legally binding international treaty, the UNFCCC, which commits us to fighting climate change in ways that are equitable. Climate change is claimed to be high on the political agenda in almost all countries. Business and finance are scrambling to call themselves 'climate-friendly'. Art, literature, and popular culture abound with representations of the climate crisis. You cannot open a newspaper without being confronted with yet another frightening story about the acceleration of the crisis. And yet: emissions are higher than they have ever been, and current policies and action put the world on track for 2.7C of warming by 2100 (Climate Action Tracker 2021; UNEP 2021). With all this talk, thought, and effort, why are we still failing so badly?

One plausible explanation is that maintaining a global carbon economy, feeding cultures of never-ending consumption, is in the interests of those with the most power; that is, those best positioned to extract maximum profit from the continued use of fossil fuels. These people influence politics and policymaking both by providing direct support to their most favoured candidates and parties, and by financing major employers and investors in domestic economies. Their potential mobility, that is, their ability to relocate their business to new places, pushes politics to serve their interests: for example, overlooking their tax avoidance, or providing state subsidies for fossil fuel extraction (Chomsky 2016). And the profit-motive makes the drive for more and more economic growth continuous and inexorable. What has fed the capitalist growth imperative is the use of natural resources, including fossil fuels and carbon sinks. Do the imperatives and institutions of global capitalism explain our climate failures? Is climate change the 'cancer stage of capitalism'? (Barry 2011; Hamilton 2004).

The view that politics, policy, and culture are driven by, and ultimately serve, economic forces is at the heart of Karl Marx's theory of history (Cohen 1978; Marx 2000). At the dawn of capitalism, the Industrial Revolution made it possible for a small class of people to extract profit from natural resources laboured on by workers. Marx argued that the growth-oriented logic of capitalism fuels ever more exploitation of workers (whose wages do not reflect the value they add to resources through their labour) leading eventually to the downfall of capitalism and revolution to establish socialism, and then communism.[14]

If global capitalism is the blocker of routes out of the climate crisis, should we take aim at capitalism by becoming Marxists? Care is needed here. On many accounts of Marx's vision of a communist society, industrial processes have developed to such a point that true freedom for all, that is, freedom from 'alienating' work in a society in which labour is 'life's prime want' (Marx 2000), is secured by political processes and structures. On these accounts, the alienation suffered by workers under capitalism disappears under communism but only because the means by which people can convert natural resources into goods and services have evolved in a way that frees everyone from drudgery. Under communism, industrial processes of production persist, and the nonhuman natural world remains a resource for unlimited human use and consumption.

For this reason, some green thinkers have rejected Marxian routes out of the climate crisis. For example, Jonathan Porritt remarks of capitalism and communism that:

> Both are dedicated to industrial growth, to the expansion of the means of production, to a materialist ethics as the best means of meeting people's needs, and to unimpeded technological development . . . From a viewpoint of narrow scientific rationalism, both insist that the planet is there to be conquered . . . (Porritt 1984: 44)

Porritt gathers together capitalism and communism as varieties of what he calls the 'super ideology of industrialism' (Porritt 1984: 44).[15] For Porritt, and many green thinkers, the road to a future free from climate crisis must be mapped in new ways that make good on the shared failures of left- and right-wing politics in the domain of the environment. Hence the motto of many Green political parties is: 'neither left nor right but forward'.

One of the fundamental planks of a new green approach is a rejection of the idea of endless economic growth with its implicit assumptions that the natural resources of the Earth are unlimited. In a resurgence of themes from the first wave of environmental theory in the 1970s, which highlighted the *Limits to Growth* (Meadows et al. 1972), some contemporary theorists have advocated 'degrowth' as a necessary paradigm shift to get us out of the climate crisis and into a more just and flourishing society (Anderson and Bows 2011; Hamilton 2004; Hickel 2021; Kallis 2011; Kallis et al. 2020). Degrowth is planned and purposeful economic contraction with the aim of slowing down economic growth. This would mean measuring the success of public policy, and the political flourishing of society, in terms of something other than GDP; and measuring the success of lives using a standard other than 'whoever dies with the most stuff wins' (Barry 2011).

It is important here to note that calls for degrowth apply at the global level, that is, to the overall growth of the global economy. These calls hardly ever apply uniformly across all regions. The impacts and severity of climate change are – and will continue to be – far worse in some parts of the world than others: climate resilience is not evenly spread. And responsibility for climate change, and for shouldering the burdens of taking action on it now, is not shared equally across all of humanity. As we saw in Chapter 5, whatever principles of responsibility for climate change we adopt, all roads lead to Rome: countries that industrialised early and are more developed are morally required to act on climate change first. If calls for degrowth were to apply uniformly in a way that ignores these facts, they would demand that the least climate resilient countries of the world, with the least responsibility for climate change, should slow their economic growth at the same time as the richest countries, which bear responsibility for the climate crisis. This would be morally outrageous (Kashwan et al. 2020). Slowing economic growth in Chad means death, hunger, and illness for countless people, now and into the future. Slowing economic growth in the UK means a lower standard of living for most people, and less profit for shareholders of companies trading there.[16] Advocates of degrowth do not argue that rates of degrowth should be constant everywhere. Indeed, climate justice might require that 'green growth' must be supported in regions with the least resilience to, and responsibility for, climate change.[17] If global degrowth is the goal, justice could require rapid degrowth in some places combined with low-carbon growth in others.[18]

Degrowth as well as other proposals for routes out of the climate crisis have been taken up a variety of social movements, from grassroots groups such as Extinction Rebellion to many of the more formally organised NGOs affiliated with networks such as the Climate Action Network.[19] If the solutions we identify to make good our climate failures are fundamentally and radically opposed to the interests of the most powerful people among us and do not map onto existing political movements, then we need to know how to make change of this magnitude happen. Political theorists interested in climate justice take this question seriously. They have identified at least two options in the face of enduring and intractable climate injustice: civil disobedience, and revolution.

Can we solve the climate crisis through protest, disobedience, or revolution?

In 2018 Greta Thunberg concluded her Declaration of Rebellion with the following words:

> Today we use 100 million barrels of oil every day.
> There are no politics to change that. There are no rules to keep that oil in the ground.
> So we can't save the world by playing by the rules.
> Because the rules have to be changed.
> Everything needs to change. And it has to start today.
> So everyone out there: it is now time for civil disobedience.
> It is time to rebel. (Thunberg 2019: 12–13)

Is our real route out of the climate crisis disobedience, protest, and if necessary violent political revolution?

There is a rich history of theorising civil disobedience per se (Harris 1989). According to John Rawls' influential account:

> Civil disobedience [is] a public, nonviolent, conscientious yet political act contrary to law usually done with the aim of bringing about a change in the law or policies of the government. By acting in this way one addresses the sense of justice of the majority of the community and declares that in one's considered opinion the principles of social cooperation among free and equal men are not being respected. (Rawls 1999: 319)

Civil disobedience involves peaceful law-breaking done in the name of fidelity to the law. The civil disobedient does not aim at overthrowing the state or promoting their own narrow self-interest. Rather, the civil disobedient acts conscientiously to shine a light on existing injustices with the aim of eliminating them. Rawls' account fits very well with some classic examples of civil disobedience. Rosa Parks' refusal to give up her seat on a bus to a white man,[20] Mahatma Gandhi's Salt March,[21] and widespread refusal to pay the Poll Tax in the UK in the early 1990s are all well described in Rawls' terms.[22]

There are many examples of climate-related direct action that also prima facie satisfy Rawlsian criteria. For example, the global youth movement Fridays for Future organises and supports non-violent strike action, rallies, and marches.[23] Extinction Rebellion members do similar.[24] There is, however, an important difference between much climate-oriented civil disobedience and the classic examples from history mentioned in the previous paragraph. Whereas the Salt March, the Civil Rights movement, and the Poll Tax Protests were all directed towards injustices perpetrated within a well-defined jurisdiction (colonially occupied India, racially segregated America, and the UK under Thatcherite Conservatism), the same is not true of the protests made by Extinction Rebellion and Fridays for Future. Given the nature of climate change as a planetary emergency, calls for rectification of climate injustices are very often directed towards world leaders and 'the global economy' rather than specific pieces of legislation.

Although Extinction Rebellion and Fridays for Future advocate nonviolent action against climate injustice, protest and disobedience can take more radical forms. The peaceful action of the Suffragists to get women the vote was matched by the sometimes violent protests of the Suffragettes. Martin Luther King's calls for nonviolent protest for civil rights were matched by Malcolm X's defence of violence by black people as self-defence in the face of white oppression. The only successful insurrection led by slaves, the Haitian Revolution, was armed and bloody (Popkin 2021).

Simon Caney helps us to make sense of climate protest both as aimed at the world order, and as potentially involving violence. He defends what he calls the Right of Resistance Against Global Injustice (Caney 2020).[25] This right of resistance, says Caney, legitimises law-breaking acts of protest that attempt to change practices, policies, or political systems that create and sustain global injustice, and so have movement towards global justice as their goal (Caney 2020: 513). This right can be exercised through conduct such as rallies, sit-ins, and other forms of nonviolent protest; but it can also be exercised through sabotage involving violence against property, and riots and rebellion, which can include violence against people. Violence is permitted as part of rightful resistance, on Caney's account, if and only if resisters 'employ the least harmful means available' (Caney 2020: 522).[26]

We can push this line of thought further. What if the only effective routes out of the climate crisis involve action that would normally be ruled out by our moral principles and judgements? What if action to avert the climate crisis is morally condemnable, but not taking that action will allow egregious injustices to accumulate? Patrick Taylor Smith describes climate change in terms of 'moral pathway infeasibility' (Taylor Smith, forthcoming): it is immoral to allow the climate crisis to spiral out of control, but the action necessary to prevent this is also morally prohibited. For Taylor Smith, climate change represents a 'revolutionary context': in this context a different kind of ethical theory, a theory of justified revolution, applies. He argues that a revolution is justified when it actually succeeds and when revolutionaries genuinely represent the communities they say they speak for. On Taylor Smith's account, the stakes for climate revolutionaries could not be higher. Revolutions are violent and brutal: innocent people lose their lives, homes, and livelihoods. For Taylor Smith, these moral wrongdoings become justified if and only if the revolution succeeds. Climate revolutionaries assume grave moral risks when they take up arms: 'when one undertakes a revolution, doing wrong with the hope that the eventual consequences will compensate or outweigh it, one is not merely lucky or unlucky depending on how it works out. Rather, one is taking a risk, exposing oneself to severe opprobrium if it fails . . .' (Taylor Smith, personal correspondence). Perhaps thinking about climate revolutionaries as willing to take such risks should affect contemporaneous moral judgements of them in the moment of revolutionary action, even if subsequent generations will judge them harshly if they fail, using ethics for a non-revolutionary context.

Conclusion

This chapter has surveyed some of the ways in which political theorists are thinking about the desperate times we are in. There are no silver bullets, of course. The climate crisis feels overwhelming – because it is. To have any hope of applying the brakes, so much will have to change. Our political institutions, from parish councils to international organisations, will have to be overhauled or replaced. For most of us lucky enough to have been born in more developed countries, our comfortable, effortless, instantaneous gratifications will have to go. We will have to renew our relationships with nature. We will have to find ways to hobble the influence of money and block power-seekers from building the world in their image. What makes this so very hard is that time is running out: to have any decent chance of staying below 2C we should be seeing action on all these fronts now. And yet, the status quo persists. If only we had more time, or some way of turning back the clock on our emissions.

In the next chapter I turn to technological proposals for geo-engineering that claim to fulfil this wish.

7

Geoengineering: Saviour Technologies or Fantasies of Control?

We know that climate change has many victims, present and future. We know that the damage suffered by victims is a matter of justice, and that much of it could be avoided or reduced. We have well-articulated and persuasive accounts of where moral responsibility for seeing justice done for climate victims falls. In the short to medium term, we know that all roads lead to Rome on the question of responsibility: the world's richest countries must take the lead on aggressive mitigation, meaningful support for adaptation, and institutional overhaul to create a political and economic world in which future crises of the Anthropocene can be avoided or better addressed. We know that these actors must also rapidly scale up and roll out renewable energy technologies that enable all people of the world to satisfy their basic rights in ways that are affordable (Shue 2014c). These things are at the heart of a just transition from a fossil-fuel intensive global economy fuelled by consumer capitalism, and stoked by MNCs in the extractive industries and the states that heavily subsidise them. What we must transition to is a zero-carbon global economy, stimulated and sustained by the world's most advantaged states and people, and governed in ways that make the basic rights of present and future poor people a priority.

If we bring about a just transition we will have taken a fork in the road of human history that will count as one of humanity's greatest achievements. We will have created a political, economic, and social platform that will give our descendants the opportunity to thrive and progress without trashing the planet and our non-human co-inhabitants. If we fail we will have chosen to force our descendants down a path of ever-increasing climatic instability, crop failure and food shortages, mass displacement, conflict at all levels, disease, and water shortage. We will have chosen for them lives of hunger, thirst, illness, precarity, loss of identity, grief, humiliation, fear, and anxiety. The stakes could not be higher.

I started the previous paragraph with 'if we bring about a just transition . . .'. But there is a more fundamental question to be asked: *can* we bring about a just transition? There are two components of a just transition. The justice component requires action by responsible agents to fulfil what they owe to climate victims. The transition component requires stabilising the global average temperature at 2C (ideally, 1.5C) above the pre-industrial average. This book has so far been focused on the justice component. But if we do not achieve the transition component, the justice component could look very different. Indeed, if we do not keep global average temperature below 2C, justice could cease to be relevant to action on climate change (McKinnon 2012: 107–28).

What do we need to do to now, and in the next (say) eighty years, to effectively transition away from a fossil-fuelled global economy and keep global average temperatures below 2C or 1.5C? Many people accept that the Paris Agreement mechanisms for ratcheting up mitigation ambition will have to work overtime for us to avoid warming of over 2C by 2100. Given present commitments, even if all parties achieve their nationally determined contributions (NDCs) we may still see temperature rises of at least 2.6C by 2100 (Rogelj et al. 2016), and many climate experts now accept that there will be significant overshoot of temperature targets in the decades prior to 2100 (CAT 2016; Rogelj et al. 2015; Schleussner et al. 2016).[1]

However, it is a deeply underappreciated fact that aggressive traditional mitigation on its own is very unlikely to suffice for this.

The IPCC maintains various suites of scenarios for future climate change. These scenarios capture an array of variables relevant to the possible state of the climate in 2100 including, for example, emissions reductions, population growth and size, different values for climate sensitivity, and renewables scale-up and rollout. 87% of the IPCC scenarios that give a 66% or higher chance of staying below 2C by 2100 assume large-scale and effective negative energy technologies – NETs. For scenarios for 1.5C, it is 100% (Allen, Babiker, and Chen 2018; Smith et al. 2016)

NETs could enable us to overshoot targets for emissions reductions without exceeding the GHG budget for 2C by 2100. NETs could do this by enhancing existing carbon sinks, creating new carbon sinks, or implementing new technologies that remove carbon. If we are to bring about the 'transition' in the just transition we are very likely to have to use NETs. If emissions continue to grow as the months and years pass our options look like they will become ever more stark: deploy NETS on a global scale to stay within the carbon budget for 2C, or lower ambition and set a higher target.[2]

What if there were a third option? One that could buy us more time to get emissions under control, NETs deployed, and renewables scaled up affordably? Enter the advocates of solar radiation management (SRM). This type of proposed geoengineering would work in ways very different to NETs. Rather than removing GHGs from the atmosphere, SRM would mask their effects. By reflecting solar radiation (sunlight) away from the planet, global average temperatures could be kept lower than they would be otherwise. If we could achieve this we might then have a fighting chance of tackling the causes of climate change by emissions reductions and NETs so as to stay under 2C (or even 1.5C).

The Royal Society defines geoengineering as '[d]eliberate large-scale manipulation of the planetary environment to counteract anthropogenic warming' (Royal Society 2009a). NETs and SRM both fit this description, but in very different ways. NETs manipulate the planetary environment by removing GHGs from the atmosphere, whereas SRM deflects sunlight from the planet so as to mask the warming effect of GHGs accumulated in the atmosphere. Geoengineering technologies are a new frontier in action on climate change. In this chapter I shall survey the two most prominent technologies under development in the NETs and SRM camps; namely, bioenergy with carbon capture and storage (BECCS),[3] and stratospheric aerosol injection (SAI).[4] My interest here is in the ethical and justice questions raised by the prospect or deployment of geoengineering. Should we think of BECCS and/or SAI as saviour technologies, dangerous Promethean fantasies, or something altogether more messy?

What questions of justice and ethics are raised by bioenergy with carbon capture and storage?

BECCs combines carbon capture and storage (CCS) with energy generated from biomass (bioenergy).[5] BECCS could serve as an effective NET as a result of two carbon reducing processes. First, feedstocks grown for biomass to create bioenergy absorb CO_2 from the atmosphere.[6] Popular suggestions are miscanthus and willow trees, both of which are fast growing. Second, the CO_2 emissions created by converting biomass into energy are captured and stored in deep geologic formations.[7]

Bioenergy technologies are well developed. From biomass boilers to vehicles run on bioethanol (which can be made from crops such as sugar cane or potatoes), bioenergy is already widely used. CCS is rapidly maturing. As of 2021, there were 65 commercial CCS facilities operating, or in development, globally (an increase of 33% over 2020).[8] BECCS technology, however, is still in its infancy. There is only one large-scale facility (in Illinois), and four smaller-scale sites (all in North America) producing ethanol.[9]

Two clear challenges for BECCS as an effective NET are as follows. First, storage of CO_2 has to be reliable, secure, and long term. In particular, storage must not be susceptible to disruption as a result of climate change.[10] Second, the infrastructure necessary for

BECCS on a large scale must not create more CO_2 emissions than facilities remove. BECCS facilities would require, for example, transportation of large amounts of feedstocks to facilities on a continuous basis, and a robust infrastructure to distribute bioenergy. Ideally, BECCS facilities should remove far more CO_2 than the emissions created by the new infrastructure they necessitate.

If BECCS can meet these challenges it is, perhaps, a viable NET.[11] But does it follow from the fact (if it is one) that we could deploy BECCS as a NET that we ought to do so?

Henry Shue distinguishes three purposes carbon dioxide removal (CDR) such as BECCS could serve (Shue 2021):

(1) Enhancement-CDR would work as a complement to current mitigation efforts, giving them a boost so as to promote progress towards net zero as fast as possible. Enhancement-CDR serves the purpose of preventing further accumulation of CO_2 in the atmosphere.

(2) Remedial-CDR would address insufficient past mitigation efforts (including those that may have been enhanced by CDR). Remedial-CDR addresses any overshoot of temperature targets by reducing CO_2 accumulation in the atmosphere.

(3) Asset-rescue-CDR would rescue fossil fuel companies reserves of oil, coal, etc. from becoming unextractable in any push towards net zero.[12] Asset-rescue-CDR serves the interests of those who stand to profit from sustaining the global carbon economy by making space in the carbon budget for emissions created by the continued extraction and exploitation of fossil fuel.

Shue rejects asset-rescue-CDR as impermissible. Whatever vision we have of climate justice, we clearly must join him in this. There is no version of the just transition in which profit trumps basic rights.

Remedial-CDR is very likely to be necessary in order to avoid an increase in global mean temperatures above Paris targets by 2100. Ninety per cent of the IPCC scenarios for 1.5C by 2100 include an overshoot of 1.5C,[13] and we are also likely to overshoot the 2C target. That we are likely to be in need of remedial-CDR is an indictment of decades of missed opportunities and political cowardice: overshoot is now almost inevitable because we have made it that way.

CDR could be used not only to make up for our failures to reduce emissions, but also to boost our mitigation efforts. In fact, to have the best chance of staying below 1.5C by 2100 we must combine aggressive mitigation with enhancement-CDR: on its own, neither will be enough. However, the fact that CDR can enhance emissions reductions raises serious concerns that CDR could be treated as a substitute for emissions reductions. This worry holds even in the absence of an actual CDR global infrastructure. The way we think and talk about CDR as an imagined technology could encourage us to treat it as a substitute (first in thought, then in action) for emissions reductions: the worry is that CDR could serve as a mitigation deterrent. There are two scenarios in which this worry could be realised. First, the displacement of all emissions reductions by CDR; and second, the deferral of emissions reductions in the expectation that future CDR technology will allow us to remove CO_2 emitted today. There is not (yet?) evidence that the former scenario is playing out. But there is accumulating evidence that the second scenario of mitigation deterrence is real (McLaren 2020).

We might wonder what is wrong with the second scenario. After all, if it is likely that in thirty years we really will be able to suck out of the atmosphere the CO_2 we are injecting into it today, then why not rely on future CDR to make good our present-day emissions, especially if those emissions are enabling the world's most vulnerable people to achieve their basic rights? To understand the dangerousness of this response we must recognise that not all emissions are equal. Emissions created today could set in train positive feedbacks fit to drive climate change away from human control, making any future drawdown of CO_2 using CDR either impossible or irrelevant. As Shue puts it:

> The possibility of CDR later must not be allowed to motivate persistence in half-hearted mitigation now in the utterly vain and totally

groundless hope that CO_2 removed later would be equivalent to CO_2 emissions avoided now. It would not. (Shue 2021)

If mitigation deterrence can be contained, other ethically troubling questions await, particularly with respect to BECCS, which is the present front-runner in CDR. These questions relate to the resources that would have to be devoted to BECCS at a scale fit for it to remedy past mitigation failures, and enhance present efforts. BECCS requires crops as feedstock to generate bioenergy. Common proposals include miscanthus, sugar cane, beet, and willow. The scale on which these crops would have to be grown is staggering. The land needed to grow feedstock to support the annual removal of CO_2 by BECCS in ways that are consistent with Paris temperature target of 2C is equivalent to 40% of the world's current arable land area – which is roughly the size of the European Union (Gough et al. 2018: 4). Other commentators estimate land use for BECCS as one to two times the size of India (Anderson and Peters 2016: 183).

Furthermore, effective BECCS would require a vast new infra-structure to transport feedstock, distribute energy, store CO_2 etc., none of which exists at present. For example, Fuss et al. argue that a pipeline network of a size similar to the current natural gas network could be required (Fuss et al.: 2016), and Anderson and Peters (2016) reflect that '[t]he logistics of collating and transport-ing vast quantities of bioenergy – equivalent to up to half of the total global primary energy consumption – is seldom addressed' (Anderson and Peters 2016: 183). This raises questions about whether BECCS would reliably remove more emissions than it would create (Quiggin 2021).

An obvious question here is: whose land should be used to grow feedstock? There are enormous risks to the world's most vulnerable people in the global scale-up of BECCS (Lenzi 2018; Burns and Nicholson 2017). This need not be, although certainly could be, a repeat of colonial-type seizure of land and other resources. Instead, the world's most vulnerable people could be made offers they cannot refuse: relinquish land (perhaps for nominal payment) for bioenergy crops or face the consequences of warming at 2C and over.

Ring-fencing fertile land and diverting water to bioenergy crops could put huge pressure on remaining land and water for food crops with disastrous consequences for subsistence farmers and those reliant on cheap food to live. The numbers of people displaced by land for feedstock, and by BECCS infrastructure development, could massively swell the numbers already expected to be displaced by climate change, and the requisition of land for feedstock further shrinks the places to which displaced people can go. Such movement of people always brings conflict, disease, and suffering. And crops for feedstock create local problems of environmental justice: people working the fields, and living near facilities, could suffer a range of severe health problems as a result of exposure to these crops as they are processed (Shrader-Frechette 2015).

Monocrop feedstocks on the scale needed for BECCS would be truly disastrous for biodiversity, and we already know that we have severely exceeded planetary boundaries in that dimension (Searchinger and Hemlich 2015; Creutzig et al. 2021). The nutrient-use necessary to sustain BECCS could also push the planet to its limits: we are well beyond the zone of risk with respect to the nitrogen cycle. The vast increase in fertiliser use necessary to continuously feed the crops for BECCS facilities could poison the seas and potable water (Delucchi 2010).

The potential of effective BECCS to cause death, displacement, and ecosystem destruction is huge. And yet, there is no IPCC scenario for 1.5C by 2100 in which BECCS is not deployed, and only 13% of IPCC scenarios give us a reasonable chance of staying below 2C by 2100 without BECCS.[14] Does this mean that BECCS presents us with a fundamental dilemma? On the one hand, climate justice requires stabilising global average temperatures below 2C, which requires a (just) transition to a (net) zero global economy at pace. If we are guided by the IPCC scenarios for 2C and 1.5C, this suggests we need a rapid deployment of BECCS. So, climate justice prima facie requires BECCS. On the other hand, we know that climate justice for present and future people requires that their basic rights are protected. This involves securing access to affordable food, clean water, healthcare, affordable energy, and (perhaps) a homeland. We have seen that BECCS poses serious threats to all these rights. So, climate justice prima facie requires avoiding BECCS.

There are at least two ways out of this dilemma: we could address the potential injustices of BECCS through governance (Burns and Nicholson 2017), and/or we could examine more deeply the nature of the IPCC models that converge on BECCS as necessary for 1.5C or 2C. First, if we must move quickly to a geo-engineered world in which extremely dangerous climate change is avoided by the 'saviour technology' of BECCS,[15] then governance is required at national, regional, and international levels. Not only must governance address the potential injustices of BECCS, it must also prevent mitigation deterrence by BECCS, or the prospect of BECCS.[16] There are existing international agreements on weather modification as a weapon, and on conserving biodiversity, but they are silent on the potential injustices BECCS could cause. At present there is a governance vacuum with respect to BECCS.

A second way out of the dilemma would be to show that modelling that makes BECCS necessary for net zero has failed properly to take account of alternative ways to remain below 1.5C by 2100. The models that converge on BECCS are integrated assessment models (IAMs). As discussed in Chapter 1, IAMs model a host of social, political, and economic variables that could influence the future trajectory of climate change. Not all of these aspects of IAMs are beyond questioning, and some of them represent contestable feasibility judgements. For example, no IAMs model a degrowth pathway to 2100, and we saw in the last chapter that calls for degrowth as a route out of the climate crisis are growing louder. In their convergence on BECCS as a route to 1.5C or 2C could IAMs have missed other feasible possibilities?[17] Debate on this question is unsettled and fast evolving but there could be reasons to think that 1.5C is achievable without any NETS at all (for example, by using nature-based climate solutions).[18]

What is certain is that as each year passes – with the stock of GHGs in the atmosphere increasing – the cuts we will have to make to flows of emissions become steeper. This means that, as the years pass, the amount of enhancement- and remedial-CDR (or other non-NETs solutions) we might need becomes greater. The carbon budget for any tolerable temperature increase is running out fast and we have no scaled up NETs – or any other solutions – in place. Emergency, desperation, and the need for a backup plan create the febrile global milieu in which decisions about solar radiation management (SRM) are being made.

What questions of justice and ethics are raised by solar radiation management?

We have seen that most IPCC scenarios for aggressive mitigation to achieve the Paris Agreement's 1.5C or 2C targets by 2100 assume BECCS. And we have also seen that even if the technology becomes scalable and well established, there remain serious unanswered ethical and political questions about how BECCS deployment could impact on planetary boundaries, and the costs of that for human and other life on Earth. In this context, some scientists are calling for accelerated research into another form of geoengineering – SRM – on the grounds that it could be needed to buy time for effective and just CDR and aggressive emissions reductions.

Until relatively recently research on SRM was somewhat taboo and certainly fringe. This changed with the publication of a paper by Nobel prize-winning meteorologist Paul Crutzen in 2006 (Crutzen 2006). This paper took seriously the proposal that by spraying sulfur particles into the stratosphere we could cool the planet enough to counteract a large part of the global warming caused by climate change. This version of SRM – stratospheric sulfur injection (SSI), sometimes also called stratospheric aerosol injection (SAI) – proposes to work in virtue of the reflectivity of the sulfur particles that would be continuously sprayed into the stratosphere so as to provide a permanent cocoon that would reflect sunlight away from the plant. A world geoengineered by SAI would have milky skies and brilliant sunsets.

Crutzen's paper made an explicit call for research, which has been answered by the scientific community (especially in the

US, UK, and Europe). At the time of writing, this answer has almost entirely consisted of modelling using computers to assess the likely impact of SRM. At different resolutions, these models aim to represent what would happen if we 'turned down' the Sun. Perhaps unsurprisingly they agree that the Earth would cool. Beyond models, there have been very few outdoor experiments. At the time of writing, the most prominent programme is being run by the Keutsch Group at Harvard who are undertaking the Stratospheric Controlled Perturbation Experiment (SCoPEX). This experiment aims to deliver increased knowledge of the atmospheric chemistry of the stratosphere by releasing small amounts of calcium carbonate to be delivered by a balloon. The balloon is planned for launch from the Estrange space centre in Sweden in the near future.

Despite the fact that SRM is an entirely imaginary technology there are signs that it is catching the attention of legislators and climate diplomats: the US Senate appropriations committee recently passed a spending bill that included funding to support SRM research (Nuccitelli 2016); there have been recent US house subcommittee hearings on geoengineering; and the head of the Intergovernmental Panel on Climate Change (IPCC), Hoesung Lee, has said that Panel should be examining SRM, including its governance, very seriously (Goldenberg 2016).

Environmental political theorists have long debated the wisdom and ethics of artificial interventions in the nonhuman natural world, from 'rewilding' to the genetic modification of crops. A recurring theme is that of hubris: like Icarus who flew too close to the Sun and fell to Earth, humanity could be sowing the seeds of its own destruction with interventions in natural systems. This strand in environmental philosophy speaks, to some extent, to SRM proposals: what could be more hubristic than trying to become a 'planetary manager'? (Gardiner 2017a, 2021)

That said, in thinking about the ethics of SRM it is important to foreground what Stephen Gardiner calls 'the contextual question': in assessing the ethical acceptability of any SRM proposal, we need to know the context for which it is proposed. Some contexts are going to make SRM obviously unacceptable: would anyone really defend SRM as a way of ensuring that the world's superrich have pleasant weather? So, we must look at the context in which SRM proposals actually reside; that is, a rapidly declining carbon budget and a lack of political will for aggressive mitigation. In this context – our context – is SRM a hubristic fantasy, a necessary evil, or humanity's last hope for getting the climate crisis under control? (Callies 2019; Gardiner 2010; Gardiner and Fragnière 2018; Heyward 2015; Hourdequin 2019; McKinnon 2019; Morrow 2014; Chhetri et al. 2018; Preston 2012, 2016; Smith 2014; Whyte 2019)

In this context, major figures in the SRM research community sometimes complain that research is 'under provided', and that governance is needed to encourage more, and better supported, research.[19] The ethical questions that arise for research have been given far less attention than those that arise for deployment.[20] This may be because it is taken as obvious that there is nothing special about research into SRM that grounds distinctive ethical concerns that should inform governance of the research, especially in the early stages of modelling, lab experiments, and small-scale field testing.

The rationale for calls for more research into SRM is not that this will deliver a technology for tackling climate change that we can rely on in place of emissions reductions. In part, this is because SRM could not serve as such. All methods of SRM propose only to mask warming caused by the accumulation of GHGs in the atmosphere: SRM does nothing to reduce this accumulation or stem the continued flow of GHGs that make it worse.[21] Instead, the dominant rationale for accelerating research into SRM is that we need to buy time for effective mitigation and scaling up of BECCS (or other NETs). Given that we have good reason to expect significant overshoot of temperature targets before stabilisation at 2C or below, the argument is made that SRM could be a valuable tool for shaving the peak off these overshoots so as to protect us from their worst impacts (McMartin et al. 2014).[22] Given this rationale, the zeitgeist with respect to SRM research is that the most that is justified right now is self-regulation; at least with respect to a significant 'allowed zone' for research (Hubert,

Kruger, and Rayner 2016; Rayner et al. 2013; Royal Society 2009b; Cicerone 2006; Morrow 2017).

Notwithstanding the fact that no SRM researchers envisage it as a replacement for mitigation, political theorists have worried that SRM could in fact displace emissions reductions as a result of the so-called 'moral hazard' effect of the research. The problem here mirrors that of mitigation deterrence in the CDR case. The worry is that the prospect and/or availability of a technology that can mask the effects of climate change could create an incentive for a slowdown in emissions reductions (Hale 2012; Baatz 2016). Knowing that some of the worst effects of climate change can be masked by continued SRM, and given that the burdens of aggressive mitigation will fall hardest on those who emit most, many of whom are the world's most powerful agents, it is not hard to imagine the can of emissions reductions being kicked down the road time and again. The unintended effect of this would be to make us much more reliant on SRM than we would have been in the absence of mitigation deterrence. The higher the concentration of GHGs in the atmosphere, the more effort will be needed to remove them; and the faster the flows of GHGs into the atmosphere, the deeper the cuts needed to support stabilisation of average temperatures at a tolerable level. If research into SRM deters mitigation, then SRM deployment intended to buy time for emissions reductions could become a permanent transformation of the planetary system: the ultimate expression of the Anthropocene.

A different rationale for research into SRM appeals to what we owe to future people. On this view, we have a duty to bequeath SRM technologies to our children as an insurance policy against our failure in the present to mitigate to the extent we ought to do. On this argument, research into SRM is morally required because our actions might make SRM a necessity for future people (Parson 2017). Stephen Gardiner calls this the 'arm the future' argument (Gardiner 2010). He analyses this argument as having the following claim at its heart: if future people have to choose between deploying SRM and averting climate catastrophe, or not deploying SRM and allowing climate catastrophe to unfold, the deployment of SRM is the lesser evil. Because future people might face this nightmare scenario we need to 'arm' them with SRM technology and do the research now.

Some of Gardiner's challenges to this argument are as follows. First, doing the research could in fact make the nightmare scenario more likely (e.g. by deterring mitigation) in which case concern for future people under climate change might counsel against doing the research. Second, the prospect of a nightmare scenario justifies considering all the options we might bequeath to future people: when we consider the full mix of ways we might arm the future against catastrophic climate change SRM might turn out to be far from the lesser evil (Fragniere and Gardiner 2016). Third, the argument obscures the facts that if the nightmare scenario comes to pass it will be as a result of our moral failures, and it will happen to people other than us. The nightmare scenario is something we will have (knowingly) done to future people. In this case, 'if we force a risky geoengineering project on to future people, we might have to compensate them with a massive climate assistance and refugee programme, potentially amounting to a global safety net' (Gardiner 2010: 293).[23] If SRM is to be a 'lesser evil' at all it would have to be accompanied by a package of demanding future-oriented policies delivering benefits to future people that are higher up the list of lesser evils: compensation, climate assistance, and action to secure a less unjust world in which the vulnerability of groups we know to be more likely to be climate victims is reduced. This package would create substantial burdens for the present generation. These burdens would exceed those created by a commitment to modest geoengineering research, and seem 'likely to curb the current enthusiasm for [more SRM research] in many quarters,' restoring many of the same motivational obstacles that face conventional climate policies and introducing further moral and political objections' (Gardiner 2010: 305).

Let me return to the first of Gardiner's challenges described above. Mitigation deterrence is not the only way in which SRM research could make the nightmare scenario more likely. There are observed features of applied research programmes – understood, as they should be, as sociotechnical systems in which technologies and social, institutional, and cultural frameworks coevolve

– which give additional weight to this worry. The process of research itself, including early-stage indoor research involving modelling and lab experiments, could deliver unanticipated and unintended harmful consequences. This is sometimes known as the 'slippery slope' or 'lock in' worry (McKinnon 2019). There are many well-documented cases in which new technologies have emerged as dominant, even though other versions of that technology perform better along a number of dimensions. A well-known example is the QWERTY keyboard. Typing speeds and accuracy are far better when a Dvorak keyboard is used, and yet QWERTY remains the dominant layout (Noyes 1983). Another example is the video home system (VHS) videotape format: despite the fact that Betamax provided better resolution, VHS dominated the market. How can we explain these suboptimal outcomes?

One explanation is that the outcomes were generated by processes of socio-technical lock-in. Broadly speaking, a society has become locked in to a particular technology, system, form of organisation, or framing of an issue when the reasons for not abandoning the locked-in feature are a function of the high costs of doing this rather than the benefits and advantages of the locked-in feature itself (Jamieson 1996). Features of a society that are locked in can persist and dominate even when there are many better ways to pursue the ends, or arrange the affairs, in question.[24] Lock-in of SRM research programmes, and lock-in from any programme to deployment, could happen as a result of positive feedbacks in four categories.[25]

First, economies of scale. Any particular SRM research programme is likely to be expensive to get started; and once started, the continued funding of (and any progress made by) that programme makes it harder for alternative programmes to launch even when they have clear potential to be better than the already existing programme. At a certain point in any programme, the only way to field test the technology is actually to deploy on a global scale, even if outdoor experiments start on a smaller scale (Hamilton 2013; Klein 2014). And once research-through-deployment is happening the space for that type of field experiment for any other SRM research programme is literally already filled with the existing technology.

Second, learning effects. As any research programme advances, perhaps to the point of research-through-deployment, the opportunities for learning in ways that enable improvement and fine tuning of the technology accumulate. Alternative programmes cannot match this, which progressively weakens the case for their initiation and funding.

Third, adaptive expectations. It need not take long for a 'new normal' to take root. Human beings have a well-documented status quo bias which could operate quite quickly to adjust their preferences to any SRM research programme actually in existence even if there are potential alternatives that are better (Kahneman, Knetsch, and Thaler 1991). Perhaps only nostalgic 'old fools' with 'lighted rooms' inside their heads would mourn for lost blue skies and starry nights (Larkin 1974).

Fourth, co-ordination effects. The more research programmes in other countries are initiated and developed, the more it is to any country's advantage to accelerate their own research programme. Given that any research programme must eventually field test through actual global deployment the existence of any research programme in a national content makes deployment much more likely overall. The obvious comparison here is with the nuclear arms race.

These four sites of positive feedback, and various combinations of them, could operate both to lock-in a particular token SRM research programme (when a less dangerous token is available) and/or to lock-in to deployment as part of the research process for any SRM technology (in other words, to lock-in to deployment from SRM as a type of research programme). The nature of the investment and infrastructure needed to scale up innovations in technologically well-developed societies probably makes some lock-in of tokens and of types inevitable. But some locked-in technologies are more dangerous than others. Indeed, we are in a climate crisis in large part because our predecessors locked in to a carbon-intensive global economic structure.

A final set of worries about SRM relates to the possibility of deployment being abruptly suspended. There are many things that could cause this to happen, including war, sabotage, or natural disaster. If deployment were to be abruptly suspended, global average temperatures would be likely to rise very quickly to pre-deployment levels. Some studies suggest a similar, although less pronounced, effect on precipitation (Jones et al. 2013; Keller, Feng, and Oschlies 2014; Zhang et al. 2014). This 'termination shock' would be damaging to future people both as a result of the impacts of the temperature rises (and other changes) previously masked by deployment, but also because of the speed at which these impacts would occur (Goes, Tuana, and Keller 2011; Reynolds, Parker, and Irvine 2016; Svoboda et al. 2011). In a termination shock, climate impacts that would have taken decades or longer to materialise as a result of cumulative emissions would be felt within a matter of years, causing great damage to people affected by the shock, especially the most vulnerable (Baum, Maher, and Haqq-Mistra 2013; Keith and MacMartin 2015; MacMartin, Caldeira, and Keith 2014). The severity of the termination shock will depend on the length of the deployment, the degree of mitigation that has happened under deployment, and the resilience of natural and social systems that have developed under deployment. Multi-century deployments with little mitigation could mean that natural and human systems have next to no chance of adapting to these changes in the short term with devastating consequences for medium to long-term mitigation and adaptation action. Even advocates of research into temporary and limited deployment used only to constrain the rate of change of global mean temperature, rather than to stabilise temperature at some acceptable level (Keith and MacMartin 2015), accept that abrupt termination would cause terrible damage (Cairns 2014).[26]

The possibility of termination shock as a result of SRM deployment raises ethical questions about 'post-implementation scenarios' (Wong 2014) that are almost totally ignored by SRM researchers (McKinnon 2020; Parker and Irvine 2018). How could a global deployment of SRM be sustained over decades if not centuries to enable transition to a zero-carbon economy and declining concentrations of GHGs in the atmosphere? If SRM is not a replacement for mitigation then at some point in time deployment would need to be wound down. How do we know when the time is right and who decides? How do we avoid capture of SRM deployment technologies and infrastructure by vested interests or militaries who might be powerfully motivated to prolong deployment for their own interests?

These questions, along with those raised by worries about mitigation deterrence, the cogency of 'lesser evil' thinking, lock-in, and the many other concerns articulated by political theorists that I have not unpacked here (Lawford-Smith 2020; Morrow 2020; Roeser et al. 2020; Wolff 2020; Callies 2019; Gardiner 2010; Gardiner and Fragnière 2018; Heyward 2015; Hourdequin 2019; Morrow 2014; Preston 2012, 2016; Smith 2014; Whyte 2019), are not the domain of scientists researching SRM. In the light of these worries some civil society groups call for a moratorium on all research: a complete shutdown even of desk-based research at least until robust global governance of SRM research is established (ETC Group 2010). In the absence of a moratorium, and if scientific research into SRM continues,[27] the ethical and political questions it raises must be confronted by humanity collectively in global forums that are politically legitimate and ethically sound. At present no such forums exist and there is a real risk that SRM technology could run away from acceptable forms of governance (as has happened with other emerging technologies, for example, gene-editing technologies such as CRISPR (Jasanoff and Hurlbut 2018)). For this reason, many political theorists engaged with SRM have a focus on governance (McLaren and Corry 2021), and there has been a slew of reports on the governance of SRM in the last decade (Gardiner and Fragnière 2018; McLaren and Corry 2021; Morrow 2017; National Academies of Sciences, Engineering, and Medicine 2021; Chhetri et al. 2018; Rayner et al. 2013).

At the very least, SRM governance must include powerful oversight provisions for the continuous assessment of the state of research and its orientation towards to the public interest. There is a variety of ways in which such oversight could be achieved. For example, Lin acknowledges the need for governance of SRM research that takes account of far more than the physical risks created by any research programme, and identifies lock-in as a 'systemic concern' that must be addressed by an adequate governance framework for research (Lin 2015). A further example is Dilling and Hauser's suggestion that project proposals be legally required to state how the research will address concerns that go beyond physical risks to include 'decision-making power/responsibility for outcomes, and the societal meaning of the research' (Corner, Pidgeon, and Parkhill 2012; Preston 2012; Stirling 2008; Stirling et al. 2008). What unites specific proposals in this area, regardless of their differences of detail, is a commitment to broadening out assessment of SRM research programmes through public participation and inclusion of more marginalised perspectives (MacMartin, Caldeira, and Keith 2014).

Many political theorists, however, take ethical soundness to require far more than mere oversight. Governance proposals must contain strenuous flexibility mechanisms by which research programmes can be shackled, or even quickly shutdown, at minimal cost if research stops serving the public interest (e.g. if mitigation deterrence becomes evident) or moves beyond the control of ethically sound governance institutions (e.g. if it is captured by a military). Political legitimacy must also be secured, and is not delivered by oversight. The legitimacy of a political institution is not derived from the perceptions of those affected by it as to whether it is legitimate. What matters instead, on many accounts, is that the institution is authorised by those affected by it, that it represents their interests, and that it is accountable to them. The temporal reach of SRM proposals mean that acceptable forms of SRM governance must steer research programmes in ways that serve the interests of the most vulnerable and least powerful people in the present, and into the future. No such governance exists at present.

Conclusion

Over three decades of delays on effective mitigation have made it almost inevitable that keeping temperature rises below an acceptable threshold will involve some form of geoengineering. Almost.

It is still possible, as I write now, on 27 January 2022, that we could stay below these thresholds by aggressive GHG reductions alone if the political will is there. Given the enormous ethical dangers and uncertainties posed by CDR and SRM, then at the very least radical mitigation is our immediate imperative combined with massive upscaling of renewables. To give ourselves the best chance, demand for energy for consumption of luxury goods must be truncated and our 'growth fetish' must be cured (Hamilton 2004). With the wind of a good political will behind us, and a bit of luck with respect to dimensions of the climate system about which we are deeply uncertain, we could avoid the need for geoengineering. Geoengineering technologies are at present untested at scale, virtually unknown to most people (Burns et al. 2016; Corner, Pidgeon, and Parkhill 2012), ungoverned by international law, and there exist none of the enormously complex global infrastructures that would be necessary for the legitimate scale-up of research and development, and their deployment. Part of what it means for us to be 'the pivotal generation' (Shue 2021) is that our choices in the next decade or so will determine whether geoengineering becomes a redundant sideshow in the history of action on climate change or a legacy we force on our descendants, perhaps forever.[28]

8

Conclusion

The last three decades have not seen significant, if any, progress on climate change. The crisis worsens month by month and the future is unclear. It is tempting to try to sugar this pill somehow but adding even more disinformation (albeit well-meaning) to the climate debate will not help.[1] However there are risks in being frank about the accelerating climate crisis and how existing efforts to address it are not only inadequate but also fall far below minimum standards of justice. The biggest risk is how this could be demotivating to people – to all of us – who will have to commit to sustained and often difficult action to stop the climate crisis getting worse. To steer the planet and all its living things away from the nightmare of a 2C+ world, we will need to put unprecedented, unflinching, and insistent pressure on political, economic, and corporate leaders so as to force them to make radical changes to put us on a pathway to net zero as soon as possible and give us the best chance of staying below 2C by 2100.

But if the potency of individual agency in the face of climate change is negligible, if climate change is a 'perfect moral storm' (Gardiner 2011), if those with the most power and riches in the world continue to serve their narrow self-interest in resisting real change, and if unjust climate impacts are a symptom of deep, historical, structural injustices that have always prevailed to hurt the most powerless and weak among us, then isn't the battle already lost? If the climate crisis is as bad as it really is, how can any of us find the will to take the difficult steps that will be needed? If we are already doomed, why bother?[2]

The first – and most important – thing is that the door is not closed on the pathway to 2C by 2100: not quite yet. As Henry Shue puts it, the temporal cohort in the present are the 'pivotal generation' who could affect this shift towards a better future (Shue 2021) and we are at the 'date-of-last-opportunity' for seismic action to make this change. The second, and almost as important, thing is that even if the 'pivotal' generation turns out not to be pivotal with respect to the 2C pathway, it could still be pivotal with respect to the 2.1C, 2.5C, 3C, 3.8C etc. pathways. Any limit on warming is likely to reduce climate impacts that will kill people and destroy their lives and we should not fetishise 2C.[3] Indeed, this works to support action to keep temperature rises to a minimum below the 2C target, too (Bain and Bongiorno 2020; Jewell and Cherp 2020).

The third important thing is that we are deeply uncertain about the future. This pertains both to the climate system (e.g. the actual level of climate sensitivity as discussed in Chapter 1) and to the effects of our own actions. What might seem quixotic from one's own point of view in the moment can turn out to have been profoundly affecting to another person, who goes on to change the world.

Political theorists and ethicists have been alive to problems of despair, fatalism, and demotivation, and have addressed them in discussions of the role of hope in action to reduce climate injustice (McKinnon 2014; Moellendorf 2022). To live in hope is not to be an optimist. An optimistic person believes that some good outcome is likely to come about (conversely, a pessimist believes a bad outcome is likely to come about). In contrast, a hopeful person is uncertain that a good outcome will come about but does what she thinks will make it more likely to come about anyway. There are plenty of instances in which these dispositions are justified and/ or understandable. If a massive asteroid will hit Earth in ten days from now pessimism is justified and optimism would be weird.[4] If my dog is horribly injured by a car, I take him to the vet in the hope that he will be saved, even if the odds don't look good to my untrained eye; my hope is well formed here.

All of these dispositional states matter for mobilising action on climate change at different scales and on different timescales. If a community's goal is to create a car-share scheme within the next six months to lower their neighbourhood emissions, and initial soundings suggest enthusiasm for this, then optimism is warranted. Despair about climate change, and attendant demotivation, does not generally attach to actions people could take on these scales. Instead, it relates to the much longer-term prospects for humanity in the climate crisis, and we are right to frame some of our worries about climate change in this more expansive way.

It does not follow, though, that we are right to despair. Although the history of our action on climate change is parlous, we do not know what the future will bring. Climate futures, understood expansively, are the domain of hope. This is especially the case because, were everyone to give up now, we would create a pathway to a climate future worthy of pessimism. Our action in the present will affect, if not determine, the nature of the future and so collective giving-up becomes a self-fulfilling prophecy. The space for effective action on climate change is kept open by cultivating hope for that action (Blöser, Huber, and Moellendorf 2020; Blöser and Stahl 2019; McKinnon 2005, 2014; Moellendorf 2006).[5]

For some people, the framing in the last paragraph will be too rose-tinted. Perhaps we know enough already to make pessimism the only sane option at least with respect to coordinated, aggressive, multilateral, fair action to limit warming to well below 2C. The political and economic leaders of 'the pivotal generation' are not up to it. It's possible we will get lucky in the game of roulette we are playing with the climate system: climate sensitivity might turn out to be very low, and maybe we are, in fact, still some way off passing any climate tipping points. But we would be fools to let these possibilities dominate the way we frame the climate crisis, given the morally corrupt myopia of our 'leaders'. Pessimism is especially warranted, on this view, because it might be the case that the trajectory of emissions until 2100 means that the carbon budget for 2C is insufficient to support subsistence emissions for all people between now and the end of the century let alone the luxury emissions to which the global rich are so attached (McLaughlin 2020). With no prospect of CDR fit to enable fulfilment of the basic rights of all, the future looks particularly grim and not fit for hope.

I want to try to end on a positive note. Perhaps we can grant the framing in the last paragraph without committing to despair. A few philosophers have focused on 'radical hope' as a constructive and motivating virtue appropriate in circumstances in which entire ways of life are likely to be lost and new ways of living with meaning are unknown (Thompson 2010; Williston 2012).[6] In the face of cultural, political, and economic collapse, with all the death, destruction, and misery this will bring, how can we go on? Radical hope is a form of courage in the climate crisis. To live with this courage is to go on despite not knowing what will replace the world we know in the conviction that 'going on' can yield something worthwhile albeit unimaginable in the present (Jamieson 2014; Johnson 2021; Marvel 2018). Only by going on will we make futures worth living in and these cannot be seen from where we are right now in the downward spiral of climate crisis. As the study of how we ought to live together political theory will be needed for the work ahead.

Notes

1 Introduction: An Unprecedented Challenge

1 Examples of political institutions are the legal system, the electoral system, the economy, and the education system.

2 See https://climate.nasa.gov/evidence/; https://www.metoffice.gov .uk/weather/climate-change/what-is-climate-change

3 See https://www.clientearth.org/latest/latest-updates/stories/what-is -a-carbon-sink/

4 See https://ourworldindata.org/grapher/global-co-concentration-ppm

5 See https://ourworldindata.org/grapher/co2-concentration-long-term

6 See https://ourworldindata.org/grapher/annual-co-emissions-by-re gion?country=International+transport~Oceania~Asia+%28excl.+Ch ina+%26+India%29~CHN~IND~Africa~South+America~North+ America+%28excl.+USA%29~USA~Europe+%28excl.+EU-27%29 ~EU-27~OWID_WRL

7 See https://ourworldindata.org/grapher/temperature-anomaly?coun try=~Global

8 See https://www.carbonbrief.org/explainer-nine-tipping-points-th at-could-be-triggered-by-climate-change

9 See https://youtu.be/Ymn3LUZIBuI; https://www.carbonbrief.org /explainer-how-scientists-estimate-climate-sensitivity

10 See https://www.ipcc.ch/
11 See https://unfccc.int/timeline/ for a useful timeline.
12 A particularly miserable moment was the shameful debacle at COP15 in Copenhagen in 2009 (Vidal 2009)
13 See https://unfccc.int/process-and-meetings/the-paris-agreement/the-paris-agreement
14 See https://unfccc.int/sites/default/files/716.pdf
15 See https://youtu.be/0yfOBBgzijs
16 See https://www.unep.org/emissions-gap-report-2020
17 See https://www.metoffice.gov.uk/about-us/press-office/news/weather-and-climate/2021/2020-ends-earths-warmest-10-years-on-record
18 A more nuanced defence of the Paris Agreement is in Falkner 2016, 2019.
19 https://www.unep.org/news-and-stories/press-release/updated-climate-commitments-ahead-cop26-summit-fall-far-short-net
20 See https://carbontracker.org/carbon-budgets-where-are-we-now/

2 Why Haven't We Achieved Climate Justice?

1 See https://www.who.int/csr/disease/smallpox/en/
2 See https://www.who.int/news-room/fact-sheets/detail/climate-change-and-health; https://www.unep.org/news-and-stories/press-release/step-climate-change-adaptation-efforts-or-face-huge-disruption-un; https://reliefweb.int/report/world/global-climate-risk-index-2021
3 The seas are now governed by the United Nations Convention on the Law of the Sea (UNCLOS) which places international waters beyond sovereign control. The world's major forests are sites of contested use and ownership rights; this contest has largely been won by states enabling destruction of the forests.
4 See https://www.globalcovenantofmayors.org/
5 See https://www.vaticannews.va/en/church/news/2021-01/global-catholic-climate-movement-one-planet-summit.html
6 This anger is also present in activism, especially by young people. See Thunberg 2019.
7 Consider President George Bush Senior's notorious comment at the

Rio Summit in 1992: 'The American way of life is not up for nego-
tiation. Period.'

8 For CO_2 emitted today, 40% remains in the atmosphere after 100
   years, 30% after 1000 years, 10% after 10,000 years.
9 See Boghossian 2006; Williams 1972.
10 See https://dark-mountain.net/about/manifesto/
11 See   http://www.jameslovelock.org/the-earth-is-about-to-catch-a
   -morbid-fever-that-may-last-as-long-as-100000-years/. See also an
   interview with Mayer Hillman, https://www.theguardian.com/envi
   ronment/2018/apr/26/were-doomed-mayer-hillman-on-the-clima
   te-reality-no-one-else-will-dare-mention
12 Note that this is only to say that human extinction as a result of climate change is not a given. It is not to say that we should not take
   seriously the possibility of human extinction as a result of climate
   change. See McKinnon 2017.
13 Amartya Sen has defended a view like this with respect to justice as
   a whole. On his 'comparative' approach, we can, and ought to, rank
   different unjust sets of arrangements in the absence of reference to a
   'transcendental' ideal of justice (Sen 2011).
14 It might be objected here that democratic politics is necessary for any
   real reduction in climate injustice, i.e. that the scenario envisaged
   here is not possible. This is far from obvious. There may be scenarios
   of climate emergency in which particular instances of justice can,
   arguably, be suspended in order to secure the conditions in which
   justice is possible at all. See McKinnon 2012.

3 *Who are the Victims of Climate Injustice?*

1 We have imposed catastrophic risks on ourselves qua species in the
   past; e.g. the risk of nuclear holocaust as an outcome of the Cuban
   missile crisis. But these risks were foreseeable and foreseen in the
   development of nuclear weapons capability and the choices made by
   those involved in the crisis.
2 See https://www.spacex.com/human-spaceflight/mars/
3 See https://www.metoffice.gov.uk/research/climate/climate-impac
   ts/food-security/impacts-on-food-security
4 See Sen 2011; https://www.globalhungerindex.org/trends.html

5 See *Gender and Climate Change: A Closer Look at Existing Evidence*, Global and Gender Climate Alliance, 2016. See http://wedo.org/wp-content/uploads/2016/11/GGCA-RP-FINAL.pdf

6 See https://www.carbonbrief.org/mapped-how-climate-change-disproportionately-affects-womens-health

7 See *Climate Change Profile Bangladesh 2018*, Ministry of Foreign Affairs of the Netherlands, https://reliefweb.int/sites/reliefweb.int/files/resources/Bangladesh_7.pdf

8 There is debate about whether rights provide the best starting point for thinking about reducing injustice. For example, Onora O'Neill argues that human rights are not action-guiding: the claim that a Bangladeshi child has a human right to be free from hunger tells us nothing about which agents have a duty to act to prevent the child's hunger. O'Neill advocates for a Universal Declaration of Human Duties to replace a Universal Declaration of Human Rights (O'Neill 1996: 135).

9 See also Beitz and Goodin 2009.

10 See Duus-Otterström and Jagers 2012 for more on the distinction between positive and negative duties in the context of climate change.

11 See Adger et al. 2006; Okereke and Agupusi 2015; Thompson and Bendik-Keymer 2012.

12 See 'Who are indigenous peoples?', UN Permanent Forum on Indigenous Issues Factsheet, https://www.un.org/esa/socdev/unpfii/documents/5session_factsheet1.pdf. See also the UN Declaration on the Rights of Indigenous People, https://www.un.org/development/desa/indigenouspeoples/wp-content/uploads/sites/19/2018/11/UNDRIP_E_web.pdf

13 Here I follow the reasoning in the ILO Report on Indigenous People and Climate Change http://www.ilo.org/wcmsp5/groups/public/---dgreports/---gender/documents/publication/wcms_551189.pdf

14 See https://www.culturalsurvival.org/news/after-30-years-only-23-countries-have-ratified-indigenous-and-tribal-peoples-convention-ilo

15 See 'Kiribati's President Plans to Raise Islands in Fight Against Sea Level Rise', *Guardian*, 10 August 2020, https://www.theguardian.com/world/2020/aug/10/kiribatis-presidents-plans-to-raise-islands-in-fight-against-sea-level-rise. The Alliance of Small Island States

(AOSIS) represents Kiribati and similarly endangered island nations in the UNFCCC. See https://www.aosis.org/

16 Note that this is not to say that the people of Kiribati are not owed monetary assistance. This assistance is owed as a matter of distributive not corrective justice.

17 Here I draw on Goodin 1989.

18 This rendition of Locke's proviso – in terms of *as much* and as good, rather than *enough* and as good (as is common in other commentaries on Locke) – is taken directly from Nine.

19 Risse 2009 also makes use of this baseline in arguing for territorial rights for the people of small island states.

20 See also Byravan and Rajan 2010; Draper 2018; Eckersley 2015.

21 See https://www.unhcr.org/uk/news/stories/2019/10/5da5e18c4/climate-change-and-displacement.html

22 See https://science.thewire.in/environment/climate-change-india-rainfall-monsoons/

23 See https://www.independent.co.uk/news/world/americas/time-almost-up-island-louisiana-sinking-into-the-sea-american-indians-coastal-erosion-isle-de-jean-charles-climate-refugees-a8280401.html

24 The debate about the role played by climate change in the Syrian conflict is not settled. See https://climatemigration.org.uk/climate-conflict-syria/

25 See https://www.theguardian.com/world/2021/jan/18/sami-reindeer-herders-file-lawsuit-against-oyfjellet-norway-windfarm-project

26 For deeper analysis of the challenges and pitfalls of attempting to quantify climate displacement see Boas et al. 2019.

27 See Rigaud et al. 2018. Available at https://www.worldbank.org/en/news/infographic/2018/03/19/groundswell---preparing-for-internal-climate-migration. See also https://www.oxfam.org/en/research/forced-home-climate-fuelled-displacement

28 It is worth noting that there is also some scepticism in the literature with respect to the usefulness of the idea of a climate refugee. See White 2019.

29 For a sceptical approach to the rights of future people see Macklin 1981.

30 An additional problem for thinking about intergenerational duties is the 'non-identity' problem, as follows. Because anyone born in the

future will come into existence only as a result of choices made by people in the past, it is not possible for people yet to be born to be harmed (or benefited) by the choices of people in the past, because had people in the past not made those choices, people in the future would not come into existence. And it is always better to come into existence than never to have existed. The most influential statement of this problem is in Parfit 1984: 119–27. See also Boonin 2021; Reiman 2007.

31 This problem with a utilitarian approach to intergenerational ethics is in part why Jamieson and Mulgan focus on utilitarian virtues, and a fostering utilitarian moral code, respectively.

32 See Murphy 2000 for a general discussion of this problem.

33 See Estlund 1993 for an excellent discussion of what is buried in claims such as this, and why we have reason to be sceptical of such claims.

34 A good explainer can be found at https://www.lse.ac.uk/granthaminstitute/explainers/what-are-social-discount-rates/. See also https://grist.org/article/discount-rates-a-boring-thing-you-should-know-about-with-otters/. The statement in the text of what gets discounted using a social discount rate deliberately obscures a number of different proposals – e.g. that the future value of commodities should be discounted, that economic growth should be discounted, or that well-being should be discounted. See Broome 1992, 1994, 2012b.

35 A recent survey of economists shows that more than three quarters of them find a social discount rate of 2% acceptable (Drupp et al. 2018).

36 Making institutions – or what Rawls calls 'the basic structure' (Rawls 1999: 6–10) – the focus of duties of justice is contentious for liberal egalitarian thinkers. See Cohen 1997; Scheffler 2006; Sypnowich 2006.

37 See 'Ecological Grief: Greenland Residents Traumatised by Climate Emergency', *Guardian*, 12 August 2019. Available at: https://www.theguardian.com/world/2019/aug/12/greenland-residents-traumatised-by-climate-emergency

38 The Committee has some precedent in the Finnish Parliamentary Committee for the Future, which is mandated by the Constitution of Finland.

4 Risk, Uncertainty, and Ignorance: Challenges for Climate Policymaking?

1 There are more technical definitions of risk in the literature whereby the outcome to which the probability attaches need not be unwanted. See Hansson 2018.

2 Utilitarian theories can also be classified according to whether they treat individual acts as the unit of moral evaluation (which would mean that morality requires every individual act to be in the service of maximising utility), or whether this unit is rules to be followed by individuals deciding how to act (so that we are required to coordinate ourselves around standards for behaviour that are likely to maximise utility overall, even if every individual act does not do so). See Lazari-Radek and Singer 2017.

3 See https://www.smh.com.au/environment/climate-change/our-lit tle-brown-rat-first-climate-change-caused-mammal-extinction-2019 0219-p50yry.html

4 The qualifier 'at best' signals the fact that many human preferences are informed by irrational heuristics which do not track what we say we actually value. I shall not explore this dimension of criticism of CBA here.

5 The most nuanced defence of cost-benefit analysis techniques in climate policymaking is in Sunstein 2006. However, even Sunstein concedes that a precautionary approach will be needed for uncertain catastrophes.

6 Emphasis added.

7 There are some exceptions in international environmental law, which are badly specified, and so fall foul of this criticism. For example, the *Third North Sea Conference* (1990) states that: 'The participants . . . will continue to apply the precautionary principle, that is to take action to avoid *potentially* damaging impacts of substances that are persistent, toxic, and liable to bioaccumulate even where there is *no scientific evidence* to prove a causal link between emissions and effects.' The italicised parts of this statement show that this agreement advocates precautionary action in scenarios of ignorance.

8 For example, the direction of politicians acting as representatives of

the people, and/or by reference to fundamental moral concepts such as rights, needs, and interests.

9 Note that Gardiner refers to this principle as the 'Rawlsian Core Precautionary Principle' (Gardiner 2006).

10 See Gardiner 2006: 47. Gardiner also adds a criterion that specifies that the threats addressed by any precautionary principle must be 'realistic' (ibid., 51), e.g., not science fiction, purely imagined, paranoid, purely religiously inspired, etc.

11 For Rawls, the other (important) things, which take priority over distributional equality are equality of basic rights and liberties, equality of opportunity, and savings across generations fit to support the pursuit of a just society for each generation (Rawls 1999: 171–221).

12 To recap: climate sensitivity is the amount of global surface warming that will occur in response to a doubling of atmospheric CO_2 concentrations compared to pre-industrial times. Climate sensitivity is one of the great uncertainties of climate science: estimates range from 1.5C–4.5C. See https://www.carbonbrief.org/explainer-how-scien tists-estimate-climate-sensitivity

13 Both figures given in Monbiot 2007: 51.

14 With a range of −1 per cent to +3.5 per cent (Stern 2006: xiii–xvi).

15 It is worth noting that the content of IPCC Reports are decided by consensus among the authors. Given their often deep divergences of scientific opinion, the net effect of this method is to produce conservative statements, the lowest common denominator of scientific opinion to which all authors can agree.

5 Who is Responsible for Climate Injustice?

1 See https://carbontracker.org/carbon-budgets-where-are-we-now/

2 See Neumayer (2000) for a variant of this view, viz. that any country's total GHG allocation should be the sum of its per capita allowance minus its historical emissions.

3 For an extended discussion of the equal per capita view, and other issues related to distributive justice in the allocation of emissions see Caney 2012a.

4 The everyday and the torts examples should both be qualified with an 'all else being equal' clause. For example, I might not think that

a person with a severe learning disability owes me an apology for an insult, and there are some instances in tort law in which causing damage to an innocent victim arguably does not generate liability for compensation (Feinberg 1978: 102). These exceptions prove the rule.

5 See https://ourworldindata.org/grapher/cumulative-co-emissions?tab=chart&country=USA~CHN

6 https://ourworldindata.org/grapher/cumulative-co-emissions?tab=chart&country=USA~CHN

7 See https://ourworldindata.org/grapher/share-of-cumulative-co2?tab=chart&time=latest&country=USA~CHN

8 See https://ourworldindata.org/grapher/co-emissions-per-capita?tab=chart&country=USA~CHN

9 See https://ourworldindata.org/grapher/cumulative-co-emissions?tab=chart&country=USA~CHN~GBR

10 Eunice Foote was an amateur scientist working in the US in the 1800s. She published work in 1856 arguing that CO_2 is a GHG with the potential to heat the planet, five years before John Tyndall's independently researched paper on the same topic. Tyndall, not Foote, is routinely credited as having made this discovery. See https://www.resilience.org/stories/2019-07-30/a-foote-note-on-the-hidden-history-of-climate-science-why-you-have-never-heard-of-eunice-foote/

11 Most people would think it would be very generous of you to act in the ways specified by the demands, but given the unreliability of generosity as a motive – especially when the sacrifices involved relate to all the comforts and pleasures of living in a more developed country – what we really want are arguments to show that you can legitimately be compelled to make the sacrifices required to meet the demands.

12 It is not difficult to make this case: development, which has been driven by fossil fuels, has delivered enormous benefits in terms of health, longevity, education, etc.

13 Caney acknowledges the force of worries about the polluter pays principle, as already described, and identifies new ones.

14 Caney's view is that this allocation of remedial responsibility to the more advantaged is not unfair. This is rooted in his broader view of global justice. See Caney 2018.

15 See also Hohl and Roser 2011.

16 The Agreement legally binds states to produce NDCs periodically but it does not create legal duties with respect to the content of the NDCs.

17 There is a very large philosophical literature on agency. For an overview see Schlosser 2019.

18 Personhood is not necessarily limited to human agents: alien life forms, or advanced AI, could qualify as persons.

19 What one agent owes to another does not always have the force of morality behind it. Arguably, I do no moral wrong when, feeling petty at a Department party, I give the cold shoulder to a colleague who has respectfully criticised my work. Still, it is 'not a very nice thing to do' and a colleague with whom I am friends can take me to task on it.

20 Sometimes also referred to as 'collective' or 'corporate' agents.

21 Of course, the content of these duties is hotly debated, although not killing children just for fun is a baseline, if anything is.

22 It is worth noting that the term 'carbon footprint' was devised by marketing agents working for BP in 2004. Critics have argued that this was a deliberate manoeuvre to distract attention away from the activities of BP qua fossil fuel MNC and on to individuals as consumers (Kaufman 2020; Solnit 2021).

23 In other words, the group qua agent supervenes on its individual members: there is no difference in what the group agent does that is not a result of what some, or all, individual members do.

24 *Citizens United v. Federal Election Commission*, 558 U.S. 310 (2010).

25 For criticism of List and Pettit see Briggs 2012.

26 Husak's definition of the control requirement as it applies to criminal liability is this: 'A person lacks control over a state of affairs and neither is nor ought to be criminally liable for it if it is unreasonable to expect him or her to have prevented that state of affairs' (Husak 2010: 37).

27 How China – and perhaps, India – fit into this set is a complicating question I shall not address here.

6 *What are our Options in the Face of Climate Failure?*

1 It is easy to assume the richest 10% of people are all Elon Musks and Mark Zuckerbergs: that is, not us. To see the reality try the calculator at https://howrichami.givingwhatwecan.org/how-rich-am-i

2 See https://climateactiontracker.org/global/cat-thermometer/

3 https://climateactiontracker.org/countries/

4 I do not mean to suggest here that 'everyone else' has no duties to act in certain ways in the climate crisis. It is likely that all people stand under some obligations to do or not to do certain things if we are to get ahead of climate change. That said, there are clearly agents – the most developed states that subsidise fossil fuel extraction, and the ultra rich, for example – that need to act now, and radically, for there to be any chance of avoiding climate catastrophe.

5 Rawls was the first to coin this term (Rawls 1999). Its importance in recent work on climate justice is reflected in the fact that it features in the title of an influential 2016 edited book (Heyward and Roser 2016). Furthermore, in non-ideal scenarios of partial compliance, it might be the case that additional duties are created for those who do comply – for example, duties to 'take up the slack' created by those who do not do what they ought to do (Karnein 2014; Miller 2011).

6 Australia is a prominent example (Crowley 2021).

7 There are other ways of casting the distinction between ideal and non-ideal theory. See Hamlin and Stemplowska 2012; Lawford-Smith 2010; Swift 2008. For an argument in favour of 'engaged political theory' over non-ideal theory, see Green and Brandstedt 2021.

8 It is worth noting that the term 'carbon footprint' was coined by BP in 2004. Critics have argued that this is a new piece of propaganda from the climate denial/fossil fuel MNC nexus, aimed at shifting attention on to individuals as consumers, and away from the wrongdoing of the extractive industries (Kaufman 2020; McKinnon 2016; Solnit 2021).

9 If mutual coercion is agreed by all, then there is an argument to be made that this makes the coercion legitimate – perhaps, democratically so.

10 Although some scepticism remains. See e.g. Beeson 2010; Lepori 2019; Wong 2016.

11 For example, much environmental policymaking uses an 'ecosystem services' frame for prioritising action to protect the environment. On this approach, the value of ecosystems is to be established by assessing the ways in which they are necessary for the well-being and development of human beings.

12 For detailed critique of carbon trading schemes see Spash 2011.

13 Note here that 'subjectively defined interests' potentially captures more than 'self-interest'. A crude version of *Homo economicus* that posits self-interest as the rudder used by people to steer their choices is obviously stupid: people make choices all the time that are not in their self-interest. 'Subjectively defined interests', however, is more subtle. Making this the rudder of human decision making incorporates as potentially rational choices that do not serve the self-interest of the agent. For example, Sir Nicholas Winton's rescue of 669 Czech children from Nazi-occupied Czechoslovakia in the six months before the outbreak of war in 1939. See *Holocaust hero Sir Nicholas Winton (That's Life – 1988) – YouTube*, 1988. Winton's altruism can be understood as part of his subjectively defined interest: a way of being, and acting, that mattered to him because of who he was.

14 For an excellent overview of Marx's political thought see Wolff 2003; Wolff and Leopold 2021.

15 Care is needed in making claims like these given that Marx himself says very little about the political and economic realities of a communist society. A distinction between what Marx said and what (some) Marxists have said would be beneficial in this context.

16 All else being equal, of course. There are clearly debates to be had about how the impact of degrowth in a more developed economy like that of the UK should be distributed across British citizens in a way that is just. This would very likely mean some form of economic redistribution from shareholders to citizens.

17 See https://cdkn.org/story/greengrowth

18 The basket of policies that reflect this approach are called 'contraction and convergence'. For a climate justice-based defence see Ott and Baatz 2012. For sceptical commentary on the degrowth agenda as a strategy for climate justice-seekers see Moellendorf 2022.

19 See https://climatenetwork.org/

20 Rosa Parks, a black woman, refused to give up her seat to a white male passenger on a bus in Alabama during the Jim Crow era. See https://www.rosaparks.org/biography/

21 In 1930, Gandhi led a peaceful direct-action campaign against British colonial powers in India. The 'Salt March' took aim at the Salt Act of 1882 which prohibited Indian people from collecting or selling salt. Marchers made salt from seawater to protest British policy.

22 The Poll Tax was introduced by Margaret Thatcher's Conservative government in 1989–90. It was a flat-rate, per capita tax on every adult. Opposition to the Poll Tax led to violent riots in London, but Rawlsian civil disobedience was evident in the mass refusal to register for, or pay, the new tax. The Poll Tax was abolished in 1991 by Thatcher's Tory successor, John Major, Prime Minister.

23 See https://fridaysforfuture.org/

24 See https://extinctionrebellion.uk/ and https://rebellion.global/

25 Caney identifies two versions of this right. The first version delineates what agents in circumstances of dire need as a result of injustice may do. The second version – described in the text – relates to the eradication of institutions, processes, laws etc. that sustain global injustice.

26 For more on violence and political protest see Brennan 2018; Delmas 2018; Flanigan 2021.

7 *Geoengineering: Saviour Technologies or Fantasies of Control?*

1 Factoring in the ratcheting up of emissions reductions as per the Paris Agreement could affect this range, but it would not be unduly pessimistic (given the record of history) to be sceptical about the prospects for effective ratcheting up.

2 There are things we could do other than reducing emissions and NETs. We could forcibly sterilise 75% of the world's population. Or 75% of fertile women could refuse to have children. The former is unacceptable and the latter is unlikely. The only plausible and ethically acceptable path to staying below 2C must involve reducing emissions without violating rights.

3 BECCS is not the only proposed NET. Other proposed methods to reduce the atmospheric concentration of CO_2 include afforestation, accelerated chemical weathering of rocks, direct air capture with

storage (DACS), ocean fertilisation (to grow huge mats of carbon-gobbling algae).

4 SAI is not the only proposed SRM technology. Other proposals to increase the reflectivity of the Earth system include marine cloud brightening (MCB), mirrors in space, genetic modification of crops to increase the reflectivity of leaves, or painting roofs white. In this domain, the only methods given any serious consideration are SAI and MCB.

5 Biomass can be converted into bioenergy through different processes, for example, combustion or conversion into biofuels such as ethanol.

6 In some versions of BECCS, waste or agricultural residues, such as sugar-cane waste, is proposed as a feedstock. Proposals also exist to use algae as a feedstock.

7 Some versions of BECCS allow for embedding CO_2 in long-lived products (such as cement) as an alternative or supplement to storing it. This is known as carbon capture and use (CCU).

8 https://www.globalccsinstitute.com/resources/publications-reports -research/net-zero-and-geospheric-return-actions-today-for-2030 -and-beyond/

9 Three further large-scale BECCS facilities are under development in Japan, Norway and the UK.

10 The IPCC concludes that deep geologic storage is likely preferable to storage under the seabed, for this reason. https://www.ipcc.ch/site/as sets/uploads/2018/03/srccs_wholereport-1.pdf

11 https://www.imperial.ac.uk/grantham/publications/energy-and -low-carbon-futures/beccs-deployment-a-reality-check.php

12 The technical term for this risk is 'stranded assets'.

13 The extent and duration of the overshoot varies across scenarios, in the range of 1.56C–1.85C, for 15–70 years.

14 By 'reasonable' chance I mean 66%>. If you prefer safer odds on staying below 2C, the percentage of IPCC scenarios without BECCS decreases.

15 See https://www.carbonbrief.org/beccs-the-story-of-climate-chang es-saviour-technology

16 See McLaren et al. (2019) for a proposal on separating emissions reductions from BECCS and those from traditional mitigation in

carbon accounting as a way of combatting the substitution of the former for the latter.

17 See Fuhrman et al. (2019) for a technical discussion of why IAMs focus on BECCS might not represent the full set of feasible options.

18 See https://www.carbonbrief.org/analysis-how-natural-climate-solutions-can-reduce-the-need-for-beccs

19 See Geoengineering Research Governance Project (GRGP) Oxford Workshop on a Code of Conduct for Responsible Geoengineering Research – Anna-Maria Hubert (FCEA n.d.).

20 There are exceptions (Harvard's Solar Geoengineering Research Program n.d.).

21 Furthermore, there are dimensions of climate change other than warming that are left entirely unaddressed by SRM, for example, ocean acidification.

22 Other arguments that appear in the literature are that SAI could enable just adaptation (Horton and Keith 2016), or that SAI could, under the right circumstances, give vulnerable countries significant leverage with respect to hegemonic powers.

23 Two more of Gardiner's specific challenges to the argument relate to political legitimacy (which the argument ignores) and political inertia (which the argument could encourage).

24 The meaning of 'better' in this context depends on the nature of the locked-in feature. For example, 'better' for technologies could mean more effective and cheaper; for frames for social issues, it could mean 'fairer'.

25 These four sites of positive feedback causing lock-in of SRM are adapted from Foxon 2007.

26 It should also be noted in this context that the range of scenarios in which SRM deployment is imagined are all framed in ways that have significant consequences for assessment of the acceptability of deployment in those scenarios. In their review of the literature assessing geo-engineering proposals, Bellamy et al. provide evidence that a number of frames that could support far less favourable assessments of deployment are routinely excluded from scenarios (Bellamy et al. 2012).

27 We should not rule out the possibility that SRM research programmes will deteriorate and die away in the coming years.

28 On 'intergenerational extortion' see Gardiner 2017b.

8 Conclusion

1 In this book I have not discussed climate denial, especially the most pernicious sort that is funded by fossil MNCs and chanelled through 'think-tanks' that attack policy processes aimed at effective action on climate change. Discussion can be found at McKinnon 2016; Talisse n.d.

2 See Pearl 2019. Note George Monbiot's comment: 'We might relieve ourselves of moral agency by claiming that it's already too late to act, but in doing so we condemn others to destitution or death' (Monbiot 2019).

3 It is broadly acknowledged that the 2C target is scientifically arbitrary (Knutti et al. 2016; Randalls 2010)

4 This sentence was written before the Netflix film 'Don't Look Up' was made. It fits remarkably well with how the main protagonists change in their attitudes and demeanour as the story progresses.

5 I have been discussing hope as a dispositional state: a set of beliefs and desires that provide at least necessary conditions for acting in a certain way. But hope can also be used to describe an emotional state: a feeling of pleasant anticipation, or even excitement. I am not sure there is much place for hope in this sense as a driver of effective action on climate change. But there are other emotions that could play this role: in particular, anger. Watch Greta Thunberg addressing the UN Climate Summit in 2019 (https://youtu.be/KAJsdgTPJpU). For research suggesting that anger is motivating in the climate crisis see Reese and Jacob 2015; Stanley et al. 2021. For work that suggests different roles for anger for climate activists in the global North and global South see Kleres and Wettergren 2017. Philosophical discussions of anger are hard to come by, and many address black anger at histories and realities of racism: see Callard 2020; Lorde 1997; Srinivasan 2018. This is an area that could be greatly enriched by ethical analysis.

6 Thompson makes use of Jonathan Lear's work on radical hope in making his argument (Lear 2006). Lear's book focuses on the Crow chief's – Plenty Coups – efforts to lead his people in the aftermath of complete cultural devastation. Lear defends an interpretation of Plenty Coups' words and action in terms of 'radical hope'.

References

Abizadeh, Arash. 2014. 'A Critique of the "Common Ownership of the Earth" Thesis 1'. *Les Ateliers de l'éthique* 8(2): 33–40.

Ackerman, Bruce and James Fishkin. 2004. *Deliberation Day*. Yale University Press.

Ackerman, Frank and Lisa Heinzerling. 2004. *Priceless: On Knowing the Price of Everything and the Value of Nothing*. The New Press.

Adger, W. Neil, Jouni Paavola, Saleemul Huq, and M.J. Mace. 2006. *Fairness in Adaptation to Climate Change*. MIT Press.

Agyeman, Julian. 2013. *Introducing Just Sustainabilities: Policy, Planning, and Practice*. Zed Books

Agyeman, Julian, David Schlosberg, Luke Craven, and Caitlin Matthews. 2016. 'Trends and Directions in Environmental Justice: From Inequity to Everyday Life, Community, and Just Sustainabilities'. *Annual Review of Environment and Resources* 41(1): 321–40.

Alkire, Sabina. 2016. 'The Capability Approach and Well-Being Measurement for Public Policy'. In *The Oxford Handbook of Well-Being and Public Policy*, eds. Matthew D. Adler and Marc Fleurbaey.

Allen, Myles, Mustafa Babiker, and Yang Chen. 2018. 'Summary for Policymakers'. In *Global Warming of 1.5C, Special Report*, eds.

Valerie Masson-Delmotte, Panmao Zhai, and Hans-Otto Portner. Intergovernmental Panel on Climate Change.

Anderson, Elizabeth. 2011. 'Democracy, Public Policy, and Lay Assessments of Scientific Testimony'. *Episteme* 8(02): 144–64.

Anderson, Kevin. 2012. 'The Inconvenient Truth of Carbon Offsets'. *Nature* 484(7392): 7.

Anderson, Kevin and Alice Bows. 2011. 'Beyond "Dangerous" Climate Change: Emission Scenarios for a New World'. *Trans. R. Soc. A* 369: 20–44.

Anderson, Kevin and Glen Peters. 2016. 'The Trouble With Negative Emissions'. *Science* 354(6309): 182–3.

Arnall, Alex, Chris Hilson, and Catriona McKinnon. 2019. 'Climate Displacement and Resettlement: The Importance of Claims-Making "From Below"'. *Climate Policy* 19(6): 665–71.

Baber, Walter and Robert Bartlett. 2018. 'Deliberative Democracy and the Environment'. In *The Oxford Handbook of Deliberative Democracy*, eds. Andre Bächtiger, John S. Dryzek, Jane Mansbridge, and Mark Warren. Oxford University Press, 754–67.

Bain, Paul G. and Renata Bongiorno. 2020. 'It's Not Too Late to Do the Right Thing: Moral Motivations for Climate Change Action'. *WIREs Climate Change* 11(1): e615.

Barnosky, Anthony D. et al. 2011. 'Has the Earth's Sixth Mass Extinction Already Arrived?' *Nature* 471(7336): 51–7.

Barry, Brian. 1977. 'Justice Between Generations'. In *Law, Morality and Society*, eds. Peter Hacker and Joseph Raz. Clarendon Press, 268–84.

Barry, Christian and Robert Kirby. 2017. 'Scepticism about Beneficiary Pays: A Critique'. *Journal of Applied Philosophy* 34(3): 285–300.

Barry, John. 1999. *Rethinking Green Politics: Nature, Virtue, and Progress.* Sage, 291.

———. 2006. 'Resistance Is Fertile: From Environmental to Sustainability Citizenship'. In *Environmental Citizenship*, eds. Andrew Dobson and Derek Bell. MIT Press, 21–49.

———. 2011. 'Climate Change, "the Cancer Stage of Capitalism" and the Return of Limits to Growth: Towards a Political Economy of Sustainability'. In *Climate Change and the Crisis of Capitalism*, eds. Mark

Pelling, David Manuek-Navarrete, and Michael Redclift. Routledge, 134–47.

———. 2012. *The Politics of Actually Existing Unsustainability: Human Flourishing in a Climate-Changed, Carbon Constrained World*. Oxford University Press.

Baum, Seth D., Timothy M. Maher, and Jacob Haqq-Mistra. 2013. 'Double Catastrophe: Intermittent Stratospheric Geoengineering Induced by Societal Collapse'. *Environment, Systems and Decisions* 33(1): 168–80.

Beckman, Ludvig and Fredrik Uggla. 2016. 'An Ombudsman for Future Generations: Legimate and Effective?' In *Institutions for Future Generations*, eds. Inigo Gonzalez-Ricoy and Axel Gosseries. Oxford University Press, 117–34.

Beeson, Mark. 2010. 'The Coming of Environmental Authoritarianism'. *Environmental Politics* 19(2): 276–94.

Beitz, Charles R. and Robert E. Goodin. 2009. *Global Basic Rights*. Oxford University Press.

Bell, Derek R. 2004. 'Environmental Refugees: What Rights? Which Duties?' *Res Publica* 10(2002): 135–52.

———. 2005. 'Liberal Environmental Citizenship'. *Environmental Politics* 14(2): 179–94.

———. 2006. 'Political Liberalism and Ecological Justice'. *Analyse und Kritik* 2006(28): 206–22.

Bellamy, Rob, Jason Chilvers, Naomi E. Vaughan, and Timothy M. Lenton. 2012. 'A Review of Climate Geoengineering Appraisals'. *Wiley Interdisciplinary Reviews: Climate Change* 3(6): 597–615.

Bentham, Jeremy. 1784. *The Collected Works of Jeremy Bentham: An Introduction to the Principles of Morals and Legislation*. Oxford University Press.

Berlin, Isaiah. 2002. *Liberty: Incorporating Four Essays on Liberty*. 2nd edn. Henry Hardy. Oxford University Press.

Biermann, Frank and Ingrid Boas. 2008. 'Protecting Climate Refugees: The Case for a Global Protocol'. *Environment: Science and Policy for Sustainable Development* 50(6): 8–17.

Blöser, Claudia, Jakob Huber, and Darrel Moellendorf. 2020. 'Hope in Political Philosophy'. *Philosophy Compass* 15(5): e12665.

Blöser, Claudia and Titus Stahl, eds. 2019. *The Moral Psychology of Hope*. Rowman & Littlefield.

Boas, Ingrid et al. 2019. 'Climate Migration Myths'. *Nature Climate Change* 9(12): 901–3.

Boghossian, Paul. 2006. *Fear of Knowledge: Against Relativism and Constructivism*. Oxford University Press.

Bonsch, Markus et al. 2016 'Trade-offs Between Land and Water Requirements for Large-Scale Bioenergy Production'. *GCB-Bioenergy* 8(1): 11–24.

Boonin, David. 2021. 'Parfit and the Non-Identity Problem'. In *The Oxford Handbook of Intergenerational Ethics*, ed. S. M. Gardiner. Oxford University Press.

Bostrom, Nick. 2013. 'Existential Risk Prevention as Global Priority'. *Global Policy* 4(1): 15–31.

Bradshaw, Corey J. A. and Frédérik Saltré. 2019. 'What Is a "Mass Extinction" and Are We in One Now?' *The Conversation*. http://theconversation.com/what-is-a-mass-extinction-and-are-we-in-one-now-122535 (29 June 2021).

Brennan, Jason. 2018. *When All Else Fails: The Ethics of Resistance to State Injustice*. Princeton University Press.

Briggs, Rachael. 2012. 'The Normative Standing of Group Agents'. *Episteme* 9(3): 283–91.

Broome, John. 1992. *Counting the Cost of Global Warming*. White Horse Press.

———. 1994. 'Discounting the Future'. *Philosophy & Public Affairs* 23(2): 128–56.

———. 2000. 'Cost-Benefit Analysis and Population Cost-Benefit Analysis: Legal, Economic, and Philosophical Perspectives'. *Journal of Legal Studies* 29: 953–70.

———. 2012a. *Climate Matters: Ethics in a Warming World*. W.W. Norton & Co.

———. 2012b. 'Discounting the Future'. In *Intergenerational Justice*, ed. Lukas H. Meyer. Routledge.

Brown, Paul. 1992. 'Earth Summit: Rio Opens with Plea for Proof of Global Brotherhood'. *Guardian* 4 June.

Burns, Elizabeth T. et al. 2016. 'What Do People Think When They Think about Solar Geoengineering? A Review of Empirical Social Science Literature, and Prospects for Future Research'. *Earth's Future* 4(11): 536–42.

Burns, Wil and Simon Nicholson. 2017. 'Bioenergy and Carbon Capture with Storage (BECCS): The Prospects and Challenges of an Emerging Climate Policy Response'. *Journal of Environmental Studies and Sciences* 7(4): 527–34.

Butt, Daniel. 2008. *Rectifying International Injustice: Principles of Compensation and Restitution Between Nations*. Oxford University Press.

———. 2014. '"A Doctrine Quite New and Altogether Untenable": Defending the Beneficiary Pays Principle'. *Journal of Applied Philosophy* 31(4): 336 48.

Byravan, Sujatha and Sudhir Chella Rajan. 2010. 'The Ethical Implications of Sea-Level Rise Due to Climate Change'. *Ethics & International Affairs* 24(3): 239–60.

Cairns, Rose C. 2014. 'Climate Geoengineering: Issues of Path-Dependence and Socio-Technical Lock-In'. *Wiley Interdisciplinary Reviews: Climate Change* 5(5): 649–61.

Callard, Agnes, ed. 2020. *On Anger*. Boston Review.

Callies, Daniel Edward. 2019. 'Institutional Legitimacy and Geoengineering Governance'. *Ethics, Policy & Environment* 26(1): 324–40.

Campbell, Iona et al. 2019. 'The Environmental Risks Associated With the Development of Seaweed Farming in Europe – Prioritizing Key Knowledge Gaps'. *Frontiers in Marine Science* 6.

Caney, Simon. 2006. 'Cosmopolitan Justice, Responsibility, and Global Climate Change'. *Leiden Journal of International Law* 18(4): 747–75.

———. 2008. 'Human Rights, Climate Change, and Discounting'. *Environmental Politics* 17(4): 536–55.

———. 2010a. 'Climate Change, Human Rights, and Moral Thresholds'. In *Climate Ethics: Essential Readings*, eds. Stephen M. Gardiner, Simon Caney, Dale Jamieson, and Henry Shue. Oxford University Press, 163–80.

———. 2010b. 'Markets, Morality and Climate Change: What, If Anything, Is Wrong with Emissions Trading?' *New Political Economy* 15(2): 197–224.

———. 2012a. 'Addressing Poverty and Climate Change: The Varieties of Social Engagement'. *Ethics & International Affairs* 26(02): 191–216.

———. 2012b. 'Just Emissions'. *Philosophy & Public Affairs* 40(4): 255–300.

——. 2014. 'Climate Change, Intergenerational Equity and the Social Discount Rate'. *Politics, Philosophy & Economics* 13(4): 320–42.

——. 2016a. *Climate Change, Equity, and Stranded Assets*. Oxfam America. Research Backgrounder. https://s3.amazonaws.com/oxfam-us/www/static/media/files/climate_change_equity_and_stranded_assets_backgrounder.pdf

——. 2016b. 'Political Institutions for the Future: A Fivefold Package'. In *Institutions for Future Generations*, ed. Inigo Gonzalez-Ricoy. Oxford University Press, 135–55.

——. 2016c. 'The Struggle for Climate Justice in a Non-Ideal World'. *Midwest Studies in Philosophy* 40(1): 9–26.

——. 2018. 'Climate Change'. In *The Oxford Handbook of Distributive Justice*, ed. Serena Olsaretti. Oxford University Press.

——. 2020. 'Climate Justice' ed. Edward N. Zalta. *Stanford Encyclopedia of Philosophy*: 25.

——. 2020. 'The Right to Resist Global Injustice'. In *The Oxford Handbook of Global Justice*, ed. Thom Brooks. Oxford University Press, 509–35.

Carrington, Damian. 2021. 'IPCC Steps up Warning on Climate Tipping Points in Leaked Draft Report'. *Guardian* 23 June.

——. 2021. 'Fossil Fuel Industry Gets Subsidies of $11m a Minute, IMF Finds'. *Guardian* 6 October.

CAT. 2016. 'Global Temperatures – Climate Action Tracker'. (6 October 2021).

Ceballos, Gerardo, Paul R. Ehrlich, and Peter H. Raven. 2020. 'Vertebrates on the Brink as Indicators of Biological Annihilation and the Sixth Mass Extinction'. *Proceedings of the National Academy of Sciences* 117(24): 13596–602.

Chancel, Lucas. 2021. 'The Richest 10% Produce About Half of Greenhouse Gas Emissions. They Should Pay to Fix the Climate'. *Guardian* 7 December.

Charmes, Jacques. 2019. *The Unpaid Care Work and the Labour Market*. http://www.bollettinoadapt.it/wp-content/uploads/2020/01/wcms_732791.pdf

Chhetri, Netra et al. 2018. 'Governing Solar Radiation Management'. Washington, DC: Forum for Climate Engineering Assessment, American University.

Chiro, Giovanna di. 2008. 'Living Environmentalisms: Coalition Politics, Social Reproduction, and Environmental Justice'. *Environmental Politics* 17(2): 276–98.

Chomsky, Noam. 2016. *Who Rules the World?* Hamish Hamilton.

Christensen, Johan. 2020. 'Expert Knowledge and Policymaking: A Multi-Disciplinary Research Agenda'. *Policy and Politics* 49(3): 455–71.

Christoff, Peter. 1996. 'Ecological Citizens and Ecologically Guided Democracy'. In *Democracy and Green Political Thought*, eds. Brian Doherty and Marious de Geus. Routledge, 149–67.

Cicerone, Ralph J. 2006. 'Geoengineering: Encouraging Research and Overseeing Implementation'. *Climatic Change* 77(3–4): 221–6.

CIEL. 2019. *Plastic and Climate: The Hidden Costs of a Plastic Planet*. www. ciel.org/plasticandclimate

Climate Action Tracker. 2021. 'The CAT Thermometer | Climate Action Tracker'. https://climateactiontracker.org/global/cat-thermo meter/

Cohen, Gerald A. 1978. *Karl Marx's Theory of History: A Defence*. Princeton University Press.

——. 1997. 'Where the Action Is: On the Site of Distributive Justice'. *Philosophy & Public Affairs* 26(1): 3–30.

——. 2009. *Why Not Socialism?* Princeton University Press.

——. 2015. 'Freedom and Money'. In *On the Currency of Egalitarian Justice, and Other Essays in Political Philosophy*. Princeton University Press, 166–200.

Collins, Chuck. 2021. *The Wealth Hoarders: How Billionaires Pay Millions to Hide Trillions*. Polity.

Collins, Stephanie. 2020. 'Corporations' Duties in a Changing Climate'. In *Climate Justice and Nonstate Actors: Corporations, Regions, Cities, and Individuals*, eds. Jeremy Moss and Lachlan Umbers. Routledge, 84–101.

Corner, Adam, Nick Pidgeon, and Karen Parkhill. 2012. 'Perceptions of Geoengineering: Public Attitudes, Stakeholder Perspectives, and the Challenge of "Upstream" Engagement'. *Wiley Interdisciplinary Reviews: Climate Change* 3(5): 451–66.

Cowen, Tyler and Derek Parfit. 1992. 'Against the Social Discount Rate'. In *Justice between Age Groups and Generations*, eds. Peter Laslett and James S. Fishkin. Yale University Press, 144–61.

Creutzig, Felix et al. 2021. 'Considering Sustainability Thresholds for BECCS in IPCC and Biodiversity Assessments'. *GCB-Bioenergy* 13(4): 510–15.

Cripps, Elizabeth. 2015. 'Climate Change, Population, and Justice: Hard Choices to Avoid Tragic Choices'. *Global Justice: Theory Practice Rhetoric* 8(2): 1–22.

——. 2020. 'Individual Climate Justice Duties: The Cooperative Promotional Model and Its Challenges'. In *Climate Justice and Nonstate Actors: Corporations, Regions, Cities, and Individuals*, eds. Jeremy Moss and Lachlan Umbers. Routledge, 101–18.

Crowley, Kate. 2021. 'Fighting the Future: The Politics of Climate Policy Failure in Australia (2015–2021).*Wiley Interdisciplinary Reviews: Climate Change* 12(5): e725.

Crutzen, Paul J. 2006. 'Albedo Enhancement by Stratospheric Sulfur Injections: A Contribution to Resolve a Policy Dilemma?' *Climatic Change* 77(3–4): 211–19.

Dearden, Lizzie. 2017. 'Theresa May Prompts Anger after Telling Nurse Who Hasn't Had Pay Rise for Eight Years: "There's No Magic Money Tree"'. *The Independent.* https://www.independent.co.uk/news/uk /politics/theresa-may-nurse-magic-money-tree-bbcqt-question-time -pay-rise-eight-years-election-latest-a7770576.html

Delmas, Candice. 2018. *A Duty to Resist: When Disobedience Should Be Uncivil.* Oxford University Press.

Delucchi, Mark A. 2010. 'Impacts of Biofuels on Climate Change, Water Use, and Land Use'. *Annals of the New York Academy of Sciences* 1195(1): 28–45.

Ditlevsen, Peter. 2017. 'Tipping Points in the Climate System'. In *Nonlinear and Stochastic Climate Dynamics*, eds. Christian L. E. Franzke and Terence J. O'Kane. Cambridge University Press, 33–53.

Dobson, Andrew. 2003. *Citizenship and the Environment.* Oxford University Press.

——. 2006. 'Ecological Citizenship: A Defence'. *Environmental Politics* 15(3): 447–51.

——. 2007. 'Environmental Citizenship: Towards Sustainable Development'. *Sustainable Development* 15(5): 276–85.

Draper, Jamie. 2018. 'Responsibility and Climate-Induced Displacement'. *Global Justice: Theory Practice Rhetoric* 11(2): 59–80.

———. 2020. 'Domination and Misframing in the Refugee Regime'. *Critical Review of International Social and Political Philosophy*: 1–24.

Draper, Jamie and Catriona McKinnon. 2018. 'The Ethics of Climate-Induced Community Displacement and Resettlement'. *Wiley Interdisciplinary Reviews: Climate Change* 9(3).

Drupp, Moritz A., Mark C. Freeman, Ben Groom, and Frikk Nesje. 2018. 'Discounting Disentangled'. *American Economic Journal: Economic Policy* 10(4): 109–34.

Dryzek, John S. 2021. *The Politics of the Earth*. 4th edn. Oxford University Press.

Dryzek, John S. and Jonathan Pickering. 2018. *The Politics of the Anthropocene*. Oxford University Press.

Duarte, Carlos M. et al. 2017. 'Can Seaweed Farming Play a Role in Climate Change Mitigation and Adaptation?' *Frontiers in Marine Science* 4.

Duus-Otterström, Göran and Sverker C. Jagers. 2012. 'Identifying Burdens of Coping with Climate Change: A Typology of the Duties of Climate Justice'. *Global Environmental Change* 22(3): 746–53.

Dworkin, Ronald. 1981. 'What Is Equality? Part 1: Equality of Welfare'. *Philosophy & Public Affairs* 10(3): 185–246.

Eckersley, Robyn. 2004. *The Green State: Rethinking Democracy and Sovereignty*. MIT Press.

———. 2015. 'The Common but Differentiated Responsibilities of States to Assist and Receive "Climate Refugees"'. *European Journal of Political Theory* 14(4): 481–500.

Egglestone, Ben and Dale E. Miller, eds. 2014. *The Cambridge Companion to Utilitarianism*. Cambridge University Press.

Estlund, David. 1993. 'Making Truth Safe for Democracy'. In *The Idea of Democracy*, eds. David Copp, Jean Hampton, and John E. Roemer. Cambridge University Press, 71–100.

———. 2011. 'Human Nature and the Limits (if any) of Political Philosophy'. *Philosophy and Public Affairs* 39(3): 207–37.

ETC Group. 2010. 'Civil Society Calls for a Moratorium on Geoengineering'. https://www.etcgroup.org/content/civil-society-calls-moratorium-geoengineering

Fairbrother, Malcolm, Gustaf Arrhenius, Krister Bykvist, and Tim

Campbell. 2021. 'Governing for Future Generations: How Political Trust Shapes Attitudes Towards Climate and Debt Policies'. *Frontiers in Political Science* 3.

Falkner, Robert. 2016. 'The Paris Agreement and the New Logic of International Climate Politics'. *International Affairs* 92(5): 1107–25.

———. 2019. 'The Unavoidability of Justice – and Order – in International Climate Politics: From Kyoto to Paris and Beyond'. *The British Journal of Politics and International Relations* 21(2): 270–78.

Feinberg, Joel. 1978. 'Voluntary Euthanasia and the Inalienable Right to Life'. *Philosophy and Public Affairs* 7(2): 93–123.

Felstiner, William L. F., Richard L. Abel, and Austin Sarat. 1980. 'The Emergence and Transformation of Disputes: Naming, Blaming, Claiming . . .' *Law & Society Review* 15(3/4): 631–54.

Figueroa, Robert Melchior. 2011. 'Indigenous Peoples and Cultural Losses'. *The Oxford Handbook of Climate Change and Society*, eds. John S. Dryzek, Richard B. Norgaard and David Schlosberg. Oxford University Press.

Finkelstein, Claire. 2002. 'Is Risk a Harm?, *University of Pennsylvania Law Review* 151(3): 963–1002.

Finneron-Burns, Elizabeth. 2017. 'What's Wrong with Human Extinction?' *Canadian Journal of Philosophy* 47(2–3): 327–43.

Fishkin, James. 2018. 'Deliberative Polling'. In *The Oxford Handbook of Deliberative Democracy*, eds. Andre Bachtiger, John S. Dryzek, Jane Mansbridge, and Mark Warren. Oxford University Press, 316–28.

Flanigan, Edmund Tweedy. 2021. 'From Self-Defense to Violent Protest'. *Critical Review of International Social and Political Philosophy*.

Fox, Warwick. 1995. *Towards a Transpersonal Ecology*. Green Books.

Foxon, Timothy J. 2007. 'Technological Lock-in and the Role of Innovation'. In *Handbook of Sustainable Development: Second Edition*, eds. Giles Atkinson, Simon Dietz, and Eric Neumayer. Edward Elgar, 140–54.

Fragniere, Augustin and Stephen M. Gardiner. 2016. 'Why Geoengineering Is Not "Plan B"'. *Climate Justice and Geoengineering: Ethics and Policy in the Atmospheric Anthropocene*, ed. Christopher Preston, Rowman & Littlefield. 15–32.

Fuhrman, Jay et al. 2019. 'From Zero to Hero?: Why Integrated Assessment Modeling of Negative Emissions Technologies Is Hard and How We Can Do Better'. *Frontiers in Climate* 1.

Fuss, Sabine et al. 2016. 'Research Priorities for Negative Emissions'. *Environmental Research Letters* 115007 11(11): 1–11.

Gardiner, Stephen M. 2006. 'A Core Precautionary Principle'. *Journal of Political Philosophy* 14(1): 33–60.

——. 2010. 'Is "Arming the Future" with Geoengineering Really the Lesser Evil? Some Doubts about the Ethics of Intentionally Manipulating the Climate System'. In *Climate Ethics: Essential Readings*, eds. Stephen M. Gardiner, Simon Caney, Dale Jamieson, and Henry Shue. Oxford University Press, 284–314.

——. 2011. *A Perfect Moral Storm: The Ethical Tragedy of Climate Change.* Oxford University Press.

——. 2014. 'A Call for a Global Constitutional Convention Focused on Future Generations'. *Ethics & International Affairs* 28(3): 299–315.

——. 2017a. 'Geoengineering: Ethical Questions for Deliberate Climate Manipulators'. In *The Oxford Handbook of Environmental Ethics*, eds. Stephen M. Gardiner and Allen Thompson. Oxford University Press, 501–17.

——. 2017b. 'The Threat of Intergenerational Extortion: On the Temptation to Become the Climate Mafia, Masquerading as an Intergenerational Robin Hood'. *Canadian Journal of Philosophy* 47(2–3): 368–94.

——. 2019. 'Motivating (or Baby-Stepping Toward) a Global Constitutional Convention for Future Generations'. *Environmental Ethics* 41(3): 199–220.

——. 2021. 'Should We Embrace a "New", Expansionist Agenda for the Virtues?' In *Crisis and Critique: Philosophical Analysis and Current Events*, eds. Anne Siegetsleitner, Andreas Oberprantacher, Marie-Luisa Frick, and Ulrich Metschl. Berlin: De Gruyter, 331–42.

Gardiner, Stephen M. ed. 2021. *The Oxford Handbook of Intergenerational Ethics.* Oxford University Press.

Gardiner, Stephen M. and Augustin Fragnière. 2018. 'The Tollgate Principles for the Governance of Geoengineering: Moving Beyond the Oxford Principles to an Ethically More Robust Approach'. *Ethics, Policy & Environment* 21(2): 143–74.

Gardiner, Stephen M. and David A. Weisbach. 2016. *Debating Climate Ethics*. Oxford University Press.

'Geoengineering Research Governance Project (GRGP) Oxford Workshop on a Code of Conduct for Responsible Geoengineering Research – Anna-Maria Hubert | FCEA'.

Goes, Marlos, Nancy Tuana, and Klaus Keller. 2011. 'The Economics (or Lack Thereof) of Aerosol Geoengineering'. *Climatic Change* 109(3–4): 719–44.

Goldenberg, Suzanne. 2016. 'UN Climate Science Chief: It's Not Too Late to Avoid Dangerous Temperature Rise. *Guardian* 11 May.

Goodin, Robert E. 1989. 'Theories of Compensation'. *Oxford Journal of Legal Studies* 9(1): 56–75.

———. 2010. 'Selling Environmental Indulgences'. In *Climate Ethics*, eds. Stephen M. Gardiner, Simon Caney, Dale Jamieson, and Henry Shue. Oxford University Press.

Gore, Tim. 2020. 'Confronting Carbon Inequality'. *Oxfam International*.

Gosseries, Axel. 2016. 'What Is Enough? Sufficiency, Justice and Health'. In *Intergenerational Justice, Sufficiency, and Health*, eds. Carina Fourie and Annette Rid. Oxford University Press.

Gough, Clair et al. 2018. 'Challenges to the Use of BECCS as a Keystone Technology in Pursuit of 1.5C'. *Global Sustainability* e5(1).

Grantham Research Institute. 2018. 'How Do Emissions Trading Systems Work?' https://www.lse.ac.uk/granthaminstitute/explainers/how-do-emissions-trading-systems-work/

Green, Fergus, and Eric Brandstedt. 2021. 'Engaged Climate Ethics'. *Journal of Political Philosophy* 29(4): 539–63

Hailwood, Simon A. 2004. *How to Be a Green Liberal: Nature, Value and Liberal Philosophy*. Routledge.

Hamilton, Clive. 2004. *Growth Fetish*. Pluto Press.

———. 2013. *Earthmasters: The Dawn of the Age of Climate Engineering*. Yale University Press.

Hamlin, Alan and Zofia Stemplowska. 2012. 'Theory, Ideal Theory and the Theory of Ideals'. *Political Studies Review* 10(1): 48–62.

Hänggli, Regula and Hanspeter Kriesi. 2012. 'Frame Construction and Frame Promotion (Strategic Framing Choices)'. *American Behavioral Scientist* 56(3): 260–78.

Hansson, Sven Ove. 2018. 'Risk'. In *Stanford Encyclopedia of Philosophy*, ed. Edward N. Zalta.

Hardin, Garrett. 1968. 'The Tragedy of the Commons'. *Science* 162(3859): 1243–8.

Harrington, Luke J. and Friederike E. L. Otto. 2020. 'Reconciling Theory with the Reality of African Heatwaves'. *Nature Climate Change* 10(9): 796–98.

Harris, Paul. 1989. *Civil Disobedience*. University Press of America.

Hayward, Tim. 2006. 'Ecological Citizenship: Justice, Rights and the Virtue of Resourcefulness'. *Environmental Politics* 15(3): 435–46.

———. 2007. 'Human Rights Versus Emissions Rights: Climate Justice and the Equitable Distribution of Ecological Space'. *Ethics & International Affairs* 21(4): 431–50.

Heilbroner, Robert L. 1974. *An Inquiry into the Human Prospect*. W.W. Norton & Co.

Heyward, Clare. 2014. 'Climate Change as Cultural Injustice'. In *New Waves in Global Justice*, New Waves in Philosophy, ed. Thom Brooks. Palgrave Macmillan, 149–69.

———. 2015. 'Is There Anything New Under the Sun?' In *The Ethics of Climate Governance*, eds. Aaron Maltais and Catriona Mckinnon. Rowman & Littlefield, 133–54.

Heyward, Clare and Jörgen Ödalen. 2016. 'A Free Movement Passport for the Territorially Dispossessed'. In *Climate Justice in a Non-Ideal World*, eds. Dominic Roser and Clare Heyward. Oxford University Press.

Heyward, Clare and Dominic Roser. 2016. *Climate Justice in a Non-Ideal World*, eds. Clare Heyward and Dominic Roser. Oxford University Press.

Hickel, Jason. 2021. *Less Is More: How Degrowth Will Save the World*. Windmill Books.

Hiller, Avram. 2011. 'Climate Change and Individual Responsibility'. *The Monist* 94(3): 349–68.

Hohl, Sabine and Dominie Roser. 2011. 'Stepping in for the Polluters? Climate Justice under Partial Compliance'. *Analyse & Kritik* 33(2): 477–500.

Horton, Joshua and David Keith. 2016. 'Solar Geoengineering and Obligations to the Global Poor'. In *Climate Justice and Geoengineering:*

Ethics and Policy in the Atmospheric Anthropocene, ed. Christopher J. Preston. Rowman & Littlefield, 79–92.

Hourdequin, Marion. 2019. 'Climate Change, Climate Engineering, and the "Global Poor": What Does Justice Require?' *Ethics, Policy & Environment* 19(6): 1–19.

Hubert, Anna-Maria, Tim Kruger, and Steve Rayner. 2016. 'Geoengineering: Code of Conduct for Geoengineering'. *Nature* 537(7621): 488.

Hume, David. 1987. *Essays – Moral, Political and Literary*. ed. Eugene Miller. Liberty Fund Inc.

Husak, Douglas. 2010. 'Does Criminal Liability Require an Act?' In *The Philosophy of Criminal Law: Selected Essays*. Oxford University Press, 17–52.

Hyams, Keith and Tina Fawcett. 2013. 'The Ethics of Carbon Offsetting'. *Wiley Interdisciplinary Reviews: Climate Change* 4(2): 91–98.

Im, Eun-Soon, Jeremy S. Pal, and Elfatih A. B. Eltahir. 2017. 'Deadly Heat Waves Projected in the Densely Populated Agricultural Regions of South Asia'. *Science Advances* 3: e1603322.

Jamieson, Dale. 1996. 'Ethics and Intentional Climate Change'. *Climatic Change* 33(3): 323–36.

——. 2010. 'When Utilitarians Should Be Virtue Theorists'. In *Climate Ethics: Essential Readings*, eds. Stephen M. Gardiner, Simon Caney, Dale Jamieson, and Henry Shue. Oxford University Press 315–31.

——. 2014. *Reason in a Dark Time*. Oxford University Press.

——. 2015. 'Two Cheers for Climate Justice'. *Social Research* 82(3): 20.

Jasanoff, Sheila and J. Benjamin Hurlbut. 2018. 'A Global Observatory for Gene Editing'. *Nature* 555(7697): 435–37.

Jewell, Jessica and Aleh Cherp. 2020. 'On the Political Feasibility of Climate Change Mitigation Pathways: Is It Too Late to Keep Warming below 1.5°C?' *WIREs Climate Change* 11(1): e621.

Johnson, Ayana Elizabeth. 2021. *All We Can Save: Truth, Courage, and Solutions for the Climate Crisis*, eds. Ayana Elizabeth Johnson and Katharine K. Wilkinson. S.l.: One World.

Johnson, Craig A. 2012. 'Governing Climate Displacement: The Ethics and Politics of Human Resettlement'. *Environmental Politics* 21(2): 308–28.

Johnson, Nicole. 2013. 'Native Village of Kivalina v. ExxonMobil Corp:

Say Goodbye to Federal Public Nuisance Claims for Greenhouse Gas Emissions In Brief'. *Ecology Law Quarterly* 40(2): 557–64.

Jones, Andy et al. 2013. 'The Impact of Abrupt Suspension of Solar Radiation Management (Termination Effect) in Experiment G2 of the Geoengineering Model Intercomparison Project (GeoMIP)'. *Journal of Geophysical Research: Atmospheres* 118(17): 9743–52.

Kahneman, Daniel, Jack L. Knetsch, and Richard H. Thaler. 1991. 'Anomalies: The Endowment Effect, Loss Aversion, and Status Quo Bias'. *Journal of Economic Perspectives* 5: 193–206.

Kallis, Giorgos. 2011. 'In Defence of Degrowth'. *Ecological Economics* 70(5): 873–80.

Kallis, Giorgos, Susan Paulson, Giacomo D'Alisa, and Federico Demaria. 2020. *The Case for Degrowth*. Polity.

Karnein, Anja. 2014. 'Putting Fairness in Its Place: Why There Is A Duty to Take Up The Slack'. *Journal of Philosophy* 111(11): 593–607.

Kashwan, Prakash, Frank Biermann, Aarti Gupta, and Chukwumerije Okereke. 2020. 'Planetary Justice: Prioritizing the Poor in Earth System Governance'. *Earth System Governance* 6: 100075.

Kaufman, Mark. 2020. 'The Devious Fossil Fuel Propaganda We All Use'. *Mashable*. https://mashable.com/feature/carbon-footprint-pr-campaign-sham

Keay, Douglas. 1987. 'Margaret Thatcher: Interview'. *Woman's Own*. https://www.margaretthatcher.org/document/106689

Keith, David W. and Douglas G. MacMartin. 2015. 'A Temporary, Moderate and Responsive Scenario for Solar Geoengineering'. *Nature Climate Change* 5(3): 201–6.

Keller, David P., Ellias Y. Feng, and Andreas Oschlies. 2014. 'Potential Climate Engineering Effectiveness and Side Effects during a High Carbon Dioxide-Emission Scenario'. *Nature Communications* 5: 3304.

Kelley, Colin P. et al. 2015. 'Climate Change in the Fertile Crescent and Implications of the Recent Syrian Drought'. *Proceedings of the National Academy of Sciences* 112(11): 3241–6.

Keohane, Robert O, Melissa Lane, and Michael Oppenheimer. 2014. 'The Ethics of Scientific Communication under Uncertainty'. *Politics, Philosophy & Economics* 13(4): 343–68.

Klein, Naomi. 2014. *This Changes Everything*. Penguin Books.

Kleres, Jochen, and Åsa Wettergren. 2017. 'Fear, Hope, Anger, and Guilt in Climate Activism'. *Social Movement Studies* 16(5): 507–19.

Knutti, Reto, Joeri Rogelj, Jan Sedláček, and Erich M. Fischer. 2016. 'A Scientific Critique of the Two-Degree Climate Change Target'. *Nature Geoscience* 9(1): 13–18.

Kothari, Uma. 2014. 'Political Discourses of Climate Change and Migration: Resettlement Policies in the Maldives'. *The Geographical Journal* 180(2): 130–40.

Larkin, Philip. 1974. 'The Old Fools'. In *High Windows*, Faber and Faber, 13–14.

Latta, P. Alex. 2007. 'Locating Democratic Politics in Ecological Citizenship'. *Environmental Politics* 16(3): 377–93.

Lawford-Smith, Holly. 2010. 'Debate: Ideal Theory – A Reply to Valentini'. *Journal of Political Philosophy* 18(3): 357–68.

———. 2016. 'Difference-Making and Individuals' Climate-Related Obligations'. In *Climate Justice in a Non-Ideal World*, eds. Clare Heyward and Dominic Roser. Oxford University Press, 64–82.

———. 2020. 'Democratic Authority to Geoengineer'. *Critical Review of International Social and Political Philosophy* 23(5): 600–17.

Lazari-Radek, Katarzyna de and Peter Singer. 2017. *Utilitarianism: A Very Short Introduction*. Oxford University Press.

Lear, Jonathan. 2006. *Radical Hope: Ethics in the Face of Cultural Devastation*. Harvard University Press.

Lenton, Timothy M. et al. 2019. 'Climate Tipping Points — Too Risky to Bet Against'. *Nature* 575(7784): 592–5.

Lenzi, Dominic. 2018. 'The Ethics of Negative Emissions'. *Global Sustainability* e7: 1–8.

Leopold, Aldo. 1989. *A Sand County Almanac, and Sketches Here and There*. Oxford University Press.

Lepori, Matthew. 2019. 'Towards a New Ecological Democracy: A Critical Evaluation of the Deliberation Paradigm Within Green Political Theory'. *Environmental Values* 28(1): 75–99.

Levin, K., B. Cashore, Steven Bernstein, and G. Auld. 2009. 'Playing It Forward: Path Dependency, Progressive Incrementalism, and the "Super Wicked" Problem of Global Climate Change'. *IOP Conference Series: Earth and Environmental Science* 6(50): 502002.

Lin, Albert C. 2015. 'The Missing Pieces of Geoengineering Research Governance'. *Minnesota Law Review* 152(434): 2509–76.

List, Christian and Philip Pettit. 2011. *Group Agency: The Possibility, Design, and Status of Corporate Agents*. Oxford University Press.

Locke, John. 1988. *Two Treatises of Government*. ed. Peter Laslett. Cambridge University Press.

Lorde, Audre. 1997. 'The Uses of Anger'. *Women's Studies Quarterly* 25(1/2): 278–85.

McEldowney, John F., and Julie L. Drolet. 2021. 'Chapter 24 – Climate Change and Refugees'. In *The Impacts of Climate Change*, ed. Trevor M. Letcher. Elsevier, 537–45.

MacGregor, Sherilyn. 2006a. *Beyond Mothering Earth: Ecological Citizenship and the Politics of Care*. UBC Press.

——. 2006b. 'No Sustainability Without Justice: A Feminist Critique of Environmental Citizenship'. In *Environmental Citizenship*, eds. Andrew Dobson and Derek Bell. MIT Press, 101–26.

——. 2014. 'Ecological Citizenship'. In *Handbook of Political Citizenship and Social Movements*, ed. Hein-Anton van der Heijden. Edward Elgar.

MacKenzie, Catriona and Natalie Stoljar, eds. 2002. *Relational Autonomy: Feminist Perspectives on Autonomy, Agency, and the Social Self*. Oxford University Press.

MacKenzie, Michael K. 2016. 'Institutional Design and Sources of Short-Termism'. In *Institutions for Future Generations*, eds. Inigo Gonzalez-Ricoy and Axel Gosseries. Oxford University Press, 24–48.

McKinnon, C. 2005. 'Cosmopolitan Hope'. In *The Political Philosophy of Cosmopolitanism*, eds. Gillian Brock and Harry Brighouse. Cambridge University Press, 234–49.

——. 2011. 'Climate Change Justice: Getting Motivated in the Last Chance Saloon'. *Critical Review of International Social and Political Philosophy* 14(2): 195–213.

——. 2012. *Climate Change and Future Justice: Precaution, Compensation, and Triage*. Routledge.

——. 2014. 'Climate Change: Against Despair'. *Ethics and the Environment* 19(1): 31–48.

——. 2016. 'Should We Tolerate Climate Change Denial?' *Midwest Studies in Philosophy* 40(1): 205–16.

——. 2017. 'Endangering Humanity: An International Crime?' *Canadian Journal of Philosophy* 47(2–3): 395–415.

——. 2019. 'Sleepwalking into Lock-in? Avoiding Wrongs to Future People in the Governance of Solar Radiation Management Research'. *Environmental Politics* 28(3), 441–59.

——. 2020. 'The Panglossian Politics of the Geoclique'. *Critical Review of International Social and Political Philosophy* 23(5): 584–99.

——. 2021. 'Postericide and Intergenerational Ethics'. In *The Oxford Handbook of Intergenerational Ethics*, ed. Stephen M. Gardiner.

Macklin, Ruth. 1981. 'Can Future Generationas Correctly Be Said To Have Rights?' In *Responsibilities to Future Generations: Environmental Ethics*, ed. Ernest Partridge. Prometheus Books, 151–6.

McLaren, Duncan et al. 2019. 'Beyond "Net-Zero": A Case for Separate Targets for Emissions Reduction and Negative Emissions'. *Frontiers in Climate: Negative Emissions Technology. Policy Brief.*

——. 2020. 'Quantifying the Potential Scale of Mitigation Deterrence from Greenhouse Gas Removal Techniques'. *Climatic Change* 162(4): 2411–28.

McLaren, Duncan and Olaf Corry. 2021. 'The Politics and Governance of Research into Solar Geoengineering'. *WIREs Climate Change* 12(3): e707.

McLaughlin, Alex. 2019. 'Justifying Subsistence Emissions, Past and Present'. *British Journal of Politics and International Relations* 21(2): 263–9.

——. 2020. 'The Limit of Climate Justice: Unfair Sacrifice and Aggregate Harm'. *Critical Review of International Social and Political Philosophy* https://doi.org/10.1080/13698230.2020.1786306

MacMartin, Douglas G., Ken Caldeira, and David W. Keith. 2014. 'Solar Geoengineering to Limit the Rate of Temperature Change.' *Philosophical Transactions of the Royal Society A* 372: 20140134.

McShane, Katie. 2016. 'Anthropocentrism in Climate Ethics and Policy'. *Midwest Studies in Philosophy* 40(1): 189–204.

Maldonado, Julie Koppel et al. 2013. 'The Impact of Climate Change on Tribal Communities in the US: Displacement, Relocation, and Human Rights'. *Climatic Change* 120(3): 601–14.

Marvel, Kate. 2018. 'We Need Courage, Not Hope, to Face Climate Change'. *The On Being Project.* https://onbeing.org/blog/kate-marvel-we-need-courage-not-hope-to-face-climate-change/

Marx, Karl. 2000. 'Critique of the Gotha Programme'. In *Karl Marx: Selected Writings*, ed. David McLellan. Oxford University Press, 610–17.

Meadows, Donella, Dennis Meadows, Jorgen Randers, and William Behrens. 1972. *The Limits to Growth – Club of Rome*. Universe Books.

Met Office. 2019. *Briefing Note on Time Lags in the Climate System*. The Met Office. https://www.theccc.org.uk/publication/briefing-note -on-time-lags-in-the-climate-system-met-office/

Meyer, Lukas H. 2003. 'Past and Future: The Case for a Threshold Notion of Harm'. In *Rights, Culture, and the Law: Themes from the Legal and Political Philosophy of Joseph Raz*, eds. Lukas H. Meyer, S. L. Paulson, and Thomas Pogge. Oxford University Press, 143–59.

Meyer, Lukas H. and Dominic Roser. 2006. 'Distributive Justice and Climate Change: The Allocation of Emission Rights'. *Analyse & Kritik* 28(2): 223–49.

———. 2010. 'Climate Justice and Historical Emissions'. *Critical Review of International Social and Political Philosophy* 13(1): 229–53.

Mill, John Stuart. 1998. *Utilitarianism*. Oxford University Press.

Miller, David. 2011. 'Taking Up the Slack? Responsibility and Justice in Situations of Partial Compliance'. In *Responsibility and Distributive Justice*, Oxford University Press, 1–18.

Moellendorf, Darrel. 2006. 'Hope as a Political Virtue'. *Philosophical Papers* 35(3): 413–33.

———. 2013. *The Moral Challenge of Dangerous Climate Change*. Cambridge University Press.

———. 2022. *Mobilizing Hope: Climate Change and Global Poverty*. Oxford University Press.

Monbiot, George. 2007. *Heat: How We Can Stop the Planet Burning*. Penguin Books.

———. 2019. 'Only Rebellion Will Prevent an Ecological Apocalypse'. *Guardian* 15 April.

———. 2019. 'My Generation Trashed the Planet. So I Salute the Children Striking Back'. *Guardian* 15 February.

Moore, Michael. 2019. 'Causation in the Law'. In *The Stanford Encyclopedia of Philosophy*, ed. Edward N. Zalta. Metaphysics Research Lab, Stanford University.

Mordecai, Erin A. et al. 2020. 'Climate Change Could Shift Disease

Burden from Malaria to Arboviruses in Africa'. *The Lancet Planetary Health* 4(9): e416–23.

Morrow, D. R. 2014. 'Ethical Aspects of the Mitigation Obstruction Argument against Climate Engineering Research'. *Philosophical Transactions of the Royal Society A: Mathematical, Physical and Engineering Sciences* 372(2031): 20140062–20140062.

———. 2017. 'International Governance of Climate Engineering: A Survey of Reports on Climate Engineering, 2009–2015'. *FCEA Working Paper Series*, 001.

———. 2020. 'A Mission-Driven Research Program on Solar Geoengineering Could Promote Justice and Legitimacy'. *Critical Review of International Social and Political Philosophy* 23(5): 618–40.

Mulgan, Tim. 2017. 'How Should Utilitarians Think about the Future?' *Canadian Journal of Philosophy* 47(2–3): 290–312.

Murphy, Liam B. 2000. *Moral Demands in Nonideal Theory*. Oxford University Press.

Naess, Arne. 1990. *Ecology, Community and Lifestyle: Outline of an Ecosophy*. Cambridge University Press.

National Academies of Sciences, Engineering, and Medicine. 2021. *Reflecting Sunlight: Recommendations for Solar Geoengineering Research and Research Governance*. Washington, DC: National Academies of Sciences, Engineering, and Medicine.

———. 2011. *Understanding Earth's Deep Past: Lessons for Our Climate Future*. Washington, DC: National Academies Press.

National Research Council. 2011. *Understanding Earth's Deep Past: Lessons for Our Climate Future*. Washington, DC: National Academies Press.

Nell, Onora and Onora O'Neill. 1975. 'Lifeboat Earth'. *Philosophy & Public Affairs* 4(3): 273–92.

Neumayer, Eric. 2000. 'In Defence of Historical Accountability for Greenhouse Gas Emissions'. *Ecological Economics* 33(2): 185–92.

Nine, Cara. 2010. 'Ecological Refugees, States Borders, and the Lockean Proviso'. *Journal of Applied Philosophy* 27(4): 359–75.

Nolt, John. 2011a. 'How Harmful are the Average American's Greenhouse Gas Emissions?' *Ethics, Place and Environment* 14(1): 3–10.

———. 2011b. 'Nonanthropocentric Climate Ethics'. *Wiley Interdisciplinary Reviews: Climate Change* 2(5): 701–11.

———. 2021. 'Long-Term Non-Anthropocentric Ethics'. In *The Oxford Handbook of Intergenerational Ethics*, ed. Stephen M. Gardiner. Oxford University Press.

Nordhaus, William D. 2007. 'A Review of the Stern Review on the Economics of Climate Change'. *Journal of Economic Literature* 45(3): 686–702.

Norgaard, Kari Marie. 2011. *Living in Denial*. MIT Press.

Noyes, Jan. 1983. 'The QWERTY Keyboard: A Review'. *International Journal of Man-Machine Studies* 18(3): 265–81.

Nozick, Robert. 1974. *Anarchy, State and Utopia*. Blackwell.

Nuccitelli, Dana. 2016. 'Scientists Debate Experimenting With Climate Hacking to Prevent Catastrophe'. *Guardian* 1 June.

Nussbaum, Martha C. 2000. *Women and Human Development: The Capabilities Approach*. Cambridge University Press.

Okereke, Chukwumerije and Patricia Agupusi. 2015. *Homegrown Development in Africa: Reality or Illusion?* 1st edn. Routledge.

Okereke, Chukwumerije and Philip Coventry. 2016. 'Climate Justice and the International Regime: Before, during, and after Paris'. *Wiley Interdisciplinary Reviews: Climate Change* 7(6): 834–51.

Olsthoorn, Johan. 2018. 'Two Ways of Theorizing "Collective Ownership of the Earth"'. In *Property Theory*, eds. James Penner and Michael Otsuka. Cambridge University Press, 187–214.

O'Neill, Onora. 1996. *Towards Justice and Virtue: A Constructive Account of Practical Reasoning*. Cambridge University Press.

Ophuls, William. 1977. *Ecology and the Politics of Scarcity*. W.H. Freeman & Co Ltd.

Ostrom, Elinor. 2010. 'Polycentric Systems for Coping with Collective Action and Global Environmental Change'. *Global Environmental Change* 20(4): 550–7.

Ott, K. and C. Baatz. 2012. 'Domains of Climate Ethics: An Overview'. In *Climate Change and Sustainable Development: Ethical Perspectives on Land Use and Food Production*. Thomas Potthast and Simon Meisch eds. Springer: 23–8.

Page, Edward A. 2007. 'Justice Between Generations: Investigating a Sufficientarian Approach'. *Journal of Global Ethics* 3(1): 3–20.

———. 2012. 'Give it up for Climate Change: A Defence of the Beneficiary Pays Principle'. *International Theory* 4(2): 300–30.

———. 2013. 'The Ethics of Emissions Trading'. *Wiley Interdisciplinary Reviews: Climate Change* 4(4): 233–43.

Palmer, Clare. 2011. 'Does Nature Matter? The Place of the Nonhuman in the Ethics of Climate Change'. In *The Ethics of Global Climate Change*, ed. Denis G. Arnold. Cambridge University Press, 272–91.

Parfit, Derek. 1984. *Reasons and Persons*. Oxford University Press.

Parker, Andy and Peter J. Irvine. 2018. 'The Risk of Termination Shock From Solar Geoengineering'. *Earth's Future* 6(3): 456–67.

Parry, Ian et al. 2021. 'Still Not Getting Energy Prices Right: A Global and Country Update of Fossil Fuel Subsidies'. *International Monetary Fund*. Working Paper No. 2021/236.

Parson, Edward A. 2017. 'Starting the Dialogue on Climate Engineering Governance: A World Commission'. *Fixing Climate Governance* (8): 1–8.

Pearl, Mike. 2019. '"Climate Despair" is Making People Give Up on Life'. *Vice*. https://www.vice.com/en/article/j5w374/climate-despair -is-making-people-give-up-on-life (2 July 2021).

Popkin, Jeremy D. 2021. *A Concise History of the Haitian Revolution*. 2nd edn. Wiley.

Porritt, Jonathan. 1984. *Seeing Green*. Blackwell.

Posner, Eric A. and David A. Weisbach. 2010. *Climate Change Justice*. Princeton University Press.

Posner, Richard A. 2006. *Catastrophe: Risk and Response*. Oxford University Press.

Preston, Christopher J. 2012. 'Solar Radiation Management and Vulnerable Populations'. In *Engineering the Climate: The Ethics of Solar Radiation Management*, ed. Christopher J. Preston. Lexington Books, 77–94.

———. 2016. *Climate Justice and Geoengineering: Ethics and Policy in the Atmospheric Anthropocene*. Rowman & Littlefield.

Prins, Gwyn, and Steve Rayner. 2007. 'Time to Ditch Kyoto'. *Nature* 449: 973–75.

Purdy, Jedediah. 2015. *After Nature: A Politics for the Anthropocene*. Harvard University Press.

Quiggin, Daniel. 2021. 'BECCS Deployment: The Risks of Policies Forging Ahead of the Evidence'. *Chatham House: Environment and Society Programme*. Research paper October 2021. Available at https:// www.chathamhouse.org/beccs-deployment/04-feedstock-choice-car bon-efficiency-and-carbon-debt

Randalls, Samuel. 2010. 'History of the 2°C Climate Target'. *Wiley Interdisciplinary Reviews: Climate Change* 1(4): 598–605.

Rawls, John. 1999. *A Theory of Justice*. Revised edn. Oxford University Press.

——. 2001. *Justice as Fairness*. Harvard University Press.

Rayner, Steve et al. 2013. 'The Oxford Principles'. *Climatic Change* 121(3): 499–512.

Raz, Joseph. 1988. *The Morality of Freedom*. Oxford University Press.

Reese, Gerhard and Lisa Jacob. 2015. 'Principles of Environmental Justice and Pro-Environmental Action: A Two-Step Process Model of Moral Anger and Responsibility to Act'. *Environmental Science & Policy* 51: 88–94.

Reiman, Jeffrey. 2007. 'Being Fair to Future People: The Non-Identity Problem in the Original Position'. *Philosophy and Public Affairs* 35(1): 69–92.

Reynolds, Jesse L., Andy Parker, and Peter Irvine. 2016. 'Five Solar Geoengineering Tropes That Have Outstayed Their Welcome'. *Earth's Future* 4(12): 562–8.

Richardson, Henry S. 2000. 'The Stupidity of the Cost-Benefit Standard'. *Journal of Legal Studies* 29(2): 971–1004.

Rigaud, Kumari et al. 2018. *Groundswell: Preparing for Internal Climate Migration*. The World Bank.

Risse, Mathias. 2009. 'The Right to Relocation: Disappearing Island Nations and Common Ownership of the Earth'. *Ethics & International Affairs* 23(3): 281–300.

Ritchie, Hannah and Max Roser. 2013. 'Land Use'. https://ourworldin data.org/land-use

Roeser, Sabine, Behnam Taebi, and Neelke Doorn. 2020. 'Geoengineering the Climate and Ethical Challenges: What We Can Learn from Moral Emotions and Art'. *Critical Review of International Social and Political Philosophy* 23(5): 641–58.

Rogelj, Joeri et al. 2015. 'Energy System Transformations for Limiting End-of-Century Warming to below 1.5 °C'. *Nature Climate Change* 5(6): 519–27.

——. 2016. 'Paris Agreement Climate Proposals Need a Boost to Keep Warming Well below 2 °C'. *Nature* 534(7609): 631–9.

Routley, Richard. 1973. 'Is There a Need for a New, an Environmental Ethic'. *Proceedings of the XVth World Congress of Philosophy* 1: 205–10.

The Royal Society. 2009a. *Geoengineering the Climate: Science, Governance and Uncertainty.*

———. 2009b. Clean Technologies and Environmental Policy *Geoengineering the Climate: Science, Governance and Uncertainty.*

Sayegh, Alexandre Gajevic. 2019. 'Pricing Carbon for Climate Justice'. *Ethics, Policy and Environment* 22(2): 109–30.

Scheffler, Samuel. 2006. 'Is the Basic Structure Basic?' In *The Egalitarian Conscience: Essays in Honour of G.A. Cohen*, ed. Christine Sypnowich. Oxford University Press, 102–29.

———. 2013. *Death and the Afterlife*. Oxford University Press.

Schleussner, Carl-Friedrich et al. 2016. 'Science and Policy Characteristics of the Paris Agreement Temperature Goal'. *Nature Climate Change* 6(9): 827–35.

Schlosberg, David. 2009. *Defining Environmental Justice: Theories, Movements, and Nature*. Oxford University Press.

Schlosberg, David, Karin Backstrand, and Jonathan Pickering. 2019. 'Reconciling Ecological and Democratic Values: Recent Perspectives on Ecological Democracy'. *Environmental Values* 28(1): 1–9.

Schlosberg, David and Lisette B. Collins. 2014. 'From Environmental to Climate Justice: Climate Change and the Discourse of Environmental Justice'. *Wiley Interdisciplinary Reviews: Climate Change* 5(3): 359–74.

Schlosberg, David and Luke Craven. 2019. *Sustainable Materialism: Environmental Movements and the Politics of Everyday Life*. Oxford University Press.

Schlosser, Markus. 2019. 'Agency' ed. Edward N. Zalta. *The Stanford Encyclopedia of Philosophy.* https://plato.stanford.edu/arch ives/win2019/entries/agency/

Scott, James C. 1985. *Weapons of the Weak: Everyday Forms of Peasant Resistance*. Yale University Press.

Searchinger, Tim and Ralph Heimlich. 2015. 'Avoiding Bioenergy Competition For Food Crops and Land'. *World Resources Institute – Working Paper.* Available at: https://www.wri.org/research/avoiding-b ioenergy-competition-food-crops-and-land?mod=article_inline

Sen, Amartya. 2001. *Development as Freedom*. Oxford University Press.

———. 2011. *The Idea of Justice*. Harvard University Press.

Shalit, Avner de. 1994. *Why Posterity Matters: Environmental Policies and Future Generations*. Routledge.

——. 2011. 'Climate Change Refugees, Compensation, and Rectification'. *The Monist* 94(3): 310–28.

Sherwood, Steven C. and Matthew Huber. 2010. 'An Adaptability Limit to Climate Change Due to Heat Stress'. *Proceedings of the National Academy of Sciences* 107(21): 9552–5.

Shrader-Frechette, Kristin. 2015. 'Biomass Incineration: Scientifically and Ethically Indefensible'. In *The Ethics of Climate Governance*, eds. Aaron Maltais and Catriona McKinnon. Rowman & Littlefield, 155–73.

Shue, Henry. 1996. *Basic Rights: Subsistence, Affluence, and U.S. Foreign Policy*. Princeton University Press.

——. 2001. 'Climate'. In *A Companion to Environmental Philosophy*, ed. Dale Jamieson. Blackwell, 449–60.

——. 2010. 'Deadly Delays, Saving Opportunities: Creating a More Dangerous World?' In *Climate Ethics: Essential Readings*, eds. Stephen M. Gardiner, Simon Caney, Dale Jamieson, and Henry Shue. Oxford University Press, 146–62.

——. 2013. 'Climate Hope: Implementing the Exit Strategy'. *Chicago Journal of International Law* 13(2). https://chicagounbound.uchicago.edu/cjil/vol13/iss2/6

——. 2014a. 'Avoidable Necessity: Global Warming, International Fairness, and Alternative Energy'. In *Climate Justice: Vulnerability and Protection*, Oxford University Press, 89–109.

——. 2014b. 'Bequeathing Hazards: Security Rights and Property Rights of Future Humans'. In *Climate Justice: Vulnerability and Protection*, Oxford University Press, 163–79.

——. 2014c. 'Climate Hope: Implementing the Exit Strategy'. In *Climate Justice: Vulnerability and Protection*, Oxford University Press, 319–40.

——. 2014d. *Climate Justice: Vulnerability and Protection*. Oxford University Press.

——. 2020. *Basic Rights: Subsistence, Affluence, and U.S. Foreign Policy*. Princeton University Press (40th Anniversary Edition).

——. 2021. *The Pivotal Generation: Why We Have a Moral Responsibility to Slow Climate Change Right Now*. Oxford University Press.

Shutkin, William A. 2001. *The Land That Could Be: Environmentalism and Democracy in the Twenty-First Century*. MIT Press.

Singer, Peter. 1972. 'Famine, Affluence, and Morality'. *Philosophy and Public Affairs* 1(3): 229–43.

———. 2004. *One World: The Ethics of Globalization*. 2nd edn. Yale University Press.

———. 2006. 'Ethics and Climate Change: A Commentary on MacCracken, Toman and Gardiner'. *Environmental Values* 15(3): 415–22.

———. 2011. *Practical Ethics*. 3rd edn. Cambridge University Press.

Sinnott-Armstrong, Walter. 2010. 'It's Not My Fault: Global Warming and Individual Moral Obligations'. In *Climate Ethics: Essential Readings*, eds. Stephen M. Gardiner, Simon Caney, Dale Jamieson, and Henry Shue. Oxford University Press, 332–47.

Smith, Patrick Taylor. 2014. 'Redirecting Threats, the Doctrine of Doing and Allowing, and the Special Wrongness of Solar Radiation Management'. *Ethics, Policy & Environment* 17(2): 143–46.

———. forthcoming. *Climate Revolution: The Ethics of Radical Environmental Action*. Oxford University Press.

Smith, Pete et al. 2016. 'Biophysical and Economic Limits to Negative CO_2 Emissions'. *Nature Climate Change* 6(1): 42–50.

Solnit, Rebecca. 2021. 'Big Oil Coined "Carbon Footprints" to Blame Us for Their Greed. Keep Them on the Hook', *Guardian* 23 August.

Spash, Clive L. 2011. 'Carbon Trading: A Critique'. *The Oxford Handbook of Climate Change and Society*, eds. John S. Dryzek, Richard B. Norgaard and David Schlosberg. Oxford University Press.

Srinivasan, Amia. 2018. 'The Aptness of Anger'. *Journal of Political Philosophy* 26(2): 123–44.

Stanley, Samantha K., Teaghan L. Hogg, Zoe Leviston, and Iain Walker. 2021. 'From Anger to Action: Differential Impacts of Eco-Anxiety, Eco-Depression, and Eco-Anger on Climate Action and Wellbeing'. *Journal of Climate Change and Health* 1: 100003.

Steel, Daniel. 2014. *Philosophy and the Precautionary Principle: Science, Evidence, and Environmental Policy*. Cambridge University Press.

Steffen, Will et al. 2018. 'Trajectories of the Earth System in the Anthropocene'. *Proceedings of the National Academy of Sciences* 115(33): 8252–59.

Stern, Nicholas. 2006. *The Economics of Climate Change: The Stern Review*. HM Treasury. https://www.lse.ac.uk/granthaminstitute/publication/the-economics-of-climate-change-the-stern-review/

Stilz, Anna. 2014. 'On Collective Ownership of the Earth'. *Ethics & International Affairs* 28(4): 501–10.

Stirling, Andy et al. 2008. '"Opening Up" and "Closing Down": Power, Participation, and Pluralism in the Social Appraisal of Technology'. *Science, Technology, & Human Values* 33(2): 262–94.

———. 2008. 'Science, Precaution, and the Politics of Technological Risk: Converging Implications in Evolutionary and Social Scientific Perspectives'. *Annals of the New York Academy of Sciences* 1128: 95–110.

Sunstein, Cass R. 2002. *Risk and Reason: Safety, Law, and the Environment.* Cambridge University Press.

———. 2004a. 'Cost-Benefit Analysis and the Environment'. *John M. Olin Law & Economics Working Paper* 227 (October).

———. 2004b. 'Valuing Life: A Plea for Disaggregation'. *Duke Law Journal* 54: 385–445.

———. 2005a. *Laws of Fear: Beyond the Precautionary Principle.* Cambridge University Press.

———. 2005b. 'Cost-Benefit Analysis and the Environment'. *Journal of Risk and Uncertainty* 115 (January): 351–85.

———. 2006. 'The Catastrophic Harm Precautionary Principle'. *Issues in Legal Scholarship* 6(3): 31.

———. 2009. *Worst-Case Scenarios.* Harvard University Press.

Svoboda, Toby, Klaus Keller, Marlos Goes, and Nancy Tuana. 2011. 'Sulfate Aerosol Geoengineering: The Question of Justice'. *Public Affairs Quarterly* 25(3): 157–80.

Swift, Adam. 2008. 'The Value of Philosophy in Nonideal Circumstances'. *Social Theory and Practice* 34(3): 363–87.

Sypnowich, Christine, ed. 2006. *The Egalitarian Conscience: Essays in Honour of G. A. Cohen.* Oxford University Press.

Talisse, Robert. 'Climate Denialism and Propaganda'. https://whywear gue.libsyn.com/climate-denialism-and-propaganda-with-catriona-mc kinnon

Taylor, Matthew, and Jonathan Watts. 2019. 'Revealed: The 20 Firms Behind a Third of All Carbon Emissions'. *Guardian* 9 October.

Teichmann, Matt. 'Interview with Philip Pettit'. https://shows.acast.com /elucidations/episodes/57b49a2f0b5f3f772a760068

Thompson, Allen. 2010. 'Radical Hope for Living Well in a Warmer World'. *Journal of Agricultural & Environmental Ethics* 23(1/2): 43–59.

Thompson, Allen and Jeremy Bendik-Keymer. 2012. *Ethical Adaptation to Climate Change: Human Virtues of the Future.* MIT Press.

Thompson, Janna. 2009. 'Identity and Obligation in a Transgenerational Polity'. In *Intergenerational Justice*, eds. Axel Gosseries and Lukas H. Meyer. Oxford University Press.

Thunberg, Greta. 2019. *No One Is Too Small to Make a Difference.* Penguin Books.

Tooze, Adam. 2021. 'Chartbook Newsletter #24'. *Chartbook.* https://adamtooze.substack.com/p/chartbook-newsletter-24

Tschakert, Petra et al. 2021. 'Multispecies Justice: Climate-just Futures with, for and beyond Humans'. *WIREs Climate Change* 12(2).

Umbers, Lachlan Montgomery, and Jeremy Moss. 2018. 'Going to Alone: Cities and States for Climate Action'. *Ethics, Policy & Environment* 21(1): 56–9.

UNDP and University of Oxford. 2021. *Peoples' Climate Vote.* UNDP. https://www.undp.org/publications/peoples-climate-vote#modal-publication-download

UNEP. 2020. *Emissions Gap Report 2020.* Nairobi: United Nations Environment Programme. https://www.unep.org/emissions-gap-report-2020

———. 2021. *Emissions Gap Report 2021.* https://www.unep.org/resources/emissions-gap-report-2021

Vanderheiden, Steve. 2008. *Atmospheric Justice: A Political Theory of Climate Change.* Oxford University Press.

Vidal, John. 2009. 'Poor Nations Threaten Climate Deal Showdown at Copenhagen Summit'. *Guardian* 13 December.

Watts, Jonathan. 2020. 'Climate Worst-Case Scenarios May Not Go Far Enough, Cloud Data Shows'. *Guardian* 13 June.

White, Gregory. 2019. '"Climate Refugees" – A Useful Concept?' *Global Environmental Politics* 19(4): 133–8.

Whyte, Kyle Powys. 2019. 'Indigeneity in Geoengineering Discourses: Some Considerations'. *Ethics, Policy & Environment* 20(2): 1–19.

———. 2020. 'Too Late for Indigenous Climate Justice: Ecological and Relational Tipping Points'. *WIREs Climate Change* 11(1).

Wilcox, Shelley. 2021. 'Does Brock's Theory of Migration Justice Adequately Account for Climate Refugees?' *Ethics & Global Politics* 14(2): 75–85.

Williams, Bernard. 1972. *Morality: An Introduction*. Harper & Row.

Williams, K. D., A. J. Hewitt, and A. Bodas-Salcedo. 2020. 'Use of Short-Range Forecasts to Evaluate Fast Physics Processes Relevant for Climate Sensitivity'. *Journal of Advances in Modeling Earth Systems* 12(4): e2019MS001986.

Williston, Byron. 2012. 'Climate Change and Radical Hope'. *Ethics and the Environment* 17(2): 165–86.

Wissenburg, Marcel. 2013. *Green Liberalism: The Free And The Green Society*. Routledge.

Wolff, Jonathan. 2003. *Why Read Marx Today?*. Oxford University Press.

———. 2020. 'Fighting Risk with Risk: Solar Radiation Management, Regulatory Drift, and Minimal Justice'. *Critical Review of International Social and Political Philosophy* 23(5): 564–83.

Wolff, Jonathan and Dirk Haubrich. 2008. 'Economism and Its Limits'. In *Oxford Handbook of Public Policy*, eds. Robert E. Goodin, Michael Moran, and Martin Rein. Oxford University Press.

Wolff, Jonathan and David Leopold. 2021. 'Karl Marx', ed. Edward N. Zalta. *The Stanford Encyclopedia of Philosophy*.

Wolff, Jonathan and Avner de Shalit. 2007. *Disadvantage*. Oxford University Press.

Wong, James K. 2016. 'A Dilemma of Green Democracy'. *Political Studies* 64(1): 136–55.

Wong, Pak-Hang. 2014. 'Maintenance Required: The Ethics of Geoengineering and Post-Implementation Scenarios'. *Ethics, Policy, and Environment* 17(2): 186–91.

Wringe, B. 2012. 'Collective Agents and Communicative Theories of Punishment'. *Journal of Social Philosophy* 43(4): 436–56.

Zellentin, Alexa. 2010. 'Climate Migration. Cultural Aspects of Climate Change'. *Analyse & Kritik* 32(1).

———. 2015. 'Climate Justice, Small Island Developing States and Cultural Loss'. *Climatic Change* 133(3): 491–98.

Zhang, Zhihua, John C. Moore, Donald Huisingh, and Yongxin Zhao. 2014. 'Review of Geoengineering Approaches to Mitigating Climate Change'. *Journal of Cleaner Production*.

Index